THE WARRIORS

By Judge Ed Butler

Edited by Jonathan Porter

DEDICATION:

Dedicated to HRM Felipe de Borbon, King of Spain.

LIST OF CHARACTERS IN ORDER OF APPEARANCE

Pope Clement	Pope
Jacques De Molay	Grand Master of the Knights Templar
HRM Philip, IV	King of France from 1754-1783
Chev. Roger De Pairaud	Templar Chairman of Expansion Committee
Pope Boniface	Pope
Chev. Peter	French Templar Priory Aumonier
Don Ferdinando Lopez-Gamez,	Mayor of Macharaviaya, Spain; father of Eduardo
Eduardo Lopez-Seguin "Lalo"	Best friend of Bernardo de Galvez
James LaMarque, Headmaster	Headmaster of the Switzerland Institute for Young Men
HRM Carlos, III de Borbon	King of Spain from 1759-1788
Eldridge Gerry	Chairman, Massachusetts Committee of Supplies

Gen. Alejandro O'Reilly	Commander of military assault on Algiers
Marqui de Grimaldi	Prime Minister of Spain
Count of Vergennes	Prime Minister of France
Pierre de Beaumarchais	Author of "Barber of Seville;" Manager of Roderigue
Hortalez and Company	
Robert Morris	Signer of the Declaration of Independence; V.P. Pennsylvania Committee of Safety.
Gov. Louis de Unzaga	Spanish Governor General of Spain, before Galvez.
Capt. Felipe Miralez	Commanding Officer New Orleans Spanish Garrison
Gilbert Anoine de Saint-Maxent	Wealthiest businessman in New Orleans; French

Marie Felicite de Saint-Maxent	Daughter of Gilbert; wife of Bernardo de Galvez
Mrs. Sara Unzaga	Wife of Governor General Unzaga
Father Joseph	Rector of New Orleans Catholic Church]
Daniel Olmeda	1st Mate on ship Como No.
Capt. Fernando Garcia	Military Aide to Colonel Eduardo Lopez – wife Esmerelda
Sgt. Joel Blance	Orderly to Colonel Eduardo Lopez
Sgt. Roberto Sanchez	Squad leader of marine squad aboard the Como No
Captain Reynaldo Altruda	Captain of the Como No
Captain Christopher Butler	Captain of the Sharnbrook. Wife – Sara
Felipe de Fondesvic y Ondeano,	

Marquises de la Torre	Governor General of Cuba
Antoinette "Toni" La Salle	Eduardo Lopez' girlfriend/wife
Chief Petty Officer Galvan	CPO on the Galveston
Capt. Jose Menchaca	CO of Marine detachment on the Galveston
Lt. Col. Esteban Rincon	XO of New Orleans Presidio
Lt. Francois DeVille	French Liaison Officer
Lt. Col. Fernando "Nando" Garcia	Chief of Staff to General Eduardo Lopez.
Lt. Javier "Javi" Ramirez	Assistant to General Eduardo Lopez – wife Lynette
Sgt. Roberto "Flaco" Olivar	Orderly to General Eduardo Lopez
Col. Antonio de Guzman	Adjutant of Cartegena, Columbia Regiment
Capt. Alonzo Palmero	Navy Captain of ship from Cartagena, Columbia

Lt. Emanuel Garza	Platoon Leader, Vera Cruz, Mexico Cavalry
Sub. Lt/ Jaime Pachecko	Asst. Platoon Leader, Vera Cruz, Mexico Cavalry
Brig. Gen _____ Montemayor	CO, Vera Cruz, Mexico Military Command
Navy Lt. Ricardo Jiménez	Captain of the Cartagena ship Solitude
Sub. Lt. Andre Costas	XO of the Cartagena ship Solitude
Mario Martinez	Mint Director, Mexico City, MX
Lt. Tomas Chavez	Platoon Leader, Cavalry escort Mex. City to Acapulco
Sub. Lt. Ramon Gonzales	Asst. Platoon Leader, Cavalry escort Mex. City to Acapulco
Navy Captain Martin De Trentian	Passenger on the Sharnbrook from Havana to Le Havre, France

Rear Admiral Adonis Contreras	Commander, Spanish Central Pacific Fleet, Acapulco, Mexico
Capt. Esteban Francisco	Captain of the ship, Diligence, a 28-gun sloop.
Lt. Filemon Escobar	XO of the ship, Diligence, a 28-gun sloop.
Lt. Henri Diaz	Gunnery Officer of the ship, Diligence, a 28-gun sloop.
Frigata Lt. Manuel Sosa	Navigator of the ship, Diligence, a 28-gun sloop.
Midshipman Emilio Rangel	Supply Officer of the ship, Diligence, a 28-gun sloop.
Midshipman Pedro Saucedo	Ass't. Gunnery Officer of the ship, Diligence, a 28-gun sloop.
Captain Fidencio Luna	Captain of the Caca Fuego
Fragata Commander Marcelo Borrego	XO of the Caca Fuego
Fragata Commander Andres Valle	Gunnery Officer of the Caca Fuego

Fragata Commander Domingo Diego	Medical Doctor of the Caca Fuego
Lt. Xavier Maldonado	Asst. Gunnery Officer of the Caca Fuego
Lt. Vicente Zerna	Navigator of the Caca Fuego
Lt. Justo Lopez	Supply Officer of the Caca Fuego
Lt. Marciano Trevino	Cargo Officer of the Caca Fuego
Sub. Lt. Eugenio de la Garza	Asst. Supply Officer of the Caca Fuego
Domingo Torres	2nd Mate of the Caca Fuego, from Mindanao, Philippines
King Kalani'opu'u.	King of Hilo, Hawaii
Rear Admiral Antonio Carlos Jobim	Commanding Officer of Subic Bay Naval Base
Major General Gaspar Valdez	Commanding Officer, Manila Philippines Presidio
Captain Joseph Acosta	Manila military escort
LT Julian Arocha	Captain of the Resolve

Sub. LT Gilberto Flores	XO of the Resolve
Jose Basco y Vargas	His Excellency, Governor General of the Philippines
Augustin de Jaurequi y Aldecoa	His Excellency, Viceroy of Peru
Brigadier General Victor Anaya	Commanding Officer, Real Felipe Fortress
Lt. Hector Delgado	Marine Platoon Commander in Peru
Sub. Lt. Emilio Cazoria	Assistant Marine Platoon Commander in Peru
Captain Jaime Rubio	Captain of the Infinity.
LT Esteban Seguin	XO of the Infinity
LT Michaela Sendejo	Gunnery Officer of the Infinity
Sub. LT Ygnacio "Nacho" Cruz	Assistant Gunnery Officer of the Infinity
Captain Justo Mirales	Captain of the Sleeping Lady – Old Treasure Ship
Fragata Captain Emilio Sosa	XO of the Sleeping Lady

Fragata Captain Eduardo Suarez	Doctor of the Sleeping Lady
LT Juan Serna	Gunnery Officer of the Sleeping Lady
LT Antonio Segovia	Supply Officer of the Sleeping Lady
Sub. LT Augustine Zuniga	Assistant Gunnery Officer of the Sleeping Lady
Captain Bennett Graham	Pirate Captain of Graham's Folly – English
Captain Benito Bonito	Pirate Captain of La Tormenta – Portuguese
Captain "Jolly Jim" Sitgraves	Pirate Captain of the Black Shark – Scottish – Black Sails
LT Rudolfo Mayor	Marine Platoon Commander, Acapulco, Mexico
Sub. LT Rafael Mendoza	Assistant Marine Platoon Commander, Acapulco, Mexico
Captain Tomas Macias	Captain of the Fortitude, 38-gun galleon, out of Acapulco

LT Marcos Montalbo	XO of the Fortitude
LT Pablo Garza	Gunnery Officer of the Fortitude
Sub. LT Amador Bizante	Assistant Gunnery Officer of the Fortitude
Sub. LT Jose Cadena	Supply Officer of the Fortitude
Captain Emilio Ponce	Captain of El Cazador
Fragata Captain Danielo Rodriguez	XO of El Cazador
Fragata Captain Antonio Hernandez	Ship's Doctor of El Cazador
LT Pedro Ruiz	Navigator of El Cazador
LT Andres Sevilla	Gunnery Officer of El Cazador
LT Nicholas Texado	Supply Officer of El Cazador
LT Pedro De Los Santos	Cargo Officer of El Cazador
Sub. LT Santiago Seguin	Assistant Gunnery Officer of El Cazador

Sub. LT Josef Serna	Assistant Supply Officer of El Cazador
Midshipman Antonio Losoyo	Assistant Cargo Officer of El Cazador
Robert Morris	Signer of the Declaration of Independence; V.P. Pennsylvania Committee of Safety.
Gov. Louis de Unzaga	Spanish Governor General of Spain, before Galvez.
Capt. Felipe Miralez	Commanding Officer New Orleans Spanish Garrison
Gilbert Anoine de Saint-Maxent	Wealthiest businessman in New Orleans; French
Marie Felicite de Saint-Maxent	Daughter of Gilbert; wife of Bernardo de Galvez
Mrs. Sara Unzaga	Wife of Governor General Unzaga
Father Joseph	Rector of New Orleans Catholic Church]
Daniel Olmeda	1st Mate on ship Como No.

Capt. Fernando Garcia	Military Aide to Colonel Eduardo Lopez – wife Esmerelda
Sgt. Joel Blance	Orderly to Colonel Eduardo Lopez
Sgt. Roberto Sanchez	Squad leader of marine squad aboard the Como No
Captain Reynaldo Altruda	Captain of the Como No
Captain Christopher Butler	Captain of the Sharnbrook. Wife - Sara
Marquises de la Torre	Governor General of Cuba
Antoinette "Toni" La Salle	Eduardo Lopez' girlfriend/wife
Chief Petty Officer Galvan	CPO on the Galveston
Capt. Jose Menchaca	CO of Marine detachment on the Galveston
Lt. Col. Esteban Rincon	XO of New Orleans Presidio
Lt. Francois DeVille	French Liaison Officer

Lt. Col. Fernando "Nando" Garcia	Chief of Staff to General Eduardo Lopez.
Lt. Javier "Javi" Ramirez	Assistant to General Eduardo Lopez – wife Lynette
Sgt. Roberto "Flaco" Olivar	Orderly to General Eduardo Lopez
Col. Antonio de Guzman	Adjutant of Cartegena, Columbia Regiment
Capt. Alonzo Palmero	Navy Captain of ship from Cartagena, Columbia
Lt. Emanuel Garza	Platoon Leader, Vera Cruz, Mexico Cavalry
Sub. Lt/ Jaime Pachecko	Asst. Platoon Leader, Vera Cruz, Mexico Cavalry
Brig. Gen _____ Montemayor	CO, Vera Cruz, Mexico Military Command
Navy Lt. Ricardo Jiménez	Captain of the Cartagena ship Solitude
Sub. Lt. Andre Costas	XO of the Cartagena ship Solitude
Mario Martinez	Mint Director, Mexico City, MX

Lt. Tomas Chavez	Platoon Leader, Cavalry escort Mex. City to Acapulco
Sub. Lt. Ramon Gonzales	Asst. Platoon Leader, Cavalry escort Mex. City to Acapulco
Navy Captain Martin De Trentian	Passenger on the Sharnbrook from Havana to Le Havre, France
Rear Admiral Adonis Contreras	Commander, Spanish Central Pacific Fleet, Acapulco, Mexico
Fragata Commande	Antonio Villarreal
Capt. Esteban Francisco	Captain of the ship, Diligence, a 28-gun sloop.
Lt. Filemon Escobar	XO of the ship, Diligence, a 28-gun sloop.
Lt. Henri Diaz	Gunnery Officer of the ship, Diligence, a 28-gun sloop.
Frigata Lt. Manuel Sosa	Navigator of the ship, Diligence, a 28-gun sloop.

Midshipman Emilio Rangel	Supply Officer of the ship, Diligence, a 28-gun sloop.
Midshipman Pedro Saucedo	Ass't. Gunnery Officer of the ship, Diligence, a 28-gun sloop.
Captain Fidencio Luna	Captain of the Caca Fuego
Fragata Commander Marcelo Borrego	XO of the Caca Fuego
Fragata Commander Andres Valle	Gunnery Officer of the Caca Fuego
Fragata Commander Domingo Diego	Medical Doctor of the Caca Fuego
Lt. Xavier Maldonado	Asst. Gunnery Officer of the Caca Fuego
Lt. Vicente Zerna	Navigator of the Caca Fuego
Lt. Justo Lopez	Supply Officer of the Caca Fuego
Lt. Marciano Trevino	Cargo Officer of the Caca Fuego
Sub. Lt. Eugenio de la Garza	Asst. Supply Officer of the Caca Fuego

Domingo Torres	2nd Mate of the Caca Fuego, from Mindanao, Philippines
King Kalani'opu'u.	King of Hilo, Hawaii
Rear Admiral Antonio Carlos Jobim	Commanding Officer of Subic Bay Naval Base
Major General Gaspar Valdez	Commanding Officer, Manila Philippines Presidio
Captain Joseph Acosta	Manila military escort
LT Julian Arocha	Captain of the Resolve
Sub. LT Gilberto Flores	XO of the Resolve
Jose Basco y Vargas	His Excellency, Governor General of the Philippines
Augustin de Jaurequi y Aldecoa	His Excellency, Viceroy of Peru
Brigadier General Victor Anaya	Commanding Officer, Real Felipe Fortress
Lt. Hector Delgado	Marine Platoon Commander in Peru

Sub. Lt. Emilio Cazoria	Assistant Marine Platoon Commander in Peru
Captain Jaime Rubio	Captain of the Infinity.
LT Esteban Seguin	XO of the Infinity
LT Michaela Sendejo	Gunnery Officer of the Infinity
	Assistant Gunnery Officer of the Infinity
Captain Justo Mirales	Captain of the Sleeping Lady – Old Treasure Ship
Fragata Captain Emilio Sosa	XO of the Sleeping Lady
Fragata Captain Eduardo Suarez	Doctor of the Sleeping Lady
LT Juan Serna	Gunnery Officer of the Sleeping Lady
LT Antonio Segovia	Supply Officer of the Sleeping Lady
Sub. LT Augustine Zuniga	Assistant Gunnery Officer of the Sleeping Lady
Captain Bennett Graham	Pirate Captain of Graham's Folly – English

Captain Benito Bonito	Pirate Captain of La Tormenta – Portuguese
Captain "Jolly Jim" Sitgraves	Pirate Captain of the Black Shark – Scottish – Black Sails
LT Rudolfo Mayor	Marine Platoon Commander, Acapulco, Mexico
Sub. LT Rafael Mendoza	Assistant Marine Platoon Commander, Acapulco, Mexico
Captain Tomas Macias	Captain of the Fortitude, 38-gun galleon, out of Acapulco
LT Marcos Montalbo	XO of the Fortitude
LT Pablo Garza	Gunnery Officer of the Fortitude
Sub. LT Amador Bizante	Assistant Gunnery Officer of the Fortitude
Sub. LT Jose Cadena	Supply Officer of the Fortitude
Captain Emilio Ponce	Captain of El Cazador
Fragata Captain Danielo Rodriguez	XO of El Cazador

Fragata Captain Antonio Hernandez	Ship's Doctor of El Cazador
LT Pedro Ruiz	Navigator of El Cazador
LT Andres Sevilla	Gunnery Officer of El Cazador
LT Nicholas Texado	Supply Officer of El Cazador
LT Pedro De Los Santos	Cargo Officer of El Cazador
Sub. LT Santiago Seguin	Assistant Gunnery Officer of El Cazador
Sub. LT Josef Serna	Assistant Supply Officer of El Cazador
Midshipman Antonio Losoyo	Assistant Cargo Officer of El Cazador

LIST OF ILLUSTRATIONS

22

ACKNOWLEDGEMENTS

Jonathan Porter has been active as the editor of this historical novel. He designed the cover and configured the book for publication on Amazon.com.

My wife, Robin Butler's assistance in proof reading was essential, as she was always able to see errors that had avoided detection by me.

23

CHAPTER 1

The Avignon Vatican

Avignon, France

June 24, 1305

The white of Pope Clement's tunic glared in the sunlight from the open window. His eyes were red from allergies, but there was a warm smile on his face as he greeted the Grand Master. Jacques De Molay genuflexed, as he bent over to kiss the Pope's ring.

"Good afternoon your Holiness. I trust you are having a good day," he said.

"Your excellency, it has been a great day, except for these pestering allergies. Please join me for a cup of wine. Be sure to join me in devouring some of these delicious pastries from the Vatican bakery. And how have you been since we last met?

"I have been in good health your Holiness, but I am discouraged that I have been unable to obtain any interest in a new crusade. It would appear that all the European monarchs are tired of battle." "That's one of the reasons I asked you to meet me here. Money is tight all over Europe, yet the Templars are rich. Since the crusades you have become the wealthiest organization in Europe. Kings owe you large sums, which makes you powerful. Many kings resent you. It behooves the Church to help you with your public image.

"Your Holiness, this wine is excellent," said the grand master, as he held his wine cup.

"The wine is from grapes grown just up the hill, said the Pope. "The vintner named it "Chateauneuf-du-Pape, after our new home in Avignon. If you like the red, you should love the white."

"Back to reality. I have two suggestions," said the Pope: "First, the Templars and Hospitallers should be combined because the Hospitallers enjoy a better public image as they are not controversial. Second, your organization needs to establish itself in other countries. King Philip, IV of France has you in his sights. I strongly suggest that you establish strong priories in other countries. If Philip moves against you, these priories in other countries could be your salvation."

"Unless your Holiness orders that we be merged with the Hospitallers, I am opposed to combining our orders. Much of our success has been due to the comradery we enjoy. This idea of merger has been bandied about has been discussed both by us and the Hospitallers and we all are against it. We have our annual Grand Convent scheduled for July 12th. I will present your suggestions to the Templars."

CHAPTER 2

Temple Church

Isle de France

Paris, France

July 12, 1305

Templars from all over France slowly entered the sanctuary. Renewing old friendships planted smiles on their faces. They shook hands and patted one another on the back. Excitement was in the air because the notice of business to be conducted at this Grand Convent stated they would be discussing a possible merger with the Hospitallers and/or branching out to other countries.

Following the opening prayers, the Grand Master called the meeting to order.

"As the first order of business I call on Chev. Robert of Avignon, the treasurer for a financial report.

From the treasurer's report it appeared that the Templars of France were the wealthiest organization in France, if not in all of Europe.

The Templars required that in order to become a knight, one must divest himself of all property. As a result, the Templars owned castles, farms, vineyards, shipping companies, mines and businesses of all varieties. Their charge from the Pope was to protect pilgrims to the Holy Land. They had constructed fortresses along the route to the Holy Land. It was at that point that they became rich. They created a fleet of ships to take people and supplies to the Holy Land. It would have been bad business to bring those ships back to Europe empty, so they became merchants, picking up and dropping off shipments all over the Mediterranean.

Becoming the first bankers of the world resulted in the bulk of their wealth. In the 14th century, travelers had to carry chests of coins when they departed on a journey. Highwaymen would lay in wait and rob them. The Templars devised a system whereby before the traveler left home, he would deposit money at a Templar facility. The Templar would provide the traveler with a Letter of Credit. That letter of credit could be debited along the way for passage, meals, etc.

They became the world's first international bankers.

"As the second order of business is the issue of whether we should merge with the Hospitallers." The debate became heated. No one spoke in favor of the suggested merger and the motion was defeated.

"As the final order of business, we need to discuss expanding our presence in Europe. Since our last battle in the Holy Land our reputation has sullied. Part of that is because of adverse comments by King Philip "the fair" about us. He hates that he owes us so much money, while his treasury shrinks. When I spoke to the Pope last month, he informed me that we should beware of King Phillip and that we should begin to disperse to other points in Europe. King Philip was powerful enough to force the Pope to move the Vatican from Rome to Avignon, so we should be prepared.

Chev. Hughes de Pairaud, a tall slender Templar with long hair and a weathered face asked to be heard.

"Your Excellency, we fought in the Holy Land alongside Templars from all the countries of Europe and enjoyed an

27

excellent friendship with them. It seems only prudent that we do the following:

1. Investigate possible sites in other countries for opening or expanding priories.

2. Review how best to redistribute our assets to protect them from seizure.

3. Discuss how best to perpetuate our order.

Discussion of this suggestion went on for hours. Finally, the Grand Master hit the gavel on the podium and called the meeting back to order.

"Based upon the discussion I have heard it is clear to me that the Templars should move forward quickly. I am naming Chev. Roger De Pairaud as Chairman of a special committee 1) to recommend locations for new priories and 2) to make suggestions of how to perpetuate our order. I am calling a special meeting of the Grand Convent for August 12, 1305 to receive and consider his report."

CHAPTER 3

Temple Church

Isle de France

Paris, France

August 12, 1305

"Your excellency", reported Chev. Roger De Pairaud, "your special committee has met and considered the issues of whether we should expand and disperse and if so, where. Our recommendations are as follows:

1. We should first expand the small priory in Switzerland, Switzerland. One, we already have Templars living and working there to assist us with the move. Second, it is adjacent to France, which will enable us to move our assets quickly across land.

2. We should work with Templars to create priories in Scotland, Spain & Portugal, because the monarchs of these countries are favorable to us.

3. We think that organizations should be established at each site to continue our goals in the event Templars become outlawed.

4. We especially recommend that a Templar School be established in Switzerland to educate Templar children and create both strong minds and strong bodies."

A somber mood existed throughout the chapel. One Templar in the back said, "It a hell of a note that an organization raised by the King of Jerusalem and originally blessed by the Pope, must sink to skullduggery to avoid the tenacles of the new Pope and a greedy king."

Fairly quickly, the Templars present voted unanimously in favor of the motion.

"All those with teaching experience see me immediately after the meeting."

CHAPTER 4

Temple Church

Switzerland, Switzerland

September 21, 1305

"Brothers", said the prior of the Switzerland Priory, "today we are honored to have with us,

Chev. Roger De Pairaud, Deputy Grand Prior. He is going to explain our new role as Templars."

"Fellow Templars, I bring you news that shouts of the new importance of this priory. Up until now, you have been only a small group whose job was to assist pilgrims to the holy land. From this day forward you shall be a shining beacon in the Templar World. The Grand Convent has voted that this priory shall create and operate a school for Templar Children and children of world leaders.

"Grand Prior DeMolay has asked that I remain here and work with you to build a school for

Templar children and children of world leaders. "I have delivered to your treasurer the sum of 100,000 Francs. We already own the dock facility at Pregny-Chambesy, a suburb of Geneva and the 50 acres adjacent to it. We hope to build a school that will graduate the smartest and best educated children in the world. We must teach them the languages of the world. They must learn their history so that they never repeat it and be strong in body and spirit. They must become masters of the sea and skilled in warfare. Our Templar children must become leaders of the world, and for that they must become gentlemen with a high sense of morality."

CHAPTER 5

Pope's Palace

Avignon, France

Sep. 7, 1307

"Good morning your majesty," said Pope Boniface. "To what do I owe this honor?"

"I am here to discuss some matters of state," replied King Philip.

"Then, please join me in my chambers and we shall enjoy refreshments."

There was a fall chill in the air, so the two men sat in overstuffed chairs on either side of a roaring fireplace. They enjoyed small talk until the servants had exited. On the table next to each had been placed a carafe of wine, cup, appetizing meat pies and fruit as well as a napkin. The pair nibbled and sipped their wine.

Wiping his hands, King Philip said: "I have had it with the Templars. They press me for payment on my debt to them, when they know that I am in financial distress. Over the past few years their popularity among the people has waned. There are stories of unchristian acts during their initiation ceremonies. They have made a fortune off my back. Had it not been for my support, they would not be so wealthy. I have a plan, and I need your help.

"What can I do my Lord?" "I plan to arrest all Templars in France for crimes against the Church and seize all their assets. You will assist me in the trial. Once they have all been found guilty, my debt will be canceled, and I will obtain enough of their gold to pay off all my bills. You will rid yourself of a troublesome group that has caused problems in the Vatican for decades."

"How can you do this all over France? Once you begin arresting them, the others will escape," said Pope Benedict.

"My operation will need advance planning so that they will all be arrested on the same date and at the same time. I will notify the Sheriff in each province to arrest them all and seize all their assets on Friday October 13, 1307.

CHAPTER 6

Temple Church

Isle de France

Paris, France

September 14, 1307

"But Grand Prior, you must use this time to get out of France. You cannot allow yourself to be arrested. King Philip is a mad man. No telling what he will do to you," said Chev. Peter, the Aumonier.

"Peter, I am planning for the bulk of Templars in France to escape with our assets. The largest group with the bulk of our assets will travel overland to our priory in Geneva, Switzerland. Recently, we formed a new priory at Balantrodoch, near Edinburg, Scotland. That group plans to create a new organization which they will call "Masons" to carry on our work. We have arranged for a convoy of our ships to depart from La Rochelle, France to carry a group to Scotland. Smaller groups will go to our priories in Lisbon, Portugal and Marbella, Spain. The latter two groups will continue to operate under the name "Knights of Christ," and both kings have agreed to transfer all our assets to the new order."

"As for me and the other grand officers, we have decided to allow ourselves to be arrested so that we can publicly denounce both the king and the pope for being the scoundrels they are. It is our moral duty to let the public know of their illegal acts."

The following day Templars all over France began packing for their permanent move, whether it be to Switzerland, Scotland, Portugal or Spain. The order had been to vacate in small groups so as not to be noticed.

CHAPTER 7

Switzerland Priory

Geneve, Switzerland

October 1, 1307

Forty-Six Templars arrived in Switzerland with 30 wagons of Templar gold, furniture, equipment and supplies. Sixteen additional covered wagons contained wives, children, and personal effects. It was a rag tag column, with horses, cows, goats, and sheep being tethered behind the wagons. The school buildings were almost completed.

One group traveled together from Paris, while others began their journey in Lyon, Bordeaux, Marseille, and Nice. By prior arrangement, the five groups met on September 30, 1307, in Bonneville, France, just a few miles south of Switzerland.

The school had been named the Switzerland Institute for Young Gentlemen. Upon their arrival a celebration erupted. Many of the Switzerland Templars had fought alongside members of the arriving cadre. They rejoiced with beer and wine.

After a bit more than an hour of celebrating they all set to the task of unloading the wagons and storing the goods. Several Templars unharnessed the horses, fed, watered and brushed them and placed them in the stable. Others placed the wagons in storage buildings.

Because the priest that the Templars dealt with in the Holy Land routinely took wives and had children, the vow of chastity was not followed by many Templars. The newly arrived Templars were accompanied by many wives and children.

Each of the 46 had a necessary skill for the Priory's school. Many were experienced teachers. Several were to become instructors of military and naval science. Others would captain the ships used to teach sailing and navigation to the students. Still others would tutor in French, German, Italian, Spanish and Portuguese. Others would work in administration, housekeeping, Construction and repair.

They had enough gold to ensure the success of the school.

CHAPTER 8

The Pope's Palace

Avignon, France

Sat. October 14, 1307

King Philip and Pope Benedict sat in large drafty room in front of an eight-foot-high fireplace which boasted a roaring fire. Huge ten-foot-high doors at the end of the room opened. A large man approached the two confidently. "May I deliver my report, your majesty?" queried the Captain of the Royal Guard.

"By all means," said the king.

"Your majesty, we captured the Templar Grand Prior and all of his grand officers. They are all in the dungeon downstairs. Unfortunately, we could find only a handful of other Templars. Our troops seized every Templar Priory, church, castle or business and there were no assets to be found other than the buildings themselves. We learned that a fleet of Templar ships departed New Rochele on October 11th. Every port has been checked but we could find no Templar ships.

"I'm going to get those bastards! They are going to wish they had never fucked with me. I'm going to burn those sons of bitches at the stake," shouted the king as he jumped from his seat and furiously waived his arms in the air.

CHAPTER 9

North America

Colonial Claims

1754

Spain was the first European country to make territorial claims in North America. Columbus was financed by Ferdinand and Isabella and hundreds of Spaniards had begun colonization before the first English arrived in 1585. Spain had laid claim to New Spain, which reached to the "Arctic Snows."

CHAPTER 10

Home of Don Ferdinando Lopez-Gamez, Mayor

Marcharaviaya, Malaga, Spain

May 14, 1761

"Lalo, Lalo, come quick. You have a letter from the Switzerland Institute for Young Men. Hurry!" said his mother, Araceli standing in the doorway.

Eduardo was just returning home from school. His mother had called him Lalo since he was a little boy. When he was a toddler, she had called him "Lalito." He kissed his mom on the cheek as he passed her in the doorway. He laid his book satchel and cap on the entry hall table and picked up the letter and tore open the envelope.

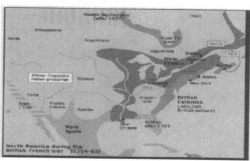

North American map 1

The letter:

"Switzerland Institute for Young Men
Geneva, Switzerland
Organized in 1305

May 1, 1761

Senor. Eduardo Lopez-Seguin

Avenida Mayor

Marcharaviaya, Malaga, Spain

Dear Senor Lopez-Seguin,

The Board of Regents of this school is pleased to inform you that it has approved a full scholarship for you, including room, board, tuition, and fees for five years of study.

It is anticipated that upon the completion of your five years of study you will be fluent in

Spanish, English, French and German, and that you will have some familiarity with Portuguese, Italian and Dutch. You will be awarded a master's degree of International Studies and will be eligible for a commission as an officer in most military branches in Europe should you elect to study military science.

You should report to the headmaster's office in Geneva, Switzerland on July 1, 1761. You will undergo a one-week orientation period during which time you will be assigned to your dormitory room, issued your uniforms and linens, sign for your books and supplies and learn what is *expected of you. You are expected to inform us not later than June 1, 1761, of your decision about attending this school. Attached for your assistance is a list of courses of instruction that will be available to you during your stay.*

Please note that you will receive instruction in both sailing and snow skiing.

Our school is on a quarter basis. At the end of each quarter, you will have two weeks' vacation to return home, visit with your family here or elsewhere. Should not wish to return home, provisions can be made for room and board during the interim. Naturally, should you remain on campus you will have access to all recreational facilities on campus and our Chamonix, France facility.

Sincerely,

James LaMarque, Headmaster"

Switzerland Institute for Young Men
Geneva, Switzerland
Founded by Knights Templars in 1305

Curriculum / required courses

Greek:	Language
	Culture
Latin:	Language
	Roman Literature
English:	Language
	History
	Art & Literature
French:	Language
	History
	Art & Literature
German:	Language
	History
	Art & Literature
History:	European
	Greek
	Roman
	Persian
	Crusades
	Ancient
	Oriental
Math:	Accounting
	Algebra
	Geometry
	Trigonometry
	Calculus
	Advanced Calculus
Science:	General Science

	Chemistry
	Biology
	Botany
	Physics
	Geology
	Anatomy
	Physiology
	Astronomy
Social Science:	Psychology
	Abnormal Psychology
	Sociology
	Penmanship
	Government & Civics
Geography:	Europe
	Asia
	North America
	South America
	Africa
	Australia & Island Nations
	Visits to towns in Switzerland, France, Italy, Germany & Austria.
Great Men:	Emperors & Kings
	Inventors & Explorers
	Warriors & Statesmen
Religion	Great Religions
Physical Fitness:	Healthy diet
	Daily calisthenics
	Downhill skiing
	Cross Country Skiing
	Ice Skating
	Tennis
	Golf
	Football (soccer)

	Swimming, lifesaving
	Sailing - 8' to 45' boats
	Self-defense - Hand to hand combat
	Track & field events
	Archery
	Knife throwing
Drafting	
Architecture	
Literature	Creative writing, Speech & Drama
Morals	Financial responsibility, & ethics
Music	Learn to play a musical instrument
Etiquette	Proper attire, & Social graces
Dancing	Periodic dances with private girls schools.
Horsemanship	Caring for horses
	Riding
	Jumping & racing
	Military formations
Sports Instruction:	Tennis
	Golf
	Downhill Skiing
	Ski Racing
	Cross Country Skiing
	Sailing
	Swimming
	Lifesaving

Optional Courses:

Italian Language	Italian History
	Italian Art & Literature
Portuguese Language	Portuguese History
	Portuguese Art & Literature

Dutch Language	Dutch History
	Dutch Art & Literature
Military Science	Military history
	Military Tactics
Military Courtesy	Map reading
	Orienteering
	First Aid
	Leadership
	Camping/cooking
	Swordsmanship
	Marksmanship
Naval Science:	Naval History
	Naval Tactics
	Naval Military Courtesy
	Rules of the Road
	Map & Chart Reading
	Navigation
	Weather
	Oceanography
	Small boat handling
	Sailing
	Seamanship
	Leadership
	Swordsmanship
	Naval gunnery
	Marksmanship
	First Aid
	Self- defense
	Hand to hand combat

"Momma, I am so excited I am going to Bernardo's to share the good news with him." Eduardo grabbed the letter and rushed out the front door. Eduardo's best friend was Bernardo de Galvez, who was one year older. These two boys grew up in Marcharaviaya, Malaga, Spain, a small village about half-way between Malaga and Granada, located just a few miles north of the Mediterranean Sea. They became fast friends. Bernardo lived with his parents two blocks north of the city hall, where Eduardo's father has his office as Mayor.

As he approached the Galvez home, he saw Bernardo sitting on the front porch steps carving a model of a two masted sloop. "Hey Bernie, I got some great news."

Galvez looked up from his ship model and said "Lalo, what is responsible for that ear-to-ear grin? Did you win the lottery?"

"No, Bernie. I just got a letter from the same school my father attended that I have been awarded a full five-year scholarship that pays for everything. I have to be there in two months. I'm so excited, I could piss in my pants. Here's the letter and enclosures. Take a look."

"Gee, Lalo this is a sweet deal. They pay for everything, and you get the best education on the continent. Have you given any thought about the military option? You could graduate with commissions in both the Spanish Army and Navy. I'm jealous. When I graduate from the Military Academy in Avila, I'll get commissioned as a sub-lieutenant, but I will not have the degree. My only advantage is that my school lasts only one year and then I am off to make my fortune. Living in Avila, and with all classes in French, I should speak French pretty good by the time I graduate. But – look at you. Since your mom's French, you grew up bilingual. When I see you after your graduation you will also be speaking German. Knowing how hard you study,

I'll bet you will be speaking Italian and Portuguese too."

"Bernie, you forget. Your father is a favorite of King Carlos, III. As a lawyer, he beat the king in court three out of three times. This forced the king to hire him as his lawyer. If I remember correctly, your father is also a general in the army. Also, let's not forget that your uncle, Jose De Galvez servs the king as Spain's Minister to the West Indies. You will get promoted because of your family ties."

"I guess we had better make hay while the sun shines, because I have to report to the Avila Military Academy on July 1st, and it's about a two week trip. I'm going to miss you," said Bernardo."

"I'll miss you too," said Eduardo. "Do you think we will see much of one another after we grow up?" "I'm hoping to get to the new world. I want to get my share of gold and silver. I want to learn about the native Indians in New Spain. Perhaps there is a fortune to be made there. You have any goals now?" asked Galvez. Lalo replied "My goal is to graduate from this school and learn as much as possible while there.

With a proper education I can only hope that the right opportunities come my way that will lead to success. Hey, my dad should be home in a few minutes, so I must go tell him the good news. Hasta luego, Bernie."

"*Hasta la vista*, Lalo."

As Eduardo walked past City Hall, he noticed that the lights were still on in his father's office. He stopped at the library across the street to check out a book for his

49

homework assignment. While waiting for his father's return home, he started his homework. He had just completed his homework when his father came in the door. His mother greeted him at the door with a kiss on the cheek. "Would you like a cup of wine, darling" she asked. "*Si, como no*," he replied.

Matias Galvez was a large man with a chiseled face. That face had deep wrinkles from sun exposure as an army officer. He was extremely strong, with a very little pot belly protruding over his belt. He had retired from the Spanish Army as a general and had become a lawyer. He won three cases against the King's lawyer, so the king now kept him on a retainer. He was a very popular mayor of Marcharaviaya.

As she handed Matias his wine, his mom said, "Lalo's got some great news for you."

"*Digame* Lalo", said his father, "What's up?"

"Papa, your alma mater has offered me a full five-year scholarship. Everything is paid for except my travel expense. I am so happy that I can follow in your footsteps. And now, I can get a commission in either the army or navy when I graduate."

"Lalo, I am so proud of you. You have always been a good student, working hard in all your classes. What a wonderful reward for all your effort. If you plan on going into the military upon graduation let me suggest that you qualify for both army and navy commissions. There may come a time when this dual commission could work in your favor. Just a word of advice from an old general. I am delighted that you will be following in my footsteps."

"Will you and mama come see me? I will have two weeks off between quarters. If I have to come home, my travel time will use up much of my holiday."

"Your mother and I will accompany you to the campus and we will visit at the end of each quarter, except for Christmas – unless one of us is sick or there is some emergency. We want you home for the holidays. You already have a leg up on many of your classmates since you already speak French. You can spend that time on another subject."

"Going away to school is your first step toward manhood. Now is the proper time to hand down to you what my father handed down to me and his father before him for many generations. This signet ring was given to our ancestor, by Templar Grand Master DeMolay before his arrest in 1307. Our ancestor was the second headmaster of your school. The design on the signet ring represents the arms granted to our ancestor, which was approved by the Pope beforehand. During his career, he always applied his ring to hot wax to seal his correspondence.

CHAPTER 11

Bourbon Family Compact

Paris, France

August 15, 1761

On August 15, 1761, the kings of France and Spain
agreed that if either was at war, the other would come to
their aid militarily. HRM Carlos, III de Borbon (20
January 1716 – 14 December 1788) was King of Spain
from 1759 – 1788. HRM Louis, XVI de Bourbon (23
August 1734 – 21 January 1743) was King of France from
1754 -1783. King Carlos, uncle of King Louis, was the
senior man in the family as Carlos was 18 years older.
This was the third time that French and Spanish kings of
the Borbon family had entered into mutual security
agreements.

HRM Carlos, III de Borbon   HRM Louis, XVI de Bourbon

CHAPTER 12

Avila Military Academy

Avila, Castile & Leon, Spain

October 6, 1761

The Royal Military Academy of Avila was where young officers of the Spanish Army were instructed in the principles of modern warfare. There, he became a member of the "Mystery of Avila" a select group of young officers who were referred to by the establishment cadre of officers as the "Beardless Ones." The old officers believed that promotions should be based upon seniority or bravery in battle. The young men were of the opinion that promotions should be based upon merit.

"Bernardo, quick. Come over here. I have found the red group."

Cadet Galvez dismounted his horse, tied him to a tree branch, and rushed over to his classmate, Cadet Jaime Gonzales. Jaime grew up in Marbella, Spain, just a few miles from Galvez' home- town. His father was Don Antonio Gonzales, the Count of Gaucin, a small village near the Malagan border with Cadiz. They were both 16 years old. Jaime ignored his noble family and just acted as one of the guys. Bernardo liked him because he maintained no airs.

From behind the huge boulder the two could see a small military group of men setting up camp in a clearing beneath the hills. Bernardo immediately jerked his hand back from the hot boulder which he leaned his hand on. Their assignment as members of the blue team had been to scout for elements of the red force. "Let's ride back to headquarters and finish this exercise," said Bernardo."

The late afternoon sun was blinding the two riders as they rode back to the exercise headquarters near the military academy. Jaime said "Can you believe that we are almost officers? Graduation is next Friday." He wiped the sweat from his forehead with his handkerchief. "My parents are bringing my girlfriend Monica to graduation. I can hardly wait to see them all."

"My family is coming too," said Bernardo. "Unfortunately, I have no girlfriend for them to bring. Here in Avila, I was so damn busy studying French this past year, I didn't have time for girls."

"Well, you might not have done well with women, but you are finishing second in our class of 122. Do you know where you are being assigned," asked Jaime.

"*Si*, I originally got my first choice. I was going to the new world. After a two week visit with my family, I was to leave and then I was to travel to Barcelona by coach. There I was to meet up with a ship that will transport me to Havana, Cuba. My C.O. in Havana was to give me my assignment. Last Wednesday, those orders were deferred. Now, I am to report to the C.O. of the Castilian Calvary Regiment for assignment. They are currently massing on the Portuguese border while diplomatic discussions are ongoing. It doesn't look like I am going to get to use my newly learned French anytime soon," said Bernardo, with a grin on his face.

CHAPTER 13

Switzerland Institute for Young Men

Chamonix, France Campus

February 22, 1762

Eduardo wiped the snow from his eyes as he got back on his feet. Apparently, all he had injured was his pride. His skies were tangled up making it difficult for him to regain his balance. Finally, his skies were pointed downhill, and he was ready to finish his run. Using his two ski poles he pushed his body downhill with his skies in the snow-plow configuration. Six inches of new snow last night allowed his skies to glide down the hill. Slowly he opened the tips of his skies from snowplow to parallel. His speed increased rapidly. He remembered that to control his turns he must unweight his body, plant his skies to the right – unweight his body -plant his skies to the left, etc.

He at first rebelled against being required to participate in ski school at the resort. Now he was glad he had paid attention. After a week and a half of school, he was beginning to feel that he had it down.

His ski buddy for the day was Daniel Whitelock, son of an English Earl, who said "when we get to the bottom, let's get something warm to drink. I'm freezing."

The pair reached the bottom of the hill with no more falls. They took off their skies and stuck them upright into the snow with their poles. At the outdoor café near the ski lift they found a table. They both ordered hot chocolate. Although freezing cold, the sun was warm on their faces.

The wind was perfectly still, so they were comfortable sitting there.

Daniel said, "I can't believe I am sitting here watching four mules going in circles to tow skiers up the mountain. It's like a grist mill, except there is a rope with loops every so many feet so that the skier can put his hand through the loop and be towed up the hill. I never even heard of skiing before I got to this school."

"When I saw that they taught skiing here," Eduardo said. "I did some research. Russians were using skies in 6,000 BC. China cave paintings from 5,000 BC show men on skies. Archeologists have discovered evidence that the Finns and Laplanders used skies in the 16th century. This school began ski instruction just a few years ago in 1749 following the Danish Norwegian Army using skies in a military exercise in 1747. On our next trip here, we get to ride the huge sleigh up to the top of the mountain and ski all the way down. That should be a thrill."

"I've enjoyed our time at the ski area, but I dread that boat ride back to the campus. Lake Geneva was rough, and I was seasick the whole way," said Daniel.

"If the wind stays calm like today, the boat ride home should be smooth," replied Eduardo.

CHAPTER 14

Treaty of Paris

Paris, France

February 10, 1763

The Seven Years War began in 1756 between the English colonists and their Indian allies on one side and the French and their native allies on the other. In North America it was called the French and Indian Wars. These wars were a fight for territory in the new world. France was the big loser and Spain was the big winner. By the

Map of Eastern North America 1

terms of the treaty,

France ceded to Britain all the mainland of North America east of the Mississippi, excluding

a. New Orleans

b.   The West Indian islands of Grenada, Saint Vincent, Dominica, and Tobago; and

c.   all French conquests made since 1749 in India or in the East Indies.

2. Britain, in return, restored to France

a. the West Indian islands of Guadeloupe, Martinique, Marie-Galante, and Désirade;

b.   the islands of St. Pierre and Miquelon off Newfoundland.

c.   the West African colony of Gorée (Senegal); and Belle-Îleen-Mer off Brittany.

d.   Saint Lucia to France.

3. Spain at the same time

   a.   recovered Havana and Manila,

   b.   ceded East and West Florida to the British, and

   c.   Louisiana, including New Orleans, in compensation from the French.

To summarize, England was given all of North America north of the Gulf of Mexico and east of the Mississippi River, and Spain was given all the land west of the Mississippi River, including what is now Mexico.

CHAPTER 15

Switzerland Institute for Young Men

Geneva, Switzerland

June 1, 1766

"Lalo, your Valedictorian's speech was wonderful," said his mother. We are so proud of you,

You grew up speaking French and Spanish and now you are also fluent in English, German and Italian. You are one of only three students to be commissioned in both the Spanish Army and Navy.

"Son, with a master's degree in international studies you can go to work just about anywhere," his father interjected.

"I've been in contact with Bernardo. His request that I be assigned to him was approved. After my two weeks leave, I am to report to the harbormaster at Cadiz for the next ship to Havana, from where I will be forwarded to Chihuahua, Mexico, New Spain.

CHAPTER 16

Between Chihuahua, Mexico & Pecos River, Tejas

New Spain

November 1, 1770

Sweat trickled down Bernardo's neck and under his arms. This heavy wool Spanish officer's uniform was not designed for the heat and humidity in this part of New Spain. His cavalry battalion had been riding for three days following an Apache raiding party. Big Texas cloudless skies offered no protection from the sun, and there was no wind to cool the skin. They had left the fort at Chihuahua riding northeast seeking the Apache war party that had raided the fort at Ruidoso on the Rio Bravo River. They killed seven and wounded four and stole all the horses.

They found the tracks of a Texas longhorn cattle herd crossed the trail of the Indians. Captain Galvez assumed that the raiding party had temporarily changed into a hunting party to enjoy a feast. On the banks of the creek at Casa Piedra, they found the abandoned Apache camp site from the night before, with cattle bones strewn throughout.

Traveling through the mountainous area was slow and difficult. Peaks in the area ranged from 7,500 to 8,500 feet. He had guessed correctly that the Apache would follow the cattle until they decided on their next target.

As Captain Galvez leaned against the massive boulder, he reached into his bag and pulled out his looking glass. From his vantage point about 3,500 feet above the bend in the Pecos River he could see an Indian encampment in the area near the river. The reports of about 300 hostiles seemed accurate. They had apparently decided to stay in the area for a while to collect Buffalo hides.

"Sgt. Menendez," Galvez shouted.

"Yes Sir," Sgt. Menendez answered.

"Ask all officers and non-coms to meet me under that big Oak Tree in 15 minutes."

Captain Galvez rested on a large rock. Within a week of his 1762 graduation from the Military Academy he was in Portugal fighting on the front line. His Corunna Cavalry Regiment had been cited for gallantry and he had received a promotion from Lieutenant to Captain. He finally arrived in New Spain in 1765, but he was assigned to his uncle's group visiting the Viceroy. It was not until 1769 that he got into action. It was in that year that he was named second in command of The Army of Vizcaya under Colonel Lope de Cuellar. Months later he was named to succeed Cuellar. This was his first mission since being named commandant. His battalion consisted of about 125 men.

Captain Galvez walked over to the large oak tree. Assembled under the shade of the oak were his officers and non-coms:

Executive Officer Captain Tomas Menendez

Supply Officer   Lt. Mario Bermudez

C.O. of Company A   Lt. Carlos Mendoza

X.O. of Company A   Sub Lieutenant Eduardo Lopez

C.O. of Company B   Lt. Roberto Aragones

X.O. of Company B   Sub. Lt. Antonio Garza

C.O. of Company C   Lt. Angel Garcia

X.O. of Company C   Sub. Lt. Gorge Hernandez

Battalion First Sgt.   Sgt. Miguel Mendez

Bugler   Cpl. Esteban Cantara

Cherokee Indian Scout   Running Wolf

"Gentlemen, we have a dilemma. The enemy we have been chasing is within sight, and a clear target for an attack tomorrow. The first problem is that we are running out of food. The second issue is that we are greatly outnumbered – almost three to one. The men are tired, hungry and burning up with heat. Should we desire to return to the fort, we would be within military regulations. If we attack, we must be aware that the men are tired and hungry."

"Several factors are in our favor. First, and most importantly, we will have the element of surprise. I propose that if we attack, we do so at about 4:00 a.m. when they are all asleep except the sentries. Second, we have pistols and muskets. I want to see how you men feel about an attack tomorrow. Take a few minutes to discuss it among yourselves, then let me know what you think."

Galvez stepped back over to his observation point to see if there was any new activity in the Indian encampment below. He wondered how his friend Lalo would handle himself in his first battle.

"Sir, we're ready for you," shouted Newly promoted Captain Emilio Gonzales, the executive officer. "The officers and non-coms believe that our men are strong enough to attack this encampment. We feel that after the battle we can slaughter a few longhorns and have a feast," he continued.

"O.K. Men, gather round and listen to my plan," said Galvez.

"Lt. Aragones, maintaining concealment you will take B company upriver about ½ mile and cross the river. Before leaving our present position, you will instruct your men to remove their spurs or anything that my rattle or make noise. They will pad the hooves of their horses, and they will maintain strict silence. We want to surprise these Indians. Tie up your horses 1000 yards from the Indian camp and leave a squad of men to guard them. You will camp in the woods just north of the Indian camp. At 3:45 a.m. you will send out scouts to dispatch the sentries that are posted around the north edge of the camp. Also, at 3:45 the remainder of your company will quietly mount their horses and slowly make their way to within 10 feet of the edge of the woods. At exactly 4:00 a.m. the bugler will sound the charge at which time a detail will cut the Indian's horses loose and the remainder of the company will attack the village. This is a raiding party so there are no women and children to worry about.

"Lt. Garcia, you will take C Company south down river about ½ mile and cross. Your men will follow the same instructions so that the redskins don't hear us coming. Your men will occupy the rocks to the south of the encampment. Tie up your horses until it is time for the attack.

"I will lead Company A. We will follow Lt. Aragones and continue on until we find concealment due east of the encampment. At 4:00 a.m. all hell is going to break loose. Any Questions," asked Galvez?

Fortunately, clouds began moving into the area in the late afternoon. By nightfall, the clouds were so thick that there was no moon or stars to be seen. It was very dark.

Smoke rose from dozens of fires. A cool breeze wafted through the encampment. A dog barked at an Indian who was going to the latrine, but otherwise all was quiet at 3:59 a.m. As predicted, one minute later, all hell broke loose. With the sounding of charge by the bugler, the serene camp erupted into chaos. The Indian horses were scattered to the wind. One hundred thirty-five soldiers shouted as they urged their mounts into the camp. Some horses rode through the middle of a tent. As the natives peered from their tent, some were shot while others were hacked by cavalry sabers. Fires were trampled, causing some tents to ignite. After about 20 minutes of fighting, the battle was won. The Apache's surrendered.

Lt. Mendoza, Commander of Company A was shot in the throat by an arrow and died, as well as two privates. His X.O. stepped up without his platoon missing a beat. He led his men to the northernmost part of the wooded area to the north of the camp. Maintaining silence, his platoon rested until the appointed time. When the bugle blew, all hell broke loose. About 20 redskins from tents on the northeast side of the village ran towards the woods. The soldiers were deep enough in the timbers that they could not be seen.

"They just ran into our arms," reported the XO. "Two of them ran east of us and got away. One of them got a me on the arm with a sharp hatchet, but we got the blood stopped."

"Lalo, I am promoting you to full Lieutenant and assigning you to command Company A," said,

Galvez. "You performed well in your first test under fire."

Twenty-eight Indian raiders were killed, with 71 injured. A total of 36 prisoners were taken. Galvez' battalion also retrieved 204 stolen horses and 2,000 Pesos worth of buffalo and antelope hides. While one detachment was collecting weapons in the camp, another group killed two longhorns. While the captured Indian raiders watched, Galvez and his men enjoyed a Texas Barb-que. All the way back to the presidio they enjoyed full stomachs.

Viceroy Croix reported to Madrid that Galvez demonstrated "glorious action." His second battle against the Apache's resulted in a similar victory, yielding a recommendation that he be promoted. Within six months he had been promoted to temporary Lt. Colonel. In October 1771 he encountered 5 Apache braves who were looking for trouble. Somehow, he miraculously defeated all five hostiles. He was left with an arrow in his left arm and two wounds in his chest from lance thrusts.

CHAPTER 17

Chihuahua, Mexico

October 3, 1772

"So, Lalo," Lt. Colonel Galvez asked, "how do you like the new world?

"Colonel, it is an honor to serve my country, but there are lots of things I miss," answered Lalo.

"What do you miss the most" asked Galvez.

"Pretty Spanish women – or perhaps I should say European women. How long has it been since we had a good serving of Paella or a decent cup of wine? What would you pay to attend a decent concert? Wouldn't you enjoy a cup of coffee on La Gran Via while People watching?

"Well Lalo, your prayers have been answered. We are being shipped home. After a month-long leave, we are both ordered to report to Pau, France. We are being assigned to the Royal Canabria Regiment. It is anticipated that Spain and France will be fighting England, and it is up to us to learn the French army way of doing things. This will give us both a chance to fine tune our French.

"Where in hell is Pau, France," Lalo inquired?

"Just few miles from the Spanish border near Pamplona," Bernardo responded.

"When do we leave," asked Lalo, with a large smile on his face?

CHAPTER 18

Committee of Safety

Boston, MA

December 23, 1774

The Boston Committee of Safety feared that American colonists were going to be forced into battle with the English army. The committee sent the following letter to obtain guns, ammunition and supplies.

Joseph Gardoqui & Sons

Bilboa, Spain

December 23, 1774

Dear Mr. Gardoqui,

The Boston Committee of Safety would like to purchase from you the following, F.O.B. Boston:

> *500 muskets*
> *500 bayonets*
> *900 pistols*
> *25,000 pounds of gunpowder*
> *100 sabers*
> *300 tents*

Please advise your best price and estimated shipment date. Once we receive your invoice, we will provide payment to your factor.

Sincerely,

Jeremiah Lee, Chairman

CHAPTER 19

Office of Joseph Gardoqui, & Sons

Bilboa, Spain

February 15, 1775

In response to the letter from the Boston Committee of Safety, Joseph Gardoqui dispatched the following letter to Boston:

Mr. Jeremiah Lee, Chairman

Boston Committee of Safety

Boston, Massachusetts

February 15, 1775

Dear Mr. Lee,

With regard to your letter dated December 23, 1774, I must tell you that at this moment I cannot fulfill your entire order. The gunpowder was shipped on January 9, 1775, via a Dutch ship. I have the following which I can ship immediately:

300 muskets

300 bayonets

600 pistols

Please advise if you with me to ship the above or await shipment of the full order. In the meantime, I will continue my efforts to fill your order.

Cordially,

Diego Gardoqui

On July 5, 1775, Elbridge Gerry submitted another order to Gardoqui on behalf of the Massachusetts Committee of Supplies.

On July 29, 1775, 14 tons of gunpowder arrived in Philadelphia from Spain, which was immediately shipped to the rebels besieging Boston.

. . .

American privateers were given "most favored nation" status and sanctuary at Spanish ports. Captain John Paul Jones used La Coruna, Spain as his headquarters for 18 months.

CHAPTER 20

Shipboard in Mediterranean

off Algiers, Algeria

July 10, 1775

General Alejandro O'Reilly was an Irishman commanding the Spanish king's military commander for the assault on Algiers. He was tall, with carrot red hair. He came down the ladder where the staff doctor was treating patients. He stopped at Bernardo Galvez's cot.

"How is Col. Galvez doing? When can he return to duty," asked the general?

The army doctor finished the bandage on Bernardo's right thigh. "Sir", said the medic, "I think his wound should heal without a problem. I suspect that he is going to have a permanent limp, however. He is very lucky that the medic got to him as soon as he did. His first aid saved the colonel's life. He should be restored to duty within six weeks," replied the doctor.

"How about Captain Lopez? How is his shoulder wound," asked General O'Reilly? "The sword went clean through his left shoulder. It missed any major artery. It should heal quickly. He will probably be unable to raise his left arm above his shoulder. Militarily, he should be able to return to duty in about a month. I doubt that he will be able to hold a musket properly, but he will heal," replied the army doctor, a captain.

As the doctor moved on to tend to other patients, General O'Reilly stood between Bernardo and Eduardo. "I can't fucking believe it," said the general. "I had the largest armada since William the Conqueror and 26,000 well trained soldiers and got clobbered by ignorant Arabs. Those stupid boat pilots landed my artillery at the wrong damn beach. All my fucking cannons were either stuck in mud near the beach or axel deep in sand. How the hell is a commander supposed to win a battle without artillery?"

"Because of your respective bravery, and because you two carried out a perfect diversion that would have spelled victory had not our main force been trapped, I am giving battlefield promotion to both of you. Lt. Colonel Galvez, you are now a full colonel. Captain Lopez, you are now a Lt. Colonel. Also, I'm awarding each of you the *Croix de Guerra Medal* for gallantry in battle. When we return to Cartagena you will both be assigned to the Military Hospital for treatment.

CHAPTER 21

Boston, Massachusetts

January 1, 1776

 New Spanish muskets from Joseph Gardoqui and Sons of
Bilbao, Spain began arriving in Boston to replace those
that had been confiscated by the English at Lexington and
Concord. Some of these muskets were distributed to
some Massachusetts Continental Regiments.

CHAPTER 22

Robert Morris

New Orleans, LA

April 1776

Oliver Pollock, a friend of governor Unzaga of Louisiana, served in April 1776 conducting secret meetings between Louisiana Governor Luis de Unzaga, Patrick Henry, Governor of

Virginia and Robert Morris, a merchant who had been doing business in Havana for years. They met to devise the method by which French and Spanish aid was to be delivered to the Americans.

CHAPTER 23

Kings of Spain and France Agree to support American Colonists

Paris, France

May 1, 1776

At the instruction of their respective kings, Prime Minister of Spain, Marquis de Grimaldi, and the Count of Vergennes, Prime Minister of France met with Pierre Beaumarchais, author and composer of the opera, *The Barber of Seville*, in Paris on May 1, 1776.

"Monsieur Beaumarchais," said Marquis de Grimaldi, "we appreciate that you have agreed to serve as manager of our new company. You must keep the activities -even the existence of this new company secret. We have opened a bank account for this new company. Each of our sovereigns has deposited one million Livres into this account. Additional deposits are expected in the future. You will receive orders of payments from Count Vergennes and myself. Here are the first invoices for payment. Both invoices are from Joseph Gardoqui & Son in Bilbao, Spain for muskets, musket balls, gun powder, uniforms, tents, knives, medical supplies, etc. One shipment of these military goods is to be shipped to the Governor General, Spanish Louisiana in New Orleans. The other goes to the Committee of Safety in Philadelphia.

CHAPTER 24

New Orleans, Louisiana

June 1, 1776

A Spanish ship loaded with military supplies from Joseph
Gardoqui and Sons arrived in the port of New Orleans,
Louisiana. During the three years before Spain declared
war on England, it

provided credit to the rebelling colonists totaling 8 million
Reales for weapons, food, military and medical supplies.

CHAPTER 25

Declaration of Independence Signed

Philadelphia, PA

July 4, 1776

Representatives of the 13 English colonies in North America joined together and signed the Declaration of Independence from England. As a result, a state of war existed between England and its colonists.

CHAPTER 26

Royal Palace

Madrid, Spain

July 12, 1776

"King Carlos will see you now, Colonel" said the young man as he opened the door to the king's chamber. Bernardo gave Edwardo an encouraging look as he stood up. "Good luck Bernie," said Eduardo. I hope it's not bad news. The strong winds rattled the windows that peered outside to the gloomy day. The throne room was bright with the glow of hundreds of candles. King Carlos, III de Borbon, King of Spain, was dressed in a light blue silk outfit over a linen shirt with fine lacework around the neck and cuffs.

"Please join me in my lounge area behind the throne, Colonel Galvez" said King Carlos, as he stepped down from the throne and extended his hand to Galvez in friendship. The king was very tall – about six and ½ feet tall, but he would win no beauty contests. His bulbous nose caused many to say he was ugly. As the two shook hands, King Carlos gently wrapped his left arm around Galvez shoulder and led him behind the throne. Behind the throne was a lounge. A table with four chairs was under the large window. Between the dining area and the throne were several comfortable chairs and tables with candles.

King Carlos indicated that they would sit at the table, which held a carafe of wine and two pewter cups. A servant filled their cups and backed out of the area with a bow.

"*Salud*, Colonel Galvez," toasted the king as he raised his cup. "Today, your life has changed for the better."

"*Salud*, your majesty. To what do I owe this honor," replied Galvez? They each took a sip of wine from their cups and placed them on the table.

"Colonel Galvez, although you and I have never met, I have kept up with you since you were a child. Your uncle Jose, the Spanish Minister to the West Indies, has been one of my closest advisors since you were a baby. I have had your father, Matias, as one of my advisors since he beat me in court three times in a row. As you know, he currently serves as my Viceroy to the Americas. Not only do they keep me updated as to your career, but your commanding officers have informed me of your military prowess."

"His excellency Unzaga, Governor General of Louisiana has asked me to replace him, as his health is failing. May I call you Bernardo? Bernardo, I am appointing you Governor General of Louisiana. What I tell you now is to go no further. King Louis XVI of France and I have decided that we will support the independence of the Americans. As you know, we have been at war with England for most of the past 600 years. A free America would become a major trading partner with New Spain. We want East and West Florida returned to us.

"Immediately after your arrival you are to start preparing for war. The first two things for you to do when you arrive is build up your defenses in New Orleans and recruit a militia to supplement the garrison. I am beefing up your command. I have ordered the Commanding general in Havana to immediately dispatch another platoon of riflemen, six cannon and crews and two caravels. The transport ship delivering those reinforcements has also been assigned to you. One caravel is to patrol Lake Ponchetran and the other shall patrol near the mouth of the Mississippi, unless you reassign it.

King Carlos continued "I have also taken notice of Lt. Colonel Eduardo Lopez, the young man you have kept under your wing for the past several years. Why have you mentored him?"

"Well, your majesty, there are several reasons," replied Galvez. First, he is brilliant. He was first in his class where we grew up in Marcharaviaya. He was parliamentarian at your alma mata, the Switzerland Institute for Young Men, where he qualified for commissions in both the army and navy, and he speaks five languages fluently. He has proved himself in battle. More importantly, he is my best friend and I know I can rely on him."

"All good reasons, Colonel," said the king. I am promoting him to full Colonel and assigning him as your Chief of Staff. You may share what is said in this meeting with him alone. "Now listen closely," said King Carlos. "King Louis and I have each given 1,000,000 Livres to support the Americans. The money is on deposit in Paris. Much more will be provided later. We have engaged the firm of Gardoqui & Hijos from Bilbao, Spain to secure muskets, musket balls, ammunition, tents, blankets, uniforms, boots, medical supplies and ship them to America. Many of these supplies will come to you in New Orleans. You will need secure warehouses to store these goods until they are forwarded to George

Washington's troops. You will also need to secure barges and bargemen to get those supplies upriver.

"From New Orleans," he continued, "you will supply the Spanish outposts at Fort Arkansas and Fort San Carlos, but the bulk of these military supplies will be shipped up the Ohio River to Ft. Pitt, which many maps still show as Ft. Duquesne. From time to time, you may be asked to deliver goods to Gen. George Rogers Clark at Ft. Nelson on the Ohio river. The British have established military outposts near New Orleans: upriver in Manchac, Baton Rouge and Natchez.

The English also have forts in both Mobile and Pensacola, the latter being a super fort. The

British have spies in New Orleans, so we must appear to be neutral in their war with the Americans until time to strike."

"You can count on Colonel Lopez and me, your majesty," said Governor Galvez.

"Governor, I wish you the best. Please ask Colonel Lopez to join me as you leave," requested the king.

. . .

"Colonel Lopez, let me congratulate you. I have appointed your friend Bernardo de Galvez as the Governor General of Louisiana. At his request I have named you as his Chief of Staff and promoted you to the rank of Colonel effective immediately. Before you report to New Orleans, I have a special assignment for you. You will not be traveling with Governor Galvez.

"Dr.[1] Benjamin Franklin, a United States delegate to France is scheduled to return to

Philadelphia in 10 days from Le Havre, France on a Spanish ship. This ship will be transporting the arms, ammunition and military supplies from Joseph Gardoqui and Son out of Bilboa, Spain to Philadelphia. Dr. Franklin speaks very little Spanish. My reports indicate that none of the officers on his ship speak English. I am appointing you as a special *aide de camp* for Dr. Franklin. You will serve not only as his interpreter, but you will also ensure that he travels are worry free. I want you to impress upon Dr. Franklin that Spain is a loyal ally of the United States. You are authorized both an aide of your choice and an enlisted orderly.

"I am providing you with this letter, personally signed and sealed by me to assist you in your task. It should help smooth your journey," said the king.

That evening Eduardo stayed up late making notes about his new assignment. Who would he select as his aide? As his orderly? What will he have them do on the long voyage? Whoever he selected as his orderly, he must have something productive for them for the long voyage. He decided that he would select several books on the military and the new world. His orderly could stay busy reading.

The books he selected for his orderly dealt with military history, Colonial Spain, and Conquistadors. Those books ought to help him become a better soldier.

He thought to himself that being appointed to do anything for the king was important. So, he decided to purchase a leather-bound journal and that he would make daily

---

[1] Benjamin Franklin was awarded an honorary Ph.D. degree from St. Andrews University in 1759. Oxford University also awarded him a Ph.D. degree in 1762.

entries of his travels, his activities and the individuals he met. Subconsciously, he might have thought that someday he would write a book about his adventures.

CHAPTER 27

Fort Pitt

August, 1776

General Charles Henry Lee, second in command to
General George Washington, sent Captain George
Gibson, with a group of 16 colonists, from Ft. Pitt to New
Orleans, to obtain weapons, gunpowder, supplies from
Spain that had arrived in June 1776.

CHAPTER 28

New Orleans, LA

September 1, 1776

The first ship load of military supplies arrived in New Orleans from the Gardoqui firm in Bilbao, Spain on September 1, 1776, including 9,000 pounds of gunpowder. Governor General Unzaga had them stored in the military warehouse adjoining the military base.

"The first shipment of military goods arrived today," said the note to Robert Morris. Now, it was his job to get these goods where they are needed.

Robert Morris was a signer of the Declaration of Independence, Vice President of the Pennsylvania Committee of Safety and a member of the Continental Congress.

From that date until the end of the American Revolutionary War, military goods arrived in New Orleans from Spain on a regular basis. Those goods were transshipped up the Mississippi and Ohio Rivers to supply General George Rogers Clark at Fort Nelson and to Fort Pitt to supply General Washington's troops. An additional 1,000 pounds of gunpowder was received in Philadelphia from Spain.

CHAPTER 29

Madrid, Spain

November 25, 1776

HRM Carlos, III ordered General Galvez to secretly collect information about the British. Later, General Galvez was ordered to render secret help to the colonists.

The following month an order was issued by Minister of the Indies, Jose Galvez, to Governor

General Unzaga of Louisiana, instructing him to support the Americans.

CHAPTER 30

New Orleans, Louisiana

December 23, 1776

Bernardo stood at the railing of the ship overlooking the port of New Orleans. He was amazed at the width of the muddy Mississippi. As the ship was securing its lines to the dock, he could see a Spanish Army platoon was there to greet him. No sooner was the gangway lowered to the pier, a handsome, well dressed young man came aboard and walked directly to where he was standing on the quarterdeck.

"Governor Galvez, I presume," he inquired.

"Yes, I am Governor Galvez. How may I be of service to you," he responded? While they conversed two soldiers rolled out a red carpet from the end of the gangway.

"Your excellency, Governor Unzaga has prepared a welcome ceremony for you. If you are ready now, he asks that you please tip your hat to him."

Following the tip of his hat he headed toward the gangway. As he entered the gangway, a small band struck up a military tune. The thud of the bass drum reverberated through the docks. As he stepped onto the pier Governor General Louis de Unzaga, the man he was replacing, extended his hand in friendship.

"*Beinvenidos*, your excellency. Welcome to your new home. I hope you had a pleasant voyage, "said Governor Unzaga. "Allow me to present Captain Felipe Morales, Commandant of the garrison of New Orleans.

Captain Morales saluted and clicked his heels together. "It is indeed a pleasure to meet you your excellency. I have heard so much about you I look forward to serving you. If it pleases your excellency, the garrison is ready for your inspection."

"Also, this is Captain Arnaldo Ponce. He was the captain of the transport recently assigned to New Orleans. I have appointed him Commodore of your fleet," added Governor Unzaga.

The garrison consisted of one company of infantry – now with four platoons, a kitchen detail, hospital group consisting of one doctor, one medic and an orderly. In addition to Captain Morales, each of the four platoons were commanded by a Lieutenant. Both the executive officer and the doctor had been reassigned and their respective replacements had not arrived. The garrison relied upon Doctor Philip La Salle, a French doctor who had practiced in New Orleans for 20 years.

"Company . . . Attention . . . Present Arms," Shouted Captain Morales. With that command the Spanish soldiers snapped to attention and held their weapons in front of them to salute Governor Galvez. "Order arms. Open ranks . . .March. Prepare for inspection. Platoon A, Attention. Platoons B, C and D, parade rest," ordered Captain Morales.

As he inspected the garrison, the band struck up another military song. Governor Unzaga was to his left and Captain Morales followed behind on his right. Galvez was disturbed at what he found: Dirty uniforms, muddy shoes, unshaven faces. A few of the men reeked with the smell of alcohol. It appeared that none of the muskets had been cleaned recently. All this he put in the back of his mind for when he took over.

When he had concluded the inspection of the garrison, Governor Unzaga again shook Galvez hand. "Governor, my aide will now escort you to your quarters. Your luggage will be delivered this afternoon. I will leave you this afternoon to get unpacked and settled into your temporary quarters. My cook will have your dinner delivered about 6:00 p.m. I would be honored if you would be my guest for lunch tomorrow. Afterwards, we can discuss the logistics of the change of command.

"Lunch tomorrow sounds good to me, "Galvez replied. "Excellent, I will send my coach for you at noon. Please dress casually. There are so few times that we can dress comfortably these days.

As you know, the day after tomorrow is Christmas. One of our local merchants has asked me to bring you with me Christmas evening for a party at his mansion outside the city. This will give you an opportunity to meet some of the people you will be dealing with."

CHAPTER 31

Home of Gilbert Anoine de Saint-Maxent

Outskirts of New Orleans, LA

December 25, 1776

The stately Saint-Maxent estate was about six miles past the city limits toward Lake Ponchetran.

It sat on a five-hectare wooded lot guarded by massive iron gates emblazoned with the Saint Maxent arms. Spanish Moss hung from the massive ancient oaks which lined the gravel driveway to the house. As his carriage approached the house it entered a circular driveway surrounding a pond from which sprayed several streams of water. In the clear pond water dozens of colorful Koi fish glided gracefully through the water.

When his carriage stopped at the entrance, a young Black boy dressed in silken livery opened his carriage door and extended his hand to help the governor from the carriage. He was in disbelief in what he saw. This mansion rivaled those of the nobles living in Madrid. The mansion was constructed in French Colonial style. The main house was built like an upside-down U. The entrance steps to the front door were carved from alabaster. The tall oak front door opened into a large entry hall. Off to the left was a coat room. Straight ahead was an enormous ball room, beautifully decorated. Along its mirrored walls were sconces. Nine crystal chandeliers provided enough candlelight to brightly light the hall.

"Lord Bernardo de Galvez, Governor General appointee of His Majesty's Colony of Louisiana" he was announced as he entered the ballroom. His keen eye spotted a well-dressed gentleman of about 50 walking toward him from across the ballroom.

"Governor Galvez, we are delighted that you have honored us with your presence tonight," said Gilbert Anoine de Saint-Maxent, as he extended his right hand in friendship. Maxent was about 5' 11" with a full head of salt and pepper hair and a thin mustache to match. He was rakishly handsome, at about 40-45 years of age. His eyes were clear crystal, which gave him an exotic look. His skin was tan and weathered and he had a strong French accent. He had made his fortune in furs, being the financial sponsor of Fort San Carlos at St. Louis. The furs were shipped downriver to New Orleans, then later to France. As the richest merchant in Louisiana, when the French were required to turn over West Florida to Spain, he had elected to pledge his allegiance to the Spanish crown and stay in New Orleans.

"I am delighted to be here in your magnificent mansion. It is the finest I have seen in the new world," Bernardo responded. Galvez had decided when he arrived that he must make friends with Monsieur Saint-Maxent, because his money could help Galvez in his duties to the crown. "Well then, let me give you a tour. The two walk-in fireplaces in the ball room are from a castle in Bayeux, Normandy, France that was owned by one of my ancestors who was the 5th Duke of Normandy and grandfather of William the Conqueror. Here, sticks your nose in the dining room. The crystal chandeliers in the dining room are from Venice. The two dining room fireplaces were retrieved from a Knight Templar priory in Cyprus. The oriental rugs throughout the home were manufactured at dozens of locations. I purchased most of them in either Constantinople or Cairo. The large painted oriental chest in the parlor was acquired by my grandfather, when he was French Ambassador to Hong Kong. Next is my study. The paneling is mahogany, which was imported from Nigeria. This fireplace was from my childhood home in Caen, Normandy France. Unfortunately, my childhood home burned while I was away at school."

"While we're here in my study, let me pour you a drink. I have something to discuss with you. Please have a seat.

Galvez sat – no, sank into the overstuffed leather armchair. He couldn't remember when he had sat in something so soft. Galvez eyes scanned the beautiful study. Heads of African animals, paintings by the masters, ancient tapestries, crossed swords and a shield with the family arms lined the walls. The bookcases contained leather bound classics, with trinkets from around the world. Saint-Maxent poured him a cup of Cognac Brandy into a delicate crystal glass. Galvez favored his native rum, wine and beer, but sipped the brandy appreciatively.

Mr. Maxent sat in a huge, padded chair behind a desk that was clear except for his writing pad, ink and salt.

"Governor, I am so rich that money is not my prime mover anymore. My agents in France tell me that France is about to go to war with England, and that Spain will be pulled into the fray.

Please bring me up to date with what you know."

"Monsieur, I too hear rumors," said Galvez. My job is to protect Spanish lands and population, and those foreigners like you who have sworn allegiance to our king. I can only say that I spend my days training my men to be ready in the event of war.

91

"Governor, it has come to my attention that you are storing military goods in a riverfront warehouse. I can only assume that these goods are for the Americans. All I want to do is help. I own several warehouses and two merchant ships. If my warehouses, my ships and my servants will be of assistance to you in the future, they are at your disposal. Just let me know when you need money. I am behind you 100%."

"Why, may I ask are you willing to help a foreign power," asked Galvez.

"Governor, to me it's just good business," he said. I think the Americans have a good chance of kicking the British off the North American continent. The western hemisphere will be reduced to the Americans and the Spanish. New Orleans will be the gateway to the United States for Latin American trade and vice versa. My cooperation will put me in the catbird seat after the war. So, you see, I have a perfectly selfish motive."

"Come, let us return to the ball room," said Maxent. "I want to introduce you to some of my guests."

As he reentered the ballroom he stopped in his tracks. His eyes feasted on a beautiful blond woman of about 25 years, in a pink and white organza dress. She was surrounded by three young men, who acted like dogs with their tongues hanging out of their mouths. He became short of breath and his heart pounded. He was hooked! It was love at first sight.

"Governor, please allow me to introduce you to my daughter Marie Felicite' de Saint-Maxent. As if by magic, Felicite' was also struck. When their eyes first met, they both dove deep into the pools of the other's soul. She was about 5' 5" with light blue eyes, light blonde hair and milk white skin. Small lines under her eyes told that there had been stress in her life. In their brief meeting he learned that she was well educated; spoke French, Spanish and English and that she was not married.

As her father was pulling at his elbow to meet other guests, Galvez whispered in her ear, "May I call on you for lunch tomorrow at noon?"

"Are you dangerous," she inquired with a flirtatious glint in her eyes?

"Only as dangerous as you would propose, my lady," he responded as he bowed with his arms outstretched, while he held her eyes in his glance.

"With a playful smile on her face and the hint of a wink, she said "*porque no – hasta manana.*

CHAPTER 32

New Orleans, LA

December 26, 1776

It was a lovely winter day on the outskirts of New Orleans. The sky was clear of clouds allowing the sun to warm the air. A soft breeze tumbled the leaves on the ground. There was a smell of fried chicken in the air. Bernardo's carriage pulled up in front of the Saint-Maxent mansion promptly at the stroke of noon. A Black carriage boy opened the carriage door and extended a hand to him. Bernardo was carrying an enormous vase of beautiful colorful flowers. "Wait here, Sam," Bernardo said to his driver. The butler opened the door before he could knock.

"Good afternoon, sir. Madam Felicite is expecting you, but she will delayed for be a few moments. Please have a seat in the study. What may I bring you sir," asked the butler? Around town Bernardo normally wore his uniform or formal attire. Today, he was dressed in his finest casual wear. His custom-made tan hounds tooth jacket went well with his brown knee britches and crème colored stockings. His white shirt was the perfect backdrop for his burgundy neck ribbon.

"How about a cup of sherry," Bernardo replied? After his sherry was delivered, Bernardo was left alone. The study door was open and there was lots of activity in the Saint-Maxent home. A butler, a housekeeper, several footmen, upstairs maid, downstairs maid – there must be 25 servants in the house, not counting the gardeners and stable boys.

He looked up and Felicite was standing in the doorway. *"Bon Jour Monsieur, como tallez vous,"* greeted Felicite. Although it was winter, Felicite had dressed for the New Orleans heat. The yellow and white cotton skirt went perfectly with the pale-yellow blouse. Her outfit was accented with a blue and yellow silk scarf. The most striking part of her outfit was a wide brimmed blue hat with a yellow bow, which was about a foot wide. He could feel his heart pounding, he was so excited.

"Good afternoon, Madam Felicite. You look beautiful. Before we leave, I have a proposal to make. Your main language is French and mine is Spanish. I suggest that we communicate primarily in English, since we are both at a disadvantage in English."

"Sounds fair to me," replied Felicite – "English it is."

Bernardo's carriage drove west toward the Mississippi River. Once they reached the river they drove along the River Road. On the left were homes on large lots, with many tall oak trees. On the right was a 25-foot-high levy to prevent flooding. You could not see the river from the road. "Bernardo, where are you taking me? With the huge levy between the river and the road, the scenery on this road is uninviting."

"Just a few minutes more," he replied. "We are almost there."

The road began to rise, and the levy seemed to diminish. There was a sharp bend in the river. The land in between had been thrust upward over a million years ago. When the carriage reached its destination atop the rise, the river was 50 feet beneath them, and they could see over the woods for miles. The entire uplift was shaded by towering oaks.

"Oh, Bernardo, this is a perfect spot. We have a beautiful view. It's shady and there is a cool breeze. But I thought you asked me to lunch. Where are we going to eat," she asked with an impish grin on her beautiful face."

"Sam, show the lady what's for lunch."

Sam jumped down from the carriage and started unpacking baskets and packages. First, he unfolded and laid out a blanket for the couple to sit on as they ate. Then the napkins and tableware. Next came three bottles of champagne. As appetizers his cook had prepared stuffed deviled eggs, celery stuffed with pimento cheese, and peeled shrimp with hot sauce. The entrees were sugar cured ham and sliced chicken breast with home-made buttermilk biscuits.

"Bernardo, I must stop seeing you," she teased. You will make me fat. How and I supposed to eat all this," she asked.

"Here, my lady. Have another cup of champagne. Enjoy the sun upon your lovely face, the gentle breeze in your hair and be happy. You have yet to see the crème de la crème. Let's take a break from food and talk. I want to know everything about you."

For the next hour or so the couple talked about themselves and asked questions. Bernardo discovered that Felicite had been married before to the former treasurer of Louisiana, when it had been under French control. He had been killed in a sailing accident. Felicite had been raised in Caen, Normandy, France and attended a private girls' school in Paris. She had been in Louisiana for 2 ½ years and was unsure if she was willing to live surrounded by a wilderness. As they spoke, each of them peered into

96

the eyes of the other. Each periodically touched the other. By 3:00 p.m. it was overcast.

"And now Sam, bring out the *piece de resistance,* Maggie's home-made bread pudding with whipped cream with a pot of chicory coffee. The couple devoured this delicious dessert, with little conversation between bites.

"Bernardo, I am going to say it again. "You are bad for my waistline," as she clamped her two hands on her stomach.

"Felicite, irrespective of your waistline, I want to see you again. At the Change of Command Ceremony in town on January 1, 1777, when I am formally installed as Governor General of Louisiana, I want you at my side. Will you please be my escort," asked Bernardo?"

"Yes, my dear, but must I wait a whole week to see you," she inquired.

"Felicite, I am so sorry. As much as I would like to spend the time with you, my duties require me to stay in town. There is much to be done in preparation for the ceremony. The ceremony begins at 1:00 p.m. I will send a coach for you at 12:30. You will be seated with me on the dais a few minutes before.

"Bernardo, are you trying to whisk me off my feet? I like you and have enjoyed your company last night and today. I think we both recognize that not only are we compatible, but also that there is a spark which might be kindled leading to us being together. Yes, I want to see you again too. Before anything gets serious between us, I must speak to my father and obtain his permission to see you. If he approves, I will send you a note."

While Sam cleaned up the picnic site and loaded the carriage, the couple walked along the escarpment looking down at the muddy river. I was inevitable. Felicite looked up at Bernardo. She placed her left hand behind his head, stood on her tip toes and kissed Bernardo. It was a long, passionate kiss. Bernardo was hooked!

CHAPTER 33

Washington Crosses the Delaware Trenton, N.J.
December 25, 1776

George Washington's Continental Army has been chased from Brooklyn to Manhattan to West Point and northern New York State. He has eluded the British Army and settled his army into winter quarters at Valley Forge, Pennsylvania.

On a bitterly cold Christmas night his army of 2,400 men quietly crossed the ice filled Delaware River and marched through knee deep snow to Trenton, New Jersey, which was occupied by Hessian soldiers under contract with the English. All night the men were exposed to freezing rain, sleet and snow. They were all drenched. Many of the Americans were in summer weight uniforms. Others had no shoes and were forced to wrap rags around their feet. All of them were freezing.

Many of the drunken Germans were still celebrating Christmas, while other lay passed out on their bunks. In Europe, the day after Christmas is also a holiday. The men on guard duty slept through the noise of four cannon being placed at strategic places around town. "The Germans were aroused from their holiday stupor and came out the door of their barracks.

A few tried to prepare a cannon to fire on the Americans, but one of the American's cannon barked and the German field piece was destroyed. Other cannons would not work because the flintlocks were wet. After a short battle of muskets and bayonets, the Germans surrendered.

99

This was General George Washington's first victory of
the American Revolutionary War.

CHAPTER 34

Change of Command Ceremonies

New Orleans, Louisiana

January 1, 1777

There was a slight chill in the air on this gorgeous warm winter afternoon. The smell of lilac was in the air. Scattered clouds offered some refuge from the sun.

On the dais were the incoming Governor General of Louisiana, Bernardo de Galvez, with his escort Mademoiselle Felicite Saint-Maxent; the outgoing Governor General Unzaga, and his wife Sarah; Father Joseph the priest from the local church, Captain Felipe Miralez, and Robert Morris, who had agreed to serve as Master of ceremonies. The leaders of the community and their wives and escorts sat in chairs on either side of the dais. Servants passed drinks and snacks to the audience, as the band played a medley of military tunes. Those attending were in a festive mood and enjoyed socializing. Several guests suffered from hangovers due to too much partying the night before.

In front of the podium some 50 yards away stood the military garrison in formation. At the head of the formation was the acting Company Executive Officer and the staff. Behind them stood four platoons, the band and a color guard.

At 1:00 p.m. Mr. Morris banged his gavel on the podium and called the group to attention. "Father Joseph will lead us in a prayer to open the ceremonies." A pair of sea gulls overhead playfully cawed back and forth as the crowd stood up for the prayer.

"Next, I call upon Captain Miralez to review his troops.

"Parade the troops," ordered the Captain. With that command the color guard moved into position in front of the staff. The band struck up marching music. The acting executive officer then ordered the staff and color guard to a position in front of Platoon A. The color guard lead the parade past the reviewing stand, carrying the colors of Spain and the flag of the Louisiana Colony. Next was the staff, with their sword salute. Then came Platoon A, with its guidon carrying the platoon banner. The band was small, consisting of a trumpet, trombone, baritone, clarinet, saxophone, cymbal player, snare and bass drummer. It was probably the most unusual band he had ever seen as there was also a mouth harmonica player on the back row.

Following Platoons B, C and D were six mules pulling the six of the garrison's 12 cannon, which arrived with D Platoon.

Once the military units completed the parade, they returned to their respective positions on the parade ground.

"Governor General Unzaga will now share a few words with us," said Mr. Morris.

Governor Unzaga was about 60 years old. He was grossly overweight and balding. There was a slight tremor in his hands. He had come from a Castilian family and there was still a noticeable lisp in his accent. He was dressed immaculately, including his jewel encrusted formal sword.

He spoke for only a few minutes. He thanked all who had supported him as Governor General and spoke of his plans for retirement. Upon the conclusion of his remarks, he ordered the color guard to advance to the dais. When they arrived, he placed them behind himself at the podium.

"Governor General Nominee Galvez, please join me at the podium," requested Unzaga.

Holding a large parchment document in front of him, he stated loudly:

"Attention to orders. His Catholic Majesty, Carlos, III, King of Spain, herewith authorized that Governor General of Louisiana, Louis de Unzaga, has served this nation and this crown with steadfast devotion for in excess of 20 years. Effective on January 1, 1777, he is to be retired on pension, with the heartfelt thanks of the crown. He is to be replaced on January 1, 1777 by Governor General Bernardo de Galvez, with whom I have the utmost confidence. Signed this 12th day of July 1776.

Taking the Louisiana colony flag from the flag bearer Unzaga handed it to Galvez, saying:

"Governor General Galvez, the king has great confidence in you. I have been relieved of my duties and the king has seen fit to appoint you to take over. This flag that I pass to you is symbolic of the trust and confidence that the crown has in you and is emblematic that you now command this colony. I wish you God's speed in all your endeavors."

Galvez took the flag with both hands. He reached down to pick up a corner of the flag and said to the audience: "I kiss the flag of Louisiana and I accept the duties and obligations that go with this position. We share this

103

continent with two warring factions. As you can see, we have been provided with an additional platoon of infantry. Stationed here now also are the transport and two war ships from Havana. You can expect for the foreseeable future that our lives will be interesting."

CHAPTER 35

Aboard the *Como No?*[2]

Le Havre, France

January 15, 1777

Eduardo had selected Lt. Fernando Garcia, a distant cousin from Granada, Spain as his aide.

Fernando had recently graduated from Bernardo's alma mata in Avila, finishing in the top 1/3 of his class. He was fluent in both Spanish and French and understood a little English. He was a huge young man, measuring almost 6 ½ feet tall with a muscular physique. He kept his hair very short and was clean shaven. Fernando played the guitar. He was easy to talk to and made friends easily.

His orderly was Corporal Joel Blanco. He was six inches shorter that Lt. Garcia and outweighed him by about 10 pounds. One might say he was stocky. He had been recommended by the personnel officer in Avila because in his two years in the army, he had never been on report, and had never had a disciplinary problem.

The three of them arrived at the pier by coach. As crewmen began to unload their luggage, they stood on the pier looking at the ship that was to be their home for the next six weeks or so.

"Cpl. Blanco, report to my cabin this evening at 10:00 p.m.," ordered Eduardo.

---

[2] Como No is Spanish for "Why not?"

She sat there looking like a new shiny toy. The keel to the *Como No* was laid in July 1776. She had just returned from her maiden voyage to Philadelphia. She was a Spanish fully rigged three masted galleon. Some sailors called it a square rigger. She was 310 feet long and had a beam of 42 feet. Her draft from the keel to the waterline was 15 feet. Because of pirates and privateers, the owners had armed her with 9 cannon on each side of the main deck and two mortars on the poop deck. For this journey, a squad of Spanish marines had been added to Eduardo's command to protect the ship, its cargo and passengers. The squad of marines were in formation on the pier. Sgt. Roberto Sanchez was the squad leader.

"Sgt. Sanchez reporting with a squad of marines sir."

"Sgt., I am glad to have you aboard. We have two very important passengers on this voyage – Dr. Benjamin Franklin and Mr. Diego Gardoqui. For the duration of this voyage, you will report to Lt. Garcia. Corporal Blanco is my orderly, who reports directly to me. Should you wish to assign any duties to him, you must first clear it with Lt. Garcia. Is that understood? "Sgt., you and your men have been assigned to protect this ship. Anytime we are in port, all your men will be on the deck and in the riggings so that you can quickly respond to any trouble. When in port, there should always be one of your men in the crow's nest. When in port, food will be brought to you, but under no circumstances are you to leave your post when we are in a foreign port.

"Aye, sir. Understood."

"You are dismissed. Get your men settled below." As the marines were boarding the ship, a seaman approached them from the ship.

"Buenos noches, Colonel, *Beinvenidos a el Como No,"* said Alberto Olmeda, the first mate.[3] "We have been advised that you are the king's representative. The crew and I will do everything in our power to ensure that you have a safe and pleasant journey. You and senor Franklin have been given our two deluxe cabins. They are on either side of the captain's cabin. Senor Gardoqui and your aide have been assigned to the cabins next to you and Mr. Franklin. The ship's doctor and I will occupy the other two cabins. The enlisted men will all sleep in the crew's quarters.

Captain Altruda will receive you, Mr. Franklin, Senor Gardoqui and your aide at 8:00 p.m. in his quarters. We sail with the tide at 11:00 p.m.

They descended the short ladder off the quarter deck. In front of them was the captain's quarters. They turned to the right. Eduardo's cabin was to be on the port side of the ship. The first mate opened the door and placed Eduardo's sea bag on a chair.

"This 'il be your quarters, sir". The young lieutenant will be berthing next to you and Senor Gardoqui will be across the way next to Mr. Franklin. Will there be anything else," he asked, as he handed the cabin key to Eduardo.

"No, thank you very much," he replied as the mate shut the cabin door. Eduardo's "De Luxe" cabin was only slightly larger than a typical jail cell. Above his bunk was a port hole. At least it could be opened for fresh air. The small closet had two drawers at the bottom. Against the wall was a small writing desk with a straight back chair. Above the desk was a bookshelf about three feet long. On

---

[3] From this point all conversation in Spanish will be translated into English.

the desk was a candle, a pewter drinking cup, a towel, wash cloth, and a bar of soap. In the corner was a small table on top of which was a ceramic pitcher of water, which sat in a ceramic bowl. A full length mirrow had been attached to the back of the door to his cabin and two paintings of ships adorned the walls.

Dr. Franklin had not yet arrived, and Eduardo was exhausted from his journey. His dinner appointment with the captain was over two hours away, so he decided to rest. He could unpack and put away his things after dinner. Although he looked forward to meeting the famous Dr. Franklin, the thought of having to interpret every word said by or to Dr. Franklin was abhorrent to him. He took his flask from his carry bag and took a long drink of brandy. He was almost asleep by the time his head sank into the pillow. His mental clock awoke him at 7: 30 p.m. He quickly dressed and combed his hair. He walked across to Dr. Franklin's room only to find it empty. Where could he be? He found the first mate on the quarterdeck, but he had no information about Dr. Franklin. As Eduardo stood in front of Dr. Franklin's cabin door, Lt. Garcia and Senor Gardoqui were both exiting their cabins at the same time. Introductions were made, and the three men chatted for a few minutes. At 8:00 p.m. he knocked on the door of the Captain's Cabin and was immediately invited in. "Good evening, Captain Altruda. I am Colonel Eduardo Lopez, and this is my aide, Lt. Fernando Garcia and your other passenger is Senor Diego Gardoqui of Balboa, the owner of this ship.

"Colonel, I had been informed that you, Dr. Franklin and Senor Gardoqui will be joining us on this transport. Is there something I should know?"

"Yes, Captain. This letter will explain it to you," replied Bernardo, as he passed a parchment note to the captain.

It read:

'The Castle of Asturias

Residence of His Catholic Majesty

HRM Carlos de Borbon, III

Catholic King of Spain

January 6, 1777

To Whom it may concern:

Colonel Eduardo Lopez is my personal representative. All Spanish citizens are to treat any request from him as if that request came directly from me.

S/Carlos de Borbon, III
Catholic King of Spain

(Royal Seal)

"Colonel, this ship, my crew and I are at your disposal. Please be seated and let us have dinner. Do you know when Dr. Franklin is due to arrive? We don't want to miss the tide," said the captain.

After dinner Eduardo, Senor Gardoqui, and Lt. Garcia went on deck to walk off their meal. The cook had prepared a beef roast with potatoes, onions, carrots and peppers. For dessert they all enjoyed the blackberry cobbler.

Promptly at 10:00 Cpl. Blanco knocked on Eduardo's cabin door.

"Enter," responded Eduardo. "Stand at ease. Corporal, you have come highly recommended to me. You will handle laundry for both Mr. Garcia and I, and keep our boots shined.

When Sgt. Mendez' men exercise, you are to exercise with them. Here are three books for you to read.

When I am not in my cabin, you may use it to read. "Do you have any hobbies," asked Eduardo? "I like to fish sir – and I also do a little wood carving, but I'm not so good yet," replied Cpl. Blanco.

"Corporal, you will report to Lt. Garcia each morning after breakfast and again each evening after dinner.

It was 10:30 p.m. Clouds raced over the full moon. The crew was unfurling the sails and making ready for departure in about one-half hour. All cargo had been loaded and two carpenters were nailing down the cargo hatches. The noise of horse's hooves on cobblestones announced the arrival of a coach. As it approached the ship, Eduardo could see that the horses were all frothing at the mouth. They had been running hard for a long time. When the coach stopped near the gangway, the footman jumped off the back of the coach and started unloading Dr. Franklin's luggage. The first mate ran down the gangway to meet Dr. Franklin and grab his luggage. Dr. Franklin was gathering his hat, overcoat and cane and paying the driver. Mr Franklin followed the first mate up the gangway, where Eduardo was waiting.

"I'll stow your luggage in your cabin Dr. Franklin. Colonel Lopez can direct you to it," said the first mate in broken English.

"Good evening, Dr. Franklin. I am Colonel Eduardo Lopez, and it will be my pleasure to be your interpreter and *aide de camp* for this journey. Allow me to introduce you to Senor Diego Gardoqui of Gardoqui and sons of Bilbao, Spain – the company that has already delivered military supplies to you Americans. This is my aide, Lt. Fernando Garcia. Lt Garcia and I are here to assist you on this voyage in any way. I will serve as your interpreter. The ship's officers speak only Spanish and French. Senior Gardoqui, Lt. Garcia, and I are the only other English speakers for the voyage, besides yourself.

"Good evening, Colonel. I imagine there are dozens of other places you would prefer to be rather than taking care of an old man."

"Dr. Franklin, I am here at the request of his Royal Catholic Majesty, the king of Spain. I am deeply honored that my king has sought to rely upon me. I have also read a lot about you and look forward to getting to learn more about you. I look forward to telling my grandchildren about this trip."

As Eduardo directed Dr. Franklin to his cabin he said "We dined at 8:00 p.m. If you are hungry,

I can get you something to eat from the galley. We are scheduled to sail in about 10 minutes." "Why don't we get to know one another over a pitcher or two of beer? Meet me in my cabin in 20 minutes," said Dr. Franklin, as he closed his cabin door.

"Single up all lines," ordered the first mate.

"Let go forward," he shouted.

"Let go aft," he continued.

"Let go amidship."

The first mate turned to the captain and said, "The ship is ready for sea Captain."

111

"Very well Mr. Olmeda, take her out," said the captain. The ship entered the English Channel and sailed southwest.

After getting settled in his cabin, Eduardo began writing in his journal. Since leaving home to go to school in Switzerland, he had been keeping a journal. Every day he would include the date, place, weather and anything important that happened. If he was aboard a ship he would include the name of the ship, its home port, present position, speed, course, ports of embarkation and disembarkation, names and ranks of officers, names of hotels, inns, pubs, restaurants, food and entertainment. At each port he would discuss wares for sale, describe the beaches and mention sights to see.

CHAPTER 36

Aboard the *Como No*

North Atlantic Ocean

January 23, 1777

Dr. Franklin was dressed and standing in front of his cabin in the foyer when Eduardo opened his cabin door.

"Good morning, Dr. Franklin, I hope you slept well," greeted Eduardo.

"Nothing like a few beers to make a man sleep well, is there," responded Franklin?

The steward had knocked on their doors a few minutes before informing them that breakfast was ready to be served in the captain's quarters. Already at the table were the Captain, and two men, speaking in Spanish. Just as they were about to take their seats, Senor Gardoqui and Lt. Garcia entered.

"Eduardo told the captain that it was an honor to be a passenger on such a fine new ship. Such a ship must have been assigned to one of Spain's finest captains." The last remark put a smile on the captain's face. He then introduced Dr. Franklin, advising the captain that Dr. Franklin did not speak Spanish and only a tiny bit of French. He apologized to the captain that Dr. Franklin, Senor Gardoqui and himself would be speaking in English. "I will be glad to pass on anything you wish to say to Dr. Franklin," said Eduardo. "Dr. Franklin, King Carlos wanted you to meet directly with Senor Gardoqui. He is a partner in the Bilbao, Spain firm that has been supplying the Americans with arms. Because the Gardoqui firm erroneously sent you red uniforms which your troops could not use, he wanted the two of you to iron out any problems so that the operation would run smoothly. The king wants the Americans to know that he is behind you 100%." Eduardo had made some notes in his journal about some of Dr. Franklin's sayings.

CHAPTER 37

Aboard the *Como No*

Franklin and Gardoqui plan deliveries

Jan. 30, 1777

The *Como No* had made good progress and the seas had been favorable. So far, they had avoided the harsh winter storms that are known in the North Atlantic during this time of year. The passengers had fallen into a daily routine. After breakfast they would take a stroll around the deck wearing their coats and gloves. After time on deck, they would return to their cabins to read, write letters or other personal matters. Dr. Franklin each day at noon made several observations about the temperature, wind, etc. The three men spent their afternoons working out details. Lt. Garcia acted as secretary for the group, taking notes of decisions made.

The captain had graciously allowed Eduardo, Dr. Franklin and Senor Gardoqui to use his cabin for their afternoon discussions. Their talks centered on the type and number of each weapon required for each port of delivery. It was agreed that Senor Gardoqui's ships would make deliveries to Boston, New York, Philadelphia, Baltimore, Beaufort, N.C., and Charleston. Getting military goods to patriots in the back country was a problem.

After dinner on the second night at sea, Eduardo asked the captain if he would like Lt. Garcia to entertain them with his guitar. With a big grin on his face he said, "Colonel, what is the name of this ship? *Si, como no.*" Lt Garcia started with a few flamingo songs, and then played

115

several ballads, to which he added his voice in song. His music uplifted all present and his entertainment became a nightly performance.

Eduardo suggested they consider sending goods for the back country to New Orleans, then ship them up the Mississippi River to the Ohio, then up the Ohio River to Fort Nelson[4] and Fort Pitt. Gardoqui warned that if his ships were to be making runs to New Orleans it would add two weeks each way, which would slow down deliveries to the east coast. He asked permission to arrange for the Gardoqui goods to be transferred to an American ship for the transit from the east coast to New Orleans, which was agreed upon.

Assuring payment to Gardoqui was a major concern. After two weeks, the orders for each port and method of payment were agreed upon.

Franklin was concerned that if a Spanish ship landed at an American city that had been overrun by the British, that the entire cargo would be lost. Discussions about safeguards occupied all of two days. They celebrated the end of four weeks of the voyage by executing the following:

MEMORANDUM OF UNDERSTANDING BETWEEN THE AMERICAN COMMITTEE OF SAFETY

AND JOSEPH GARDOQUI AND SONS

Feb. 21, 1777

This agreement made and entered into on this the 21st day of February in the year of our Lord 1777 is designed to cover the agreement between the American Committee of

---

[4] Present day Louisville, KY

*Safety (hereinafter sometimes referred to as "Committee"
or "The Committee" and Joseph Gardoqui and Sons of
Bilbao, Spain (hereinafter sometimes referred to as
"Gardoqui") concerning the provisioning of military
goods to North America. This agreement is entered into
upon the high seas and is to be interpreted under the laws
of Spain.*

1. *Gardoqui agrees to accept orders for weapons and
materials from the Committee; to fulfill those orders as
expeditiously as possible; and to ship them on one of its
ships or a ship leased to it to one of the following ports:*

a. *Boston, Massachusetts*

b. *New York, New York*

c. *Philadelphia, Pennsylvania*

d. *Baltimore, Maryland*

e. *Beaufort, North Carolina*

f. *Charlestown, South Carolina.*

2. *Gardoqui presently has six cargo ships at its disposal.
It hopes to be able to fill orders within two weeks of
receipt and to send a ship to one of the American ports
every two weeks.*

3. *Gardoqui agrees to contract with an independent
shipping company to make deliveries to New Orleans,
Louisiana from east coast ports.*

4. *For each order, the Committee will provide the
following:*

a. *Name of Committee contact person for each port,*

b. *Name of back-up Committee contact person for each
port,*

c. *Password for Gardoqui to use at each port,*

d. *Countersign for Committee members to repeat to Gardoqui at each port.*

e. *Location of alternative port and contact person*

5. *To guard against loss by theft, Gardoqui agrees that once it has acquired the goods ordered it will have those goods guarded 24 hours each day until loaded upon the transport vessel.*

6. *From the time the goods leave Gardoqui's warehouse, it will provide an associate to accompany the goods until delivered in America. This associate will ensure that all the goods are loaded and that none are unloaded at a port before arriving in America.*

7. *To conceal the true identity of the military goods being transported, muskets will be labeled as "tools"; gunpowder will be labeled as "lead;" uniforms will be labeled as "men's clothing" and other items will be labeled with innocent nomenclature.*

8. *Gardoqui's crew will be informed that stiff prison sentences will be meted out for discussing their cargo, destination, etc. For security reasons no crew member shall be allowed ashore at any port visited until all goods have been offloaded and transported away from the dock.*

9. *No visitors shall be allowed on the ship before departure, or at any port stop enroute or at the port of delivery until all goods have been transported away from the port.*

10. *To inhibit the opening of the shipping containers by inspectors, Gardoqui will ensure that the goods for the committee are loaded first at the bottom of the hold.*

Upon those crates will be placed a large piece of heavy machinery.

11. Before entering any American port, Gardoqui agrees that it will lay offshore until dark, at which time it will send a small boat ashore to make discreet inquiries to determine if the Americans are in control of the port.

12. If the British control the port, the Captain will host the quarantine flag and proceed to the alternative port.

13. If the Americans control the port the Captain will flashlights twice toward shore. The

Committee representatives will respond with three flashes of light if all is well. The Committee will send representatives to the ship where the Captain will be informed where to dock, etc.

14. If the ship encounters the English, it will attempt to outrun the English ship and proceed to the nearest American port for sanctuary.

15. The Committee agrees to provide security for the ship and dock from the time of the ship's arrival until all Committee goods have been unloaded.

16. To avoid detection and possible confiscation of Gardoqui's ship, the Committee agrees that it will take all possible steps to:

a.   Utilize a dock that is not usually busy and away from prying eyes,

b.   Unload in late afternoon or evening,

c.   Cover all cargo on the dock or in wagons,

d.   Utilize a storage area as close as possible to the dock to avoid the amount of time the cargo is in the public eye, and

e. *Limit the number of Americans who are aware in advance of the arrival of the ship or its cargo.*

17. *To minimize the possibility of discovery, no cargo will be unloaded until the Committee's horses and wagons are on the pier. The goal is to offload directly from the ship to the wagon. Gardoqui will provide tarpaulins to cover the cargo.*

18. *At all times when the ship is in port, whether at the pier or anchored in the harbor, two lookouts will be stationed in the crow's nest.*

19. *Once all goods have been offloaded from the vessel, delivery shall be deemed complete, and the Committee representative shall execute a "Receipt of Goods and Order for Payment" and promptly deliver said receipt and order to the Gardoqui representative.*

20. *Gardoqui will then deliver the "Receipt and Order For Payment" to Monsieur Beaumarchais in Paris for payment.*

21. *Once all deliveries have been made, Gardoqui is free to book passengers and cargo for their return crossing to Europe.*

CHAPTER 38

Aboard the *Como No*

Franklin & Eduardo discuss gulf stream

Feb. 12, 1777

It was just after noon. The sun was out and there was a modest breeze from the south, which brought warmer temperatures. With the wind there were modest seas, with small white caps.

Several dolphins played in the ship's wake. Seeing them was supposedly a good sign. With the wind and waves the ship was pitching, rolling and yawing. Eduardo walked on deck and saw Mr. Franklin making his observations while trying to steady himself by holding onto the railing.

"Well Dr. Franklin, you and senor Gardoqui have concluded all your business. Do you feel that a weight has been lifted off your shoulders," asked Eduardo?

"Colonel, yes, it is nice that this issue has been solved for the moment. In our revolution there are so many other issues. We have been unable to interest the Canadian colony or those of East and West Florida to join us in the revolution. The fort at St. Augustine, Florida would sure be useful."

"I worry that our revolution may fail," he continued. "Last year was horrible, militarily. Our army was forced to retreat from Brooklyn to Manhattan and then to upstate New York with the red coats on their heels all the way. Had the Lord not provided a heavy fog in Brooklyn, our leaders would all be in jail by now. General Washington continued to evade battle until Christmas. His army crossed the frozen Delaware River and surprised the Hessian soldiers in Trenton with an impressive victory. Even so, I am afraid that our army and our citizen soldiers may not be strong enough to eject the English from North America. The support we are receiving from Spain and France may just be what we need to route the redcoats."

"You're sure doing your part to provide your army with the tools it needs to fight," responded Eduardo.

"I need to spend more time on my personal business," replied Dr. Franklin. I have been away so long. I can't expect the business to run itself. Before the war, I went into partnership with print shops in Beaufort, N.C., Charlestown, S.C. and on two islands in the Caribbean. Yet, when we arrive in Philadelphia, I must meet with the Committee of Safety and report our progress. My wife complains that she feels like a widow because I am away so much of the time."

"Dr. Franklin, may I ask you why you take these measurements every day," asked Eduardo.

"All my life I have been interested in what was going on around me and how things like temperature, humidity, etc. affect our daily lives, and what improvements can be made to the things we use to make them better. Let me give you an example. As a printer, I read many hours each day. As an old man, I need magnifying glasses to read as my glasses are for distant vision. I invented bifocal glasses with magnification limited to the bottom half of the lens with the top half for distant vision.

"Sometimes, you discover something that wasn't in your sights when you start an inquiry. This is my 7th crossing of the Atlantic between American and Europe. On each voyage at noon, I make my observations. I do it at noon because it is at noon each day when the Captain makes an entry into the ships log of our latitude and longitude. I record the time, ambient temperature, temperature of the water, humidity, barometric pressure, wind speed and direction, and ship's current speed and direction. I also note any discoloration of the water and any flotsam or

Sargasso weed present."

"In 1775 I notified the English Admiralty that I had discovered a huge Gulf Stream that crossed the Atlantic. The stream is highly visibly because of its muddy consistency. I informed them that this current traveled at about four to five knots[5]. In my written report to them I suggested very strongly that when transiting from Europe to America they should avoid the current against them, and when traveling in the opposite direction they should utilize the current to add four to five knots to their speed. They thanked me and filed my report. It doesn't appear that they have informed the English fleet about the Gulf Stream, but our captains use it daily. I gave a chart of the Gulf Stream to Senor Gardoqui on the evening of our departure. He told me that he had provided it to the Captain. Once we reach Philadelphia, I will provide him with chart copies for all his captains. We appear to be making excellent time."

As Dr. Franklin walked away, Eduardo noticed that Lt. Garcia was sitting on deck writing. He approached him and inquired "What are you so diligently writing, Fernando?"

---

[5] nautical miles per hour equals about 1 1/8 miles per hour.

"Sir, I have been keeping a daily journal of our passage. I make note of the weather, sea state, activities on the ship, any injuries or sickness, discipline meted out and the daily discussions with Dr. Franklin."

"May I see it, please?"

After only a few minutes, he said: "Fernando, this is fantastic. I am so glad you took it upon yourself to create this journal. I have been so busy with Dr. Franklin that I didn't even think about my report to headquarters about this voyage. Would it be possible for you to make a duplicate copy of your journal, which we could label "Official Report," he asked?

"Sure, Colonel, I would be glad to prepare a duplicate. And I'll make entries in both journals for the duration."

"In my stored luggage there are several blank journals which I was going to deliver to General Galvez. If you follow me, I will give you the blank journal now.

That evening before dinner in the captain's cabin, Eduardo rose. In English he said:

"Gentlemen, I wish to propose a toast. My aide Lt. Fernando Garcia has been extremely diligent on this voyage. He has acted as secretary of the important meetings between Dr. Franklin and me for more than a month. He has written drafts of our progress all along the way, and he has maintained a daily log of our voyage. Please join me in toasting Captain Fernando Garcia, who is just now discovering that he has been promoted." He raised his cup and shouted "Here, Here!"

For the ship's captain, first mate and doctor, he repeated the same toast in Spanish.

"Captain Garcia, you are out of uniform. I will be my honor to place upon your shoulders the insignia of a Captain. Congratulations."

CHAPTER 39

Philadelphia, PA

Franklin introduces Eduardo to Philadelphia
gentry/Committee of Safety Mar. 2, 1777

The Captain docked the ship at an isolated pier across the
Delaware River from the Philadelphia dock. All four
passengers were lined up along the railing observing the
docking procedures. The marines rushed to their assigned
positions topside.

"It appears that our committee members have kept a keen
lookout," said Dr. Franklin. They have sent a coach for
me and wagons for the cargo. I understand that you
gentlemen will stay onboard and supervise the unloading.
Colonel, please ask the captain how long the ship will
remain in port. Tomorrow, I will send a coach to the pier
to pick you up and drive you to a lovely inn near my
home. Tomorrow evening you two will be the guests of
honor at a very secret reception. We must be careful.
The British have spies around every corner. Our party
will be held at the Philadelphia Masonic Temple, out of
sight and hearing of their spies."

It was just after 2:00 a.m. the following morning when the
last wagon of supplies left the pier. With the Captain's
blessing Senor Gardoqui gave the crew and the marines
enough beer for every man to get drunk. He also told
them that tomorrow was a day of rest. Except for the
cooks, nobody had to work.

As promised, the following morning a coach appeared
with a jolly Dr. Franklin. He had spent time with his wife

and had been updated on the news of both his family and the war. As they rode to the inn, Dr. Franklin updated Eduardo and Senor Gardoqui on the status of the war. There was little to report.

After getting checked in and getting their luggage to their respective rooms, the four men went into the pub that was connected to the inn. Corporal Blanco was instructed to remain on the ship.

"Never too early for a beer," said Dr. Franklin," as they toasted the revolution. Eduardo informed the group that the ship captain was expecting several days delay before returning to

Bilbao. "When the square sail on first mast blew out during that storm we encountered, it damaged some of the rigging. They are already working on it, but they also have cargo and passengers to load. He said to check back in three days," said Eduardo. "That gives Senor Gardoqui, Capt. Garcia, and I some time to sightsee in your famous city, Dr. Franklin," said Eduardo.

"Gentlemen, my carriage will pick you up promptly at 7:00 p.m. You have a pleasant evening in store for yourselves," said Mr. Franklin, as he used his cane to get up from the pub chair. As he exited the pub, he touched the handle of his cane to his hat, bidding them farewell.

St. John's Lodge of the Free and Accepted Masons was located downtown Philadelphia at 1

North Broad Street. It was an imposing three story building. At the second-floor level was a Masonic emblem that was at least three feet high and about the same width. As they entered the reception hall, a 20-piece string orchestra was playing softly.

127

"This is a very impressive venue," Dr. Franklin. "How in the world did you get this private organization to allow you to have this function in their building," asked Eduardo?

"Sometimes, it's not what you know, but who you know. You see, I served as Grand Master of this lodge of Masons in 1734. While I was living in London, I served as Grand Master of the Grand Lodge of England in 1760. Do either of you know anything about the Masons," asked Dr. Franklin?

"I believe that when the Knights Templar were attacked by King Philip "The Fair" in 1307 one group of them migrated to Scotland, where they converted to the Masonic order," responded Eduardo.

"That's what I thought too," added Senor Gardoqui. As good aides do, Captain Garcia remained quiet.

"You young men are very knowledgeable. Where did you learn of the connection between the Templars and the Masons," inquired Dr. Franklin?

"We are both graduates of the Switzerland Institute for Young Men in Geneva, Switzerland, sir. I might add that King Carlos is also an alumnus of that school. It was founded in 1307. For all these centuries, the headmaster has always been a Templar. One of my ancestors was a founder and served as its second headmaster. What do you know about the Templars, Dr, Franklin, Eduardo asked?

"When I was serving as Grand Master of the Grand Lodge of England, in 1760, I made a trip to Edinburg, Scotland. My main reason for the trip was to meet with scientists and men of learning. At that time, I was an active member of "Men of Enlightenment." There were a large number of geniuses in Edinburgh. While I was in Edinburg, one afternoon I took a coach to visit Rosslyn Chapel. I spent several hours there. It appears that the Templar who became the founder of the Masonic Order was Lord Sinclair. His sarcophagus was in the church. It was amazing to see Templar icons and Masonic icons both emblazoned upon it. This chapel was a short walk away from Lord Sinclair's castle. He had donated the land and paid to have the chapel built. The chapel walls, columns and doors also contained several markings of both Templars and Masons.

"The evidence was strong that there was a connection between the two organizations. I came away with a bigger question. Above the entrance to the chapel is carved an ear of corn," finished Dr. Franklin. "The chapel was started in 1446. At that time there was no corn in Europe. Europeans did not see corn until after they started to colonize North America. What this tells me is that Templars were in North America many years before Columbus."

Gently guiding Eduardo and Senor Gardoqui, Dr. Franklin said, "it's now time for the receiving line." Dr. Franklin stood first in line so he could introduce the local gentry to their guests. Lt Garcia stood to the right of Senor Gardoqui.

"Let me present the Honorable William Bradford. He is both an esteemed lawyer and a learned judge. Judge Bradford, it is my pleasure to present to you, Colonel Eduardo Lopez, a personal representative of His Royal Majesty, Carlos, III de Borbon, King of Spain; and Senor Diego Gardoqui, a partner in the firm of Joseph Gardoqui and Sons of Bilbao, Spain; and Capt. Fernando Garcia,

129

aide to Colonel Lopez. They are providing supplies to our patriots.

"Colonel, please inform his majesty of our appreciation for his assistance," said Mr Bradford. Senor Gardoqui, thank you and your company for working to supply us. Lieutenant, it is a pleasure to meet you. I hope you remain safe," said Mr. Bradford.

The reception line moved slowly. Each guest had a question or two or perhaps just wanted to make conversation. Among the other dignitaries with whom he chatted were:

John Dickenson, known as the "Penman of the Revolution" because he sent 12 letters from farmers in 1767-1768. He was a member of both the 1st and 2nd Continental Congress.

Thomas Mifflin, the first governor of Pennsylvania.

Robert Morris, who signed the Declaration of Independence, The Articles of Confederation and the Constitution. He was known as the "Financier of the Revolution." Mr. Morris was seated with Dr. Benjamin Rush, a signer of the Declaration of Independence.

Oliver Pollock. In early 1777, Governor Galvez appointed Oliver Pollock "commercial agent" of the United States for New Orleans. The two chatted amiably for a few minutes.

Both Eduardo and Senor Gardoqui were at ease with this distinguished gathering. There were about 50 in attendance. Each hand was shaken and a short conversation with each was conducted. Many of the wives asked questions.

When the reception line was concluded Dr. Franklin took the podium. "Distinguished guests, please charge your cups for a toast. Waiters throughout the gathering filled the champagne cups.

"My illustrious friends, please join me in a toast to our two distinguished guests," toasted Dr. Franklin. With his toast the orchestra did a string version of ruffles and flourishes to honor their guests.

"As is customary, I am now going to call on our guests one by one to bring greetings – Colonel Lopez, why don't you regale us first," inquired Dr. Franklin.

"Ladies and gentlemen, I am tremendously honored that you have organized this fabulous reception for Senor Gardoqui and myself. It was indeed an honor to travel with your Dr. Franklin by ship from Europe. He is indeed a very interesting and brilliant man. I am deeply impressed with the stature of all the guests in this room. I am looking at the future leadership of the new American nation. I am here as a personal representative of King Carlos of Spain. He asked me to assure you that Spain is your ally, and that he will do everything reasonably possible to ensure that you defeat the English. There is no love lost between Spain and England. Over the past 600 years we have been at war with each other for over 400 of those years. They are our natural enemies. In a few days I will depart Philadelphia on a journey to New Orleans, where I have been named by King Carlos as the Aide de Camp to General Bernardo de Galvez, Governor General of Louisiana. To provide weapons and supplies to the Americans living in the back country, we will be sending them up the Mississippi and Ohio Rivers to Virginia[6] and

---

[6] Ft. Nelson was in what is now Louisville, Kentucky. At the time in

131

Ft. Pitt. Thank you for all your courtesies, he said as he turned to take his seat on the dais. The audience all stood and applauded.

Senor Gardoqui took the podium. "My elegant friends – and I call you elegant as I look at the lovely women, adorned with beautiful jewelry, and the gentlemen, all dressed to the T. I am truly thankful for the honor you have bestowed upon me by including me with Colonel Lopez as an honoree. On our voyage Dr. Franklin and I, with the assistance of Colonel Lopez, arrived at an agreement that will safeguard the supplies that my firm is supplying to you, and speed up deliveries. Did you know that on May 1, 1776, my King Carlos and King Louis LVI each donated 1,000,000 Livres to assist your revolution? Or, that they agreed to spend more as needed? Did you know that on September 1, 1776, shipments of supplies from my firm arrived here in Philadelphia and in New Orleans? Ladies and gentlemen, those supplies departed Bilbao, Spain weeks before your Declaration of Independence was signed. We are honored to have served the Borbon family in Spain for over 200 years. King Carlos has instructed us to do everything within our power to assist you. My presence here tonight is evidence of our intent to support you until the end of your revolution. My ship will not depart for at least three days. Should any of you have matters you would like to discuss with me I will be staying at the Bull and Bear Inn. Thank you for a wonderful evening, which I shall never forget. Thank you."

question, Louisville was located in Kentucky County, Virginia.

CHAPTER 40

Pub at the Bull and Bear Inn

Philadelphia, Pennsylvania

March 7, 1777

The pub was dark from the lack of windows and from the dark mahogany walls. The smell of spilled beer was strong, but not as irritating as the smoke from pipes and cigars. Eduardo and Senor Gardoqui had met for a farewell beer. Each of them was much better dressed than any of the other patrons in the pub.

"Eduardo, my ship sails this afternoon. You will be pleased to know that I have successfully negotiated an agreement for shipment of our goods from the American east coast to New Orleans. This shipping company has also been approved to carry mail and passengers on behalf of the crown. Should you need to make a shipment to Havana or Vera Cruz, he will deliver it for you. I arranged a booking for you, your aide and your orderly on the *Sharnbrook*, a three master, which departs Philadelphia the day after tomorrow. Our cargo is being transferred to the *Sharnbrook* as we speak. Your voyage could be about a month long. It depends on how many stops the captain makes. He covers all the major ports on the coast. The captain was named Christopher Butler. He owns a fleet of eight transport ships which mainly ply the east coast from Boston to Charleston. He has had trouble with pirates for years, so your transport ship will be heavily armed," concluded Senor Gardoqui.

"Diego, it has been great traveling with you. We have so much in common. We are both graduates of the Switzerland Institute for Young Men. I have enjoyed our chats and working together. I hope we have the opportunity to be together in the future. I'll be in New Orleans for the foreseeable future. I hope you have fair winds, smooth sailing and following seas."

"I too have enjoyed our comradery, Eduardo. I wish you well in New Orleans. If you are ever in the north of Spain, please contact me. He stood and walked to the door. As he opened the door, he turned and said, "*Adios amigo – Vaya Con Dios*", turned and left.

That afternoon Eduardo visited a bookstore, where he purchased three books, stationary, envelopes, postage stamps, pen, ink, salt, newspapers from Philadelphia, New York, Baltimore and Charleston, and a box of dominos. The headlines of the Charleston, S.C. newspaper told of the British Attack on Charleston Harbor on Feb. 13 and how the Americans won a decisive victory. Eduardo thought to himself that it was strange that so far in 1777 there had been little military activity in the colonies for a war that was supposedly raging. As a matter of courtesy, Eduardo always passed his newspapers on to Fernando and then to the captain.

At a confectionary shop a few doors down the street, he purchased a small chocolate cake, cookies, hard candy, caramel chews and jellybeans. He had a serious sweet tooth, and these sweets would take out some of the pain of traveling.

Dr. Franklin had recommended that he have dinner at the City Tavern, the best restaurant in town. He took Capt. Garcia with him. They both ordered the house specialty, prime rib of beef with potatoes and carrots and peach cobbler for dessert. The food was great, as was the service, but Eduardo was uncomfortable sitting on a bench rather than a chair with a comfortable back.

As they walked back to their inn, they agreed to go sightseeing on their last day in Philadelphia.

After a nightcap in the pub, Eduardo went upstairs and wrote a long letter to his parents.

After breakfast the following morning, Eduardo placed his letter in the mailbox. He and Capt. Garcia hired a carriage to take them to Independence Hall. There they explored the interior of the building and viewed a copy of the Declaration of Independence. Just outside the front entrance to Independence Hall was the famous Liberty Bell. At a nearby tea shop, they stopped for coffee and pastries. They visited several art galleries and shops. After eating too much for lunch at a downtown pub, they strolled down the waterfront to view the ships in port.

"Fernando, it's about time to head back to the inn and pack for our journey tomorrow. Please ensure that Sgt. Blanco will be ready to embark tomorrow after breakfast.

Captain Butler, upon agreeing to take cargo to Spanish speaking New Orleans went to the same bookstore and purchased two books: *English – Spanish Dictionary*, and a *Spanish Primer*. He wanted to be able to ask for a beer, ask for directions to the bathroom and to be able to say "please" and "thank you."

It was past midnight when Eduardo finished updating his journal and blew out the candle.

CHAPTER 41

The *Sharnbrook*

Philadelphia, PA

March 9, 1777

A coach dropped Colonel Lopez and his entourage and their luggage near the gangway of the *Sharnbrook*. It was a handsome three masted schooner. Captain Butler was on the deck and saw them arrive. He walked down the gang plank.

"Good afternoon gentlemen. I'd expect that you are my passengers to New Orleans," queried Captain Butler? Captain Butler was six feet tall and was a large man. He had a full head of brown hair. His face was weathered and wrinkled for a man of about 35 years of age, due to his life at sea. His suit was neatly pressed and clean. As he greeted his new passengers, he sprouted a wide smile.

"That we are captain. I am Colonel Eduardo Lopez. This is my aide, Capt. Fernando Garcia, who will regale you with his guitar during our voyage, and my orderly, Sgt. Joel Blanco. Are you ready for us to board?

"First, "he shouted to the first mate on deck. Get some hands down here to collect this luggage." He led the group up the gangway. "Colonel, you and the Captain will have the two staterooms near my cabin. Your orderly will be assigned a rack in the crew's quarters."

Captain Butler led them to their quarters. 'Gentlemen, if you will excuse me, I have some matters which require me on deck. We are scheduled to shove off with the tide at 4:00 p.m. Please join me in my cabin for drinks before dinner at 6:00 p.m. This gives you plenty of time to unpack and get settled in your cabin. If you want, you have time for lunch ashore. If not, you are welcome to join me at 1:00 p.m. for lunch onboard." The captain turned and went up the steps to the main deck.

Eduardo examined his cabin and thought to himself that his new jail cell was not as spacious as his home for the past six weeks. It was almost the same size but had no paintings on the wall. Fortunately, he still rated a porthole. Just then, a seaman delivered his luggage. He was finished unpacking by departure time, so he went on deck to watch them leave port. An hour after departure they were still in the Delaware River heading towards the open ocean. He rested until time for cocktails.

At 5:55 p.m. his aide tapped on his door. "Just wanted to make sure you were ready sir. Did you get to rest," asked Fernando?

"Yes, Fernando, and now I am ready for some nectar of the Gods," said Eduardo as he tapped on Captain Butler's cabin door.

"Come in," shouted Captain Butler, "the door is open." They entered a captain's cabin that was much more spacious than on the *Como No*. To the left of the entrance was a desk against the wall. His enclosed bunk was on the starboard side. On the port side was an overstuffed chair and ottoman. The entire stern was covered in windows, under which were bench seats. The huge table dominated the center of the room. There were 8 chairs around the table. There were only three table settings for dinner and Captain Butler was at the head of the table. The other end of the table was covered with nautical charts, a compass and some notes.

137

"Captain, your cabin is so light with the light-colored wood. What kind of wood did you use," he asked?

"It's North Carolina Birch, which is a hardwood. I had this ship built over 10 years ago. I had found that the typical dark wood used onboard was depressing. If you'll notice, this cabin is substantially larger than you will find on the typical ship. Gentlemen, if you will inform the steward of your poison we can relax. You have a choice of rum, whisky, gin, beer or brandy."

Each of them gave their order to the steward, who poured their drinks and served them. He then served each of them a small bowl of nuts.

"Colonel, since there will be only the three of on this month-long trip, I suggest that we dispense with formalities and use our Christian names. Please call me Christopher. How should I refer to you?"

"Please call me Eduardo and Capt. Garcia's first name is Fernando," responded Eduardo.

For almost two hours, the three men chatted, mostly small talk. Their friendly conversation continued through dinner, after which Fernando got out his guitar and serenaded the captain and colonel while they continued to drink. "Christopher, I purchased this chocolate cake for our dessert. Please be my guest." The steward took the cake, cut off three slices and served them.

Eduardo noticed that Captain Butler had a sizeable library in his cabin including an atlas and the three volume *Encyclopedia Britannica*, published in 1768. Captain Butler said, "I also maintain charts of every port I have entered; for some that would include a map of the island and a map of the harbor. If you will notice on the back of each chart, I have made notations, including:

The name and address of the agent I used.

The cargo I offloaded & the cargo I loaded. The name of Hotel used where I got a hot bath, Other hotels available A description of the port, and the type shops available.

Best things to buy.

A description of the beach.

Current weather conditions.

The name of favorite bars, restaurants, and types of entertainment."

"Captain, I think the thing I admire most about your cabin is the huge floor model world globe," said Eduardo.

"Let me ask you a question," said Eduardo. If you are the owner of 8 ships, how can you be off on a month-long cruise?

"My younger brother, Joseph manages the business from his home in Philadelphia. He dislikes being at sea, and I hate sitting behind a desk and love being at sea. He provides my wife Sara with monthly reports on the shipping business, warehouse profits, and gift shops.

"Steward, please cut another piece of cake, put a fork on the plate and give it to Capt. Garcia," requested Eduardo. "Fernando, please give that cake to Sgt. Blanco with my compliments when he reports to you tonight."

After dinner Eduardo went on deck. The Spring cool air on his face felt refreshing. There was a near cloudless sky and a full moon. The moonlight reflected off the white caps on top of the waves. He could see the lights of several other ships approaching or departing Philadelphia. The lights from shore were still visible.

139

Eduardo had been overserved and probably also ate too much. He was feeling both tight and stuffed. He thought to himself, "This captain is a neat guy, well educated, a good conversationist, and a seasoned captain. I think we are in good hands and that the voyage will be enjoyable." He returned to his cabin and slept through breakfast the next morning.

CHAPTER 42

Philadelphia to Baltimore

Aboard the *Sharnbrook*

March 10-12, 1777

For the first time in seven weeks, Eduardo felt relaxed. He didn't have to serve as an interpreter or work on a contract. His time was his own. Capt. Garcia had agreed to continue with two copies of his daily journal, one copy of which was to be filed with General Galvez once he arrived in New Orleans, as his official report.

After breakfast he started one of his three books he had purchased in Philadelphia. He started reading *The History of the Decline and Fall of the Roman Empire* by Edward Gibbon, which was just published last year. Subconsciously, while reading, his hand would dig into a bag and come up with some jellybeans or hard candy.

Capt. Garcia was standing by the railing smoking his pipe. The first mate approached him. "Excuse me sir. I was wondering if you would be willing to play your guitar with some of our crew members. Able Seaman Hastings plays the harmonica. Seaman recruit Johnson plays a ukulele, and yeoman Green has a drum. Would you be willing to get together with them and come up with some music? We also have four guys who think they can sing. Would it be possible for you all to put on a concert?

"First, I would be delighted. You arrange a time for us all to get together and practice and let me know."

That afternoon, Eduardo and Fernando stood on the Poop Deck watching the crew go through its "Repel Boarders" drill.

That evening at dinner, Eduardo asked Christopher how the ship came to be named *Sharnbrook*.

"This is a long story but since you asked, I'll try to keep it as short as possible. Sharnbrook is a small village in Bedford County, England, which is northeast of London. When King Henry VIII established the Church of England, he confiscated most of the property of the Catholic

Church in England. The Knight Templars maintained a priory in Sharnbrook, which they called "Toft Manor." This mansion sat on 450 acres surrounded by a stone wall ten feet high. Toft Manor was huge, about 10,000 square feet interior, with 14 bedrooms. In 1450 King Henry VIII sold Toft Manor to my Butler ancestor, who was a Baronet. His descendants include the Dukes and Earls of Leinster. From that time until my great grandfather migrated to Maryland in 1631 every member of my family had arms."

"Christopher, we have a Templar connection. I graduated from the Switzerland Institute for

Young Men in Switzerland. Many Templars escaped France just days before Friday October

13, 1307, when King Philip, the Fair, had ordered their arrest and confiscation of their assets. A large group which had been instructed to construct and operate a school moved to Switzerland, where the Templars already had a priory. It was co-founded by a Templar, who is my direct lineal ancestor, who became its second headmaster. This school has been operated by the Templars since its inception, and each headmaster has been a Templar. Upon my graduation, I was knighted a Templar.

"Eduardo, we might be cousins. Through another line, I am a direct lineal descendant of King Ferdinand and Queen Isabela of Spain. But my main claim to royalty is through King Edward,

III. Through him we are descended through all the English kings back to William the Conqueror. King William was the grandson of Emperor Charlemagne. One of our family historians has concluded that we are descendants of over 400 kings and queens on our father's side, and over 300 on my mother's side. If my pedigree is so good, why am I not rich," he asked jokingly.

"Yes, we are cousins," replied Eduardo. I too descend from Ferdinand and Isabela. We have a saying in Spain: *somos primos*, which means we are all cousins. My mother is French, but her mother was a direct lineal descendant of El Cid, who of course is one of our most famous heroes. "One of my cousins has just recently began looking into our family pedigree. He discovered that we are descendants of the famous Spanish painter Diego Velazquez. Can I join your club," he asked laughingly?

That evening the three men played dominos until late; they drank; and they talked. Clearly, these three men were bonding.

The next morning, they entered Chesapeake Bay and headed almost due north. In these sheltered waters, the sea was calm. At lunch Captain Butler invited Eduardo and Fernando to join him. "I want to take you gentlemen to dinner tonight at the best restaurant in town. Their crab

143

cakes are to die for, and they serve oysters about a half-dozen ways. I eat there every time I'm in port."

As they approached Baltimore after lunch, Eduardo noticed an elevated piece of land near the entrance to the harbor. He thought to himself, this would be a great place for a fort[7]. A light rain approached from the southwest, so Eduardo went to his cabin to read.

The *Sharnbrook* snuggled up to the dock about 6:00 p.m. All the longshoremen had gone home, so unloading would have to wait until the morning. A good part of the crew was granted liberty. Capt. Garcia granted liberty to Sgt. Blanco, telling him that he was free the entire time the ship was in port.

The three good friends were already dressed for dinner. It was still misting rain and a fog was beginning to settle on Baltimore harbor. Their coach unloaded them in front of a two-story building. The sign outside said, "The Crab's Claw Restaurant – Falls Point, MD - Est. 1756." Christopher said, "You can tell from the noise that this is a great place to eat. When the people are happy, the food must be good." He could hardly be heard over the din inside. What a busy place. Roaring fireplaces at each end of the restaurant warmed the interior. Waiters carried large trays of food, while bar maids delivered wine, beer and liquor. The smell from the kitchen was wonderful. Customers talked and laughed loudly. This was a happy place.

Christopher took a sip of his large tankard of beer and ordered "peeled shrimp with hot sauce" as an appetizer.

---

[7] Fort McHenry was not constructed on this spot until 1798.

For his entre he selected "Maryland Deluxe Fried Crab Cakes" with a salad and baked, stuffed potato. Eduardo chose a dozen oysters on the half-shell and said "and I'm having your famous crab cakes also. "It all looks good to me," said Fernando. "I'll start with the Oysters *a la Maison*. They sound so good with cheese, tomato, onion, garlic and pepper. Bring me the crab cakes too."

The three had their best meal since Philadelphia. When they left the restaurant, they found themselves in a dense fog.

CHAPTER 43

Baltimore, Maryland

Aboard the *Sharnbrook*

March 13, 1777

After breakfast, Eduardo stepped out onto the deck. The fog was still present, but it was a wispy fog, with infrequent dense spots. Below on the dock, First was directing the offloading of cargo onto merchants' wagons. Eduardo and Fernando had planned to have lunch ashore and look around afterwards.

Sgt. Blanco had made friends with a young member of the crew. The two of them decided to spend their time fishing. An hour later they were already drowning worms in the water from their spot on the dock a few yards away.

Christopher had begged off having lunch with Eduardo and Fernando. He had to meet with his agent and discover the nature of his new cargo and where it had to be delivered. He had recommended the pub "Elephant and Lion" for lunch. It was located directly across the street from the governor's mansion. The menu was not as exhaustive as the evening before, but it offered some interesting choices.

Eduardo ordered a bowl of bouillabaisse and bread with a mug of beer. Fernando selected fish and chips with white wine. Both enjoyed their selections.

As they exited the pub, they were delighted to discover that the fog had lifted, the rain had stopped, and the sun was warming the day. They strolled through the downtown area, window shopping until they came upon a bookstore. Eduardo purchased newspapers from New York, Boston, Philadelphia and Charleston. He also grabbed the last copy of the *London Times*. He could now find out what was going on in the world. As he tendered payment for his newspapers, he asked the clerk "Is there a sweet shop nearby?"

"Yes sir. There is one almost behind us on the next street over," as she turned and pointed to the rear of her store.

At the candy shop Eduardo had to replace the sweets consumed in the past few days and provide for the journey to Charleston. He purchased a few chocolates which he must eat before they melted. He replenished his jellybeans and hard candy. Walking back to the ship, they enjoyed the sun on their faces. Fernando saw some cuff links in the window of a jewelry store that he couldn't live without. Just as they were within sight of the ship, they ducked into a gallery to see what kind of art was popular.

The crew finished offloading the cargo on March 15th. On the morning of the 16th, Wagons from the ship's agent began to arrive and the crew began loading the cargo. It appeared to be unsafe on deck during the loading or unloading of cargo. The holds were filled with corn, soybeans, tobacco, fruits and vegetables and live chickens. Surprisingly, there were several large crates marked "Caramel Candy."

Eduardo returned to his cabin and began another letter to his parents, which he posted the following day. He spent the day reading newspapers. He could hear Fernando and his "band" rehearsing. He silently hoped they improved.

147

That evening at dinner Eduardo asked the captain about the types of cargo he transports. "In each port I enter, I have my agents look for goods that are not readily available in other ports. I don't deal in seafood because it spoils so quickly. As an example, we purchase newspapers in each city. They are sold in other cities for three times our cost. Each town touts its own beer and booze. I buy in volume at a discount and sell for three times the retail price. In each of the major cities on the east coast I have a small inn with a pub, an agent, a warehouse, and a general store.

"So, you don't just operate ships," said Fernando.

"No, Fernando. I have a contract with the Postmaster General to deliver mail and packages to the major ports along the east coast. As out of town newspapers are being read throughout the colonies, colonists order goods from other cities. I have contracts with many of the major vendors in each city to deliver their orders. Your friend Senor Gardoqui contracted me to deliver the cargo from Spain and you to New Orleans."

"Once I deliver you folks in New Orleans, and unload your goods from Spain" he continued, "I will be a busy guy. I don't have an agent there, so I will be out myself making purchases. I plan to go back to the east coast loaded with goods not available there such as Cuban cigars, Puerto Rican Rum, Mexican Tequila, Cajun Moonshine, New Orleans Pralines, coffee, sugar, molasses, alligator hides and Indian pottery. These items will all sell quickly at a 300% - 400% profit. If Gardoqui sends my ships down here often enough, I will hire an agent and rent a warehouse.

Capt. Garcia had established a routine with Sgt. Blanco. Sgt. Blanco reported to Captain Garcia's cabin at 9:00

a.m. to receive any instructions and obtain answers to any questions. Each evening at 6:00 p.m. he was again to report. At six that evening Sgt. Blanco reported that he and his buddy had caught six fish. They had given them to the cook to share with the crew for dinner that evening.

"Congratulations sergeant. Perhaps you should consider hanging a line over the side when we get underway. You are excused."

CHAPTER 44

Voyage from Baltimore to Charleston.

Aboard the *Sharnbrook*

Departure March 18, 1777

Sea voyages can be monotonous – sometimes downright boring. Reading was the easiest way to avoid boredom. Playing games allowed one to interact with others. Listening to music also offered an escape, but if it was not pleasant music, it could make you squirm in your seat. At lunch on the third day out of Baltimore, Fernando advised that a concert would be presented on the quarter deck at 3:00 p.m. for all hands. The "musicians" had gotten their act together. With guitar, ukulele, harmonica and drum, the ensemble serenaded the crew for about 30 minutes. Surprisingly, it was a rather nice performance. Then they were joined by a four-man singing group, which included First, the first mate. Everyone was surprised at the good quality music this small group was generating.

At dinner that evening, Christopher thanked Fernando for taking the time to prepare the concert.

"Gentlemen," he said, "while we were being regaled by the London Philharmonic this afternoon, we passed my home on the outer banks of North Carolina. Let me tell you a story about this area. When I was a young man my shipping company had only four ships. At one time or another each of my ships was attacked and pillaged by Blackbeard the pirate. The colonial governor of North Carolina was a man named Eden. Governor Eden was in cahoots with Blackbeard. He got a percentage of

Blackbeard's booty. The local newspaper carried a story about my ships being pirated and quoted me as calling the governor a "Brigand. The governor ordered the Attorney General to file criminal charges against me for criminal libel."

"Governor Eden offered a pardon to any pirate who would give up pirating and live an honest life. Blackbeard took him up on his offer, signed the agreement and was pardoned. Blackbeard built a beautiful mansion next door to the governor's mansion."

"When my criminal trial came up, I was tried and found guilty. As punishment for this wicked crime, I received a severe reprimand. Even the judge knew that Eden was a crook. After I paid the costs, the case was dismissed."

"Blackbeard violated his signed oath and went back to pirating. He maintained a base on the islands that lie within the lagoon inside the outer banks. I made a visit to the Virginia governor and explained the plight of shipping companies. The Virginia governor ordered an English ship to hunt Blackbeard down and bring him to justice. I was allowed to accompany this military detachment. I led them to an island he had used in the past. Just at sunset we attacked him and his crew.

Most of them were too drunk to fight so the battle didn't last too long. I still have a mental image of Blackbeard's head hanging from the rafters of his ship."

"What a story. Are we likely to see any pirates on our voyage," asked Fernando?

"Possibly. There are not as many around as in years past. They mostly strike in the Florida straits, the Gulf of Mexico, and the Caribbean. When we get into those waters, I will double the watch. You see the canons on

151

deck, so we are prepared to defend ourselves. Also, this is one of the fastest three masted schooners on the east coast. There is a good likelihood that we can outrun most pirates."

"Shall we break out the dominos," Christopher asked?

CHAPTER 45

Charleston, SC

Aboard the *Sharnbrook*

March 25, 1777

By this time the passengers had fallen into a routine. They looked forward to each new port as a place where they could get a change in food; a place to make purchases; to walk around and get a feel for a new town; to stretch their legs and enjoy new smells; a place to write home about. The next leg of the voyage was the longest of the journey. It was estimated to take a month to circumnavigate Florida and get to New Orleans.

Eduardo had finished both his *History of the Rise* and *Fall of the Roman Empire* and Mr. Franklin's *Poor Richard's Almanac*, so he must shop for reading material as well as candy. How much was a month's worth of candy?

At dinner the evening after the ship docked in Charleston, the captain said "Gents, I would like to take you for breakfast tomorrow to a very famous restaurant. I think you will have the best breakfast you have ever had.

. . .

The coach stopped in an area that a lot of dignified people refused to visit. The sign said, "Mama's Biscuits." It was not fancy, but it appeared to be clean. The following were just a few of the selections offered:

ALL ORDERS ARE SERVED WITH MOMA'S HOME MADE BUTTERMILK BISCUITS, SOFT BUTTER AND APPLE JELLY, COFFEE OR TEA.

153

Farmers Breakfast

3 farm fresh eggs cooked to order

3 rashers of maple flavored bacon

3 sausage patties

1   slice of Virginia Sugar Cured Ham

Grits slathered in melted butter

Fried potatoes

Merchants Breakfast

Omelet made with 3 farm fresh eggs, with your choice of:

Cheese, Onion, Tomato, peppers, bacon, sausage or ham.

2   slices of Virginia sugar cured ham

Fried potatoes

Grits slathered in melted butter

Hungry Man's Breakfast

4 biscuits

Bowl of Sausage Gravy

Choice of Bacon, Sausage or ham.

Three voracious eaters sat at the table. These three gentlemen were enjoying their food so much they were talking with their mouths full. The food was delicious. They all ate so much they were uncomfortable.

Before they left, the captain ordered biscuits, gravy, ham, bacon, sausage and marmalade for their breakfast tomorrow. He was going to tell the cook to sleep late tomorrow.

"Gentlemen, I must get back to the ship, but you may keep the carriage to do your shopping. Keep it as long as you like."

After dropping off the captain, the driver took them to a tobacconist so that Fernando could buy some pipe tobacco. It was a pretty town with its lovely parks and green areas. Many buildings were trimmed in wrought iron that had been used as ballast by merchant ships arriving with little or no cargo. Eduardo asked the driver to stop at a candy store. Thirty minutes later he came out of the store burdened with four packages. "Please take us to a bookstore next, asked Eduardo."

At the bookstore he purchased four books: *The Barber of Seville*, by Beaumarchais, who was involved in the shipment of military supplies to the Americans; *Common Sense*, by Thomas Paine; *Thoughts on Government*, by John Adams; and Thomas Jefferson's *A Summary View of the Rights of British America*. He knew that the book selection available in New Orleans would be sparse. He also purchased newspapers from New York, Boston, and Philadelphia, as well as all the local papers. Fernando picked up a couple of magazines, several boxes of matches and some pipe cleaners. He asked for and received directions to a music store, where he could purchase some guitar strings and picks, as it might be years before he is where they are sold. As they were leaving the bookstore, he noticed a handsome large world atlas. This was a 1776 edition, so it would have the latest information. He went back and purchased it.

155

As their carriage neared the ship it was just afternoon. "Fernando, do you prefer to eat onboard at 12:30 or would you like to drop off our purchases and take the carriage to a restaurant for lunch?"

"Colonel, after that enormous breakfast, I am still stuffed. Our shopping has tired my body. Lunch onboard followed by a long nap sounds good to me."

"So be it. Driver, when you drop us off you are finished for the day. Eduardo handed the driver a shilling as a gratuity and said: "Thank you for your time and courtesy." In his journal that night he went into great detail about his country's breakfast.

CHAPTER 46

Charleston to New Orleans

Pirate attack

April 1, 1777

There was excitement in the air. For many onboard this would be their first venture into the Gulf of Mexico. Captain Butler, Eduardo and Captain Garcia had all gone to Easter church service at St. Michael's Anglican Church on Broad Street. As they entered the church vestibule, they passed six youngsters pulling ropes to ring the church bells. One little boy held on to the bell rope which took him four feet off the ground with each tug. He was a happy cowboy. The three men sat in the first row behind box seats.

"Gentlemen, there is only one friendly port between here and New Orleans, and that is

Savannah, GA. Hopefully, there will be no emergency onboard before we get to New Orleans. I have no cargo or mail for Savannah, so it is not my present intention to stop there.

On the first day out of Charleston the captain had the crew perform a "Fire Drill." On this drill the crew was to prepare to fight a cargo fire in the hold. After the drill was over, he gathered all hands-on deck. Standing on the poop deck, he congratulated them on the fire drill. "Men, for the next few weeks we are going to be in pirate infested waters. Each day until we enter the Florida Straits we are going to drill. It may save our lives. Every member of this crew has a job for each potential problem.

157

You need to learn where you are supposed to be for each scenario. There will be Battle Station Drills, Fire Drills, Repel Boarders Drills and Foul Weather Drills. As they sailed down the Florida coast, Ferdinand smelled orange blossoms.

As they sailed past the Florida Keys, several small boats approached the *Sharnbrook* on its port side. They had seafood, fruits and vegetables, homebrew and other items for sale. The crew had run out of fruit. Captain Butler ordered that several sails be furled, which cut the ship's speed to about 3 knots. While the first mate went down the ladder on the port side of the ship, captain Butler went to his stateroom to get some money. The small boats tied on to the *Sharnbrook* for the negotiations.

While the crew's attention was on the small boats on the port side of the ship, a pirate ship approached them fast on the starboard side. When captain Butler realized the ruse, his orders were crisp: "Unfurl all sails! Full speed ahead! Cut the lines on those small boats! Man your battle stations! Load all cannon!"

Even after all the drills, the crewmen were disorganized. As the sails unfurled the ship began to pick up speed, but the pirate ship was gaining on them. It was a two masted sloop, known for its speed. The pirate ship had gained on them so much he could see the pirates on deck.

Just then the loud report of a cannon erupted off the port beam of the ship. As if by magic, a Spanish war ship appeared. With the cannon report, the pirate ship turned sharply to reverse course and flee. As the Spanish vessel passed them on the port side, the *Sharnbrook* crew waved and shouted. After a chase of about two nautical miles, and three cannon ball hits, the pirate ship heaved to and surrendered.

Eduardo and Fernando were rowed over to the 24-gun two masted Spanish Caravel, which was commanded by Lt. Jesus Calderon.

"Permission to come aboard," said Eduardo.

"Granted," said Lt. Calderon, as he stood to attention and saluted. I am Lt. Jesus Calderon, captain of His Majesty's ship *Destiny*. How may I be of service to you," He asked.

"Lt. Calderon, I am Colonel Eduardo Lopez, and this is my aide, Captain Fernando Garcia. I have here a letter that I request you read," he said as he handed him the King's letter. After reading the letter, Lt Calderon handed it back, saying "Colonel, my crew and I are at your disposal. This is my executive officer Lt. Carlos Esteban. What are your orders," he asked?

"May we step into your quarters to talk," asked Eduardo? Without answering, Lt. Calderon bowed and extended his left arm toward his quarters.

The four officers sat around the captain's table. The captain's steward poured wine for each man.

As the steward exited the room, Eduardo said: Gentlemen, This is my aide Captain Fernando Lopez. King Carlos has appointed me his special representative to handle secret matters of state. By this letter, he has granted me royal powers. Providence has brought the *Destiny* to me. Our ship, the *Sharnbrook*, is under contract with Joseph Gardoqui and sons of Bilbao, Spain, which is also working directly with his majesty. This ship is carrying a top secret and very valuable cargo. The king has decided that escorting these merchant ships is just as important as escorting treasure ships. I am canceling your current orders. You are now assigned the primary duty of escorting the *Sharnbrook* to New Orleans. You will be

159

reassigned to Governor General Bernardo De Galvez in New Orleans."

"First, we must identify each pirate and put them in shackles. They will be divided up and placed in the brigs of all three ships. Captain Garcia and your executive officer will select crew members from both our ships to crew the pirate ship. My aide, captain Garcia will act as captain of the pirate ship. Your Lt. Esteban will serve as his executive officer. Carpenters from both our ships will sail aboard the pirate ship and make repairs while we are underway. Four of my marines will be assigned to the pirate ship for security. Lt. you will assign two of your men who have legible handwriting to make a complete inventory of the pirate vessel, including number of cannons, cannon balls and other weapons and a complete inventory of their cargo. This should be complete by our arrival in New Orleans. Take down the skull and crossbones and run up the Spanish flag. I understand that with the transfer of men from our respective ships to the pirate ship, and the dispersal of prisoners, some time will be needed. I will return to my ship. When you are ready to get underway, send up the "ready" flag. We travel to New Orleans in convoy. Any Questions?" "Sir," asked Lt. Calderon, "What do we tell our commanding officer in Havana?"

"Governor General Galvez and I will both advise him of your official change in duties," answered Eduardo.

"Lt. Calderon, you, Lt. Esteban and your two sub-lieutenants are invited to dine with us on the *Sharnbrook* this evening at 7:00 p.m.

As the two seamen rowed Eduardo back to the *Sharnbrook*, he knew that one of his recommendations to the king was going to be that all merchant ships carrying supplies for the Americans should be escorted through Spanish waters – from the Georgia -Florida border to New Orleans and back to the border. He thought that some might say that escorting that ship back to the east coast was unnecessary. The counterargument was that it was carrying official mail and possibly official passengers and prevented a ship being used by His Majesty from being hijacked.

"Permission to come aboard sir," requested Eduardo.

"Permission granted," replied Captain Butler. Let's go to my cabin. I have a million questions."

"Captain Butler, your chestnuts have officially been pulled out of the fire. You can relax until we get to New Orleans, because now you will be escorted by the Spanish navy and a captured pirate ship, which will soon be outfitted as a ship of Governor General Galvez' fleet. I think I can swing it so that you will also have an escort back to the Florida-Georgia line, and that all your ships delivering goods along the Spanish Main will likewise be escorted by the Spanish navy. Capt. Garcia will be leaving us, as he is taking command of the captured pirate ship. Four of my marines and some of your seamen will also be transferred to man it and provide security. Please ask the steward to prepare a special meal tonight, and that will have four officers from the *Destiny* as our guests tonight. I have asked Fernando to get the band and choir to entertain our young Spanish officers tonight. He will leave us after the entertainment."

CHAPTER 47

Eduardo arrives in New Orleans

April 12, 1777

It was a beautiful spring day in New Orleans. The white petals of the cottonwood trees provided a background for the pink and lavender rosebud trees. The smell of Magnolia blossoms sweetened the cool air. Pastel azaleas basked in the sun.

What a sight to behold. A convoy of three ships docking near the cathedral at the same time. A crowd of civilians watched intently as the three ships tied up. A dozen soldiers stood in awe. None had ever seen a pirate ship.

Standing at the rail, Eduardo saw his friend Bernardo on the pier with his hands on his hips and a smile on his face. His joy at seeing his friend for the first time in nine months, brought a tear of happiness.

In his cabin, he made a preliminary report to Bernardo of his voyage across the Atlantic with Dr. Franklin and Senor Gardoqui; of Gardoqui's agreement with Captain Butler; their transit from Philadelphia, including their attack by pirates and the intervention of Lt. Calderon. Finally, he told Galvez that he had commandeered the Spanish ship for escort duty.

"Well Done, Lalo. You handled the situation just as I would have. Thank you for adding to my fleet with your pirate ship," he said with a wide grin on his face. I too have much to tell you, but first things first. Your quarters, which are much more spacious than these, are ready for you to move in. Your aide will be assigned to the BOQ[8].

Also, BOQ quarters will be assigned to the four officers of the *Destiny*. Your orderly will be assigned a bunk in enlisted quarters for noncoms. Tonight, I am ordering a Pachanga[9] at my palace. Please invite your aide, the officers of the *Destiny*, and the captain of this ship. I am declaring that tomorrow is a holiday to celebrate your successful completion of the mission. Order that the marines must remain to guard the cargo. Tell them they will also have a holiday after the goods are unloaded and stored in the warehouse."

That evening Eduardo was overwhelmed. After months of solitude at sea, he was confronted with a room full of strangers. The garrison band played, while the guests feasted. Those who liked to drink could get their fill. Everybody who was anybody in and around New Orleans was there. Social etiquette required that the guests stand in a reception line so as to be introduced to all present. He was first introduced to Bernie's fiancé, Felicite, who was clearly the most beautiful woman there. Next was Felicite's father, Gilbert Anoine de Saint-Maxent, the richest merchant in New Orleans. Robert Morris, the millionaire, was next. They both recognized that

they had met at Dr. Franklin's reception in Philadelphia. Others included the Mayor, Cathedral priest, garrison commander, chaplain, garrison doctor, junior officers, and a handful of merchants, including their wives.

Eduardo and Fernando sat at the head table with Galvez and his fiancée, and Captain Butler. Their conversation focused on the pirate attack and their capture. Fernando discretely asked to be excused shortly after dinner. He

---

[8] Bachelor Officer Quarters
[9] Spanish for "party."

recognized that these two men had personal things to discuss.

"Enjoy your holiday tomorrow. A carriage, horse and driver have been assigned to you. You might want to ride around the town and investigate your home for the foreseeable future. You, your aide, and the officers of the *Destiny* will all take your meals at the officer's club."

"Captain Butler, we will also assign you a room in the BOQ and you are welcome to eat with us at the officer's club. Would you join me and Colonel Lopez tomorrow for lunch at the officer's club? I have some ideas I want to pass on to you."

"Captain Butler, if you will join me in my office tomorrow morning at 10:00 a.m. with the Bill of Lading from Gardoqui and Sons, I suspect there might be a few coins for you," Galvez said with a smile."

The next morning Christopher felt like a wealthy man. Galvez had paid him in gold. In addition to getting paid for the journey from Philadelphia to New Orleans, he was able to sell his private cargo to his local agent for gold and silver.

CHAPTER 48

All Officers Meeting

New Orleans

April 14, 1777

"Good morning gentlemen. I see that the unloading of the pirate ship is almost finished. It should take three days to unload the *Sharnbrook* and get the cargo stored in the warehouse. Mr.

Morris has some cargo for you to load Captain Butler. Please don't forget to take our mail bag. We have quite a bit of business to conduct today. On the tables are pencils and paper which you might find handy.

"First, I want to thank Lt. Calderon and his crew for saving the *Sharnbrook*.

"Second, I want to compliment Captain Garcia on commanding our pirate ship from the Florida Straits to New Orleans without incident.

"Colonel Lopez is to be congratulated for getting the cargo from Le Havre France to New Orleans, while supervising the convoy.

"Captain Butler, we appreciate your cooperation in getting our precious cargo to us. So that you may more easily fulfill your agreement with Gardoqui and sons in delivering future cargos to us, I am awarding you a commission in the Spanish Navy as a ship's Captain. I am also registering your ship in New Orleans, as a Spanish ship. When you are in Spanish waters you are allowed to fly this flag, which will prevent you being unnecessarily stopped by our navy or our French allies. I am also entering into an agreement with you to carry our mail and any passengers.

"Captain, I request that you take Colonel Lopez and his entourage to Havana on the *Sharnbrook*. In Havana he will deliver letters from me and the king to the commanding Admiral requesting the transfer of three warships to New Orleans which shall be used to escort commercial ships carrying the king's secret cargo. You will not only be allowed to take their outgoing mail, but you will have the freedom of the port to purchase goods for resale. In the future, if landing in Cuba, you will also have the right to sell goods. If you are willing, Havana will become part of your regular route.

"Lt. Calderon, the *Destiny* will escort the *Sharnbrook* to Havana and remain there until the *Sharnbrook* is ready to depart. You will then escort it to the waters off the Georgia-Florida coast. Henceforth, you will be under the command of Captain Butler until separated on the Florida-Georgia coast. In the future, you will be under the command of the captain of all his Majesty's merchant ships coming into the Straits of Florida and the Gulf of Mexico destined for Spanish ports in the gulf.

"Colonel Lopez will also deliver a note from me to Cuban Governor General Felipe de Fondesviela y Ondeano, Marqués de la Torre to assuage any concern he might have that I am stepping on his toes."

"Next Saturday morning at 10:00 there will be a garrison formation of the presidio with a parade of the troops and a presentation of medals. Lt. Calderon, you and your crew will participate, so get them squared away. Please have your troops practice so that we are not embarrassed."

166

CHAPTER 49

New Orleans Presidio

Saturday, April 19, 1777

The garrison band began playing at 9:45 a.m. to warm up the crowd. New Orleans was a small town. The merchants and citizens were all aware of today's ceremony. They came from miles around to see the pomp and ceremony. In addition to the garrison were the officers and crew of not only the *Destiny*, but most of the officers and crew of the two carousels assigned to Galvez. Finally came the squad of Marines who were now assigned to the garrison.

Following the trooping of the colors came the inspection of the troops.

"Attention to Orders," announced the acting executive officer: "General Bernardo de Galvez, the Spanish Governor General of Louisiana, has seen fit to present medals to deserving members of this garrison. The honorees stand before the Governor General. The following medals were presented by General Galvez:

Colonel Eduardo Lopez	Royal & Distinguished Order Of Charles, III
Captain Christopher Butler	Navy Medal
Captain Fernando Garcia	Cross of Naval Merit

167

Lt. Jesus Calderon	Cross of Naval Merit
Lt. Carlos Esteban	Cross of Naval Merit
Crew of the *Destiny*	Campaign Medal

Immediately following the ceremony there was an informal reception at the Officer's Club.

At the Officer's Club General Galvez walked over to Captain Butler. "Chris, I hope you can see how important you are to us. In the future you can expect many more shipments. If you wish we can add Vera Cruz as one of your ports of call for mail, etc. We hope you can dedicate more of your ships to our deliveries. I can't impress upon you enough how important these shipments are. I understand that you and the *Destiny* will be shipping out tomorrow with the morning tide."

"In this envelope you will find your Captain's Commission in the Spanish Navy, a letter of introduction from me, and a copy of the registration of your ship in New Orleans as a Spanish vessel. If you will advise me in advance of the name of the ships and their captains you will be sending into the Gulf, I will also register those ships and commission those captains and dispatch them to you by next ship."

"When and if you have news that might be of interest to me, please write. Please enclose any newspaper clippings that you think I would want to see. Please have each ship headed this way bring newspapers from all major ports. By the way, I appreciate it that you saved your old newspapers for me. They help me understand the American people. If you will excuse me, I have other guests to whom I must attend," said Galvez. "May you have fair winds and following seas," he said, as he turned and walked across the room.

Robert Morris came up to Christopher and said, "Congratulations Captain, I understood that you are casting off tomorrow morning. I had hoped that we could spend some time together. I'm sorry that didn't work out. It appears that you and other ships of your company will be making regular trips to New Orleans soon. As you know, I am a factor for the Spanish Government and have a warehouse. I would like to interest you in a business arrangement whereby my company would act as your agent to purchase goods for transport and warehouse them until your next ship arrives. Many items come through this port from Mexico, Cuba, Puerto Rico and sometimes the Caribbean. In the enclosed envelope are two copies of a proposed contract for your review. If you agree, return the signed agreement and a deposit."

"Mr. Morris, this is my first trip to New Orleans, and I have had no opportunity to investigate what products exist here that might be of interest to my customers on the east coast. What kind of goods can you provide," asked Christopher?

"Cuban Cigars, rum from Puerto Rico, Mexico, Cuba and Louisiana; tequila and Mescal from Mexico, Silver from Mexico, Gold from Peru, beer and wine from each area, boots and leather goods, corn, dried beans, parrots, bolts of cloth – need I provide more," Morris asked?

"Christopher looked at the proposed agreement for about three minutes. "If you will meet me at my ship tomorrow morning at 8:00 a.m., we can seal the deal. I will give you a deposit. You can sign my copy and give me a receipt. I look forward to a prosperous relationship for us both. If you will excuse me, Colonel Lopez is waiting for me at the bar. Good evening."

169

CHAPTER 50

Eduardo & Capt. Butler meet with Cuban Officials

Havana, Cuba

April 25, 1777

Captain Butler and Eduardo were standing on the poop deck of his ship when they first spotted Morro Castle some three miles away. It was the surf crashing against its massive walls that first caught their attention. It sat atop a 200-foot cliff. As they neared the entrance into Havana harbor La Punta, the fortress on the other side of the harbor entrance came into view. Christopher was amazed when he looks along the coast to the west of La Punta. The shore was lined with military fortifications and gun batteries for as far as the eye could see. The *Sharnbrook* was flying the Spanish flag as it entered Havana harbor.

"Christopher, Morro Castle is one of the most famous fortresses in the world. It was constructed in 1589. But it is not the oldest. On the other side of the harbor is La Punta Fortress. It was the first fort in Cuba, completed in 1583. To protect the harbor the Cuban defenders would string a chain from El Morro to La Punta to deny ships entrance into the harbor."

As the *Sharnbrook* passed between the two fortresses, Eduardo pointed out a huge fortress on the left, also resting on a 200-foot hilltop. That's Cabana Castle, which is also known as Fort Charles. It was just completed a few years ago. The British occupied Havana for a year in 1762-1763. They were able to capture Morro

Castle from the land side. Cabana Castle was constructed to prevent that from ever happening again.

With only enough sail to navigate, the *Sharnbrook* eased past a battery of two guns on shore to the right making about two knots. The channel was so narrow that they could see the Treasury, Custom House, Post Office, and other public buildings along the waterfront. They docked in the Navy Yard, under the watchful eye of Atares Castle to the southwest.

"Look Eduardo, they are building another castle on that hill overlooking the city. Why so many castles," Christopher asked?

"They built it for the same reason that constructed Cabana Castle. The Spanish government wanted this to be the strongest city in the hemisphere," responded Eduardo. "Let's go check in with the harbormaster," he added.

As they departed the harbormaster's office and obtained clearance to dock in the Navy Yard, they flagged a passing carriage. "Take us to the Governor's Mansion," Eduardo directed. The Palace of Governors was located on the Plaza de Armas, which overlooked the harbor channel and Cabana Castle on the far shore.

Havana harbor, courtesy of Mappery.com 1

"Colonel Eduardo Lopez and Captain Christopher Butler to see his excellency," he stated to the receptionist. She got up and walked down a long passageway. Moments later, a middle aged Lt. Colonel approached them.

"His excellence is ready to see you gentlemen. Please follow me." At the end of the passageway, they entered two large doors decorated in gold leaf. Within was an office with four desks manned by officers and civilians handling stacks of paperwork. Their guide gently knocked on the Governor's inner door.

"Come in," said the Governor. After a cordial greeting, Governor General Felipe de Fondesvie y

Ondeano, Marques de la Torre, said "Gentlemen, I received a note from my friend Governor General Galvez asking me to receive you when you arrived. What important news do you have to share with me?"

"Your excellency, I have two letters for you. Please read this letter from Governor Galvez," as Eduardo handed Galvez' letter to the Governor.

OFFICE OF THE GOVERNOR GENERAL HIS
MAJESTY'S LOUISIANA COLONY NEW
ORLEANS, LOUISIANA

April 14, 1777

To:

His Excellency Felipe de Fondesvie y Ondeano, Marques de la Torre

Governor General of Cuba

Havana, Cuba

My dear Governor,

I hope you have been well and that this greeting finds you in good health. First, I want to share with you that I plan to marry Felicite de Saint-Maxent in New Orleans on November 1st this year. I am hopeful that you and your entourage will be able to attend as my guests.

Now to business. Colonel Eduardo Lopez, who handed you this letter is not only my Chief of Staff. Our beloved king, HRM Carlos III, has seen fit to name Colonel Lopez as his personal representative to carry out a secret mission. He is under direct orders from King Carlos not to disclose his mission to anyone but me. Colonel Lopez will present to you the letter from King Carlos, containing both his royal signature and also his wax seal. I urge you to cooperate with him and to direct your subordinates to comply with his requests.

As the Sharnbrook was making a delivery of the goods deemed vital by King Carlos, they were attacked by

173

pirates in the Florida Straits. Fortunately, they were rescued by His

Majesty's ship, Destiny. By authority of the king, Colonel Lopez commandeered the Destiny and ordered it to accompany the Sharnbrook to New Orleans.

Colonel Lopez will request that certain military assets be transferred from Havana to New Orleans. I join in that request.

The other gentleman in your office is Captain Christopher Butler, a citizen of North Carolina. Captain Butler is the owner of a fleet of 8 ships. He has been engaged by the firm of Joseph Gardoqui & Sons, in Bilbao, Spain to carry Spanish cargo and mail for Spain. This agreement was made at the express direction of King Carlos. He has been tried and tested under fire. I have great confidence in him.

Captain Butler's continued friendship is vital to the national interest of Spain. I respectfully request that you grant him "Freedom of the Port," thereby allowing him to buy and sell goods in Havana. I also strongly suggest that Havana also utilize the services of Captain Butler's company, and approve his company's ships for mail, cargo and passengers.

Starting in the very near future and lasting for the next few years, I anticipate that his ships will be making frequent deliveries to Spanish ports in the gulf. I have commissioned him as a Captain in the Spanish Navy. I have registered his ship, the Sharnbrook, as a Spanish vessel homeported in New Orleans, and I have executed a contract authorizing him to carry mail, cargo and passengers for Spain.

Your humble servant,

Bernardo De Galvez

Governor General of Louisiana.

SEAL

P.S. You might find it interesting that it was Captain Butler who brought about the capture and execution of Blackbeard the pirate.

"Colonel, please let me see the letter from the king," asked Governor Fondesvie.

"I recognize the king's signature and his seal, but I am confused. Why would King Carlos make a Colonel his personal representative? This is the job of an ambassador or minister. I find it difficult to believe that the king would entrust secret business with a field officer. Can you explain this to me," he asked?

"Your excellency, I have no way of knowing what was going on in the king's royal head when he selected me. I can only offer some possibilities."

"Please share your surmises with me," answered the governor.

"Sir, King Carlos and my father were schoolmates at the Switzerland Institute for Young Men, which was also the school from which I matriculated. From time-to-time King Carlos has appointed his friend, my father, to positions of trust. The king was also an acquaintance of my paternal grandfather. His majesty told me that he had been keeping up with my education. He knew that I had finished first in my class and that I was fluent in Spanish, English, French, German and Italian, and could struggle through Dutch and Portuguese. I can only suggest that he felt that I was mentally able, physically ready and morally
175

equipped to keep my activities secret. Putting myself in his place, if I had something that I wanted handled secretly, I would prefer a Colonel over a noble because their movements would draw less attention to British spies.'

"Well, I am impressed with you Colonel. Since the king has appointed you his personal representative, I shall refer to you as Ambassador.

"Gentlemen let's move over to the table. Antonio, please pour the wine." The three men sat around a round table. Christopher thought to himself, "How much more egalitarian can we get?" What are you requesting," asked the governor?

"Your excellency, on behalf of King Carlos, I respectfully request that the following be transferred from Havana to New Orleans:

Three ships of the line and their officers & crew.

10 able seamen to serve as replacements for death, sickness and injury.

A supply officer, Disbursing Officer and a Chaplain.

1,000 yards of line

Spare sails

12 cannons, 12 limbers

36 horses

12 saddles and bridles

500 Cannon balls and 10,000 pounds of gunpowder

One company of Marines, who will be dispatched on escort vessels for security.

Three cases of rifles and 5,000 bullets

Three dozen tents

100 beds, mattresses, blankets and linens

Increased monthly rations for 150 men

10 wagons

1,000 Livres in gold to be used to further the king's goals.

"Quite an order you have there Mr. Ambassador. I have the authority to order that everything on your list is provided. However, I think that we need to consult my military. Let's get back together here tomorrow with my Admiral, my General, and my supply officer. I don't foresee a problem, but I don't want to act without consulting them.

"Before we adjourn Captain Butler, what can you tell me about yourself other than your involvement in capturing Blackbeard the pirate?

"Your excellency, I live on the North Carolina coast. I operate 8 cargo ships that regularly ply the seas along the east coast. Because of my previous problems with pirates, all of my ships are armed with cannons and mortars. In each major city on the east coast, I maintain a warehouse and operate a general store. I am a direct lineal descendant of Ferdinand and Isabella, whose daughter, Catherine of Aragon married King Henry, VIII. As an American I am proud to assist Spain. The transfer of war ships from Havana to New Orleans to serve as escorts for my ships, will inhibit attacks by pirates, protect the king's secret cargo, and will make it much easier for me to hire crew members.

After lunch, since neither of them had ever been to Havana, Eduardo and Christopher hired a carriage for a tour around downtown. Passing a group of large guns on the ship channel, their first stop was La Punta Fortress. They took a short self-guided tour. Christopher had never seen guns as large as the four defending the harbor. They must have been 10 feet long, he thought. As they were reentering their carriage, they could hear the shouts of prisoners in the Havana Jail across the street. Street vendors selling candy got Eduardo's attention. He bought some Mazapan candy.

They drove through Old Havana, with its beautiful 16th century colonial architecture. The gem of the city was the ornate Plaza Cathedral, which was just completed in 1776. They both admired the multi-colored buildings in the Old Plaza.

Christopher asked that they stop at the Colon Market. He wanted to see what kind of goods he might purchase for this return home. He found Molasses, sugar, rum, coffee, tobacco, cigars, colorful dresses, boots, spurs, peanuts, straw hats and bags, cotton cloth and guayaberas. The prices here for cigars, rum, beer, etc. seemed to be slightly lower than in New Orleans. He decided to make some purchases, but since he didn't speak Spanish, he first would have to find an agent who spoke English. He was fascinated with the cotton guayaberas, loose fitting shirts with four pockets. They came in all colors and for sale were both long sleeve and short sleeve. He purchased a short sleeve light blue shirt.

Walking through the market toward the carriage a vendor was selling what looked like carved potatoes. "What's that Eduardo?

"Christopher, this is jicama. It looks like a cross between a potato and a turnip, but it tastes like a cross between a potato and an apple. It's very healthy and tasty too. Here, help yourself."

"Hey, this is good. Why haven't I ever heard of it before? It's juicy and has a great crunch. They will be popular in my shops."

They stopped the carriage at a park just before reentering the naval base, deciding to have some tacos from a sidewalk vendor's cart for lunch. Christopher experimented with a beef taco. He watched as the vendor placed strips of beef on top of a corn tortilla. On top he placed chopped onions, tomato and a green herb. On top of all that he added a green paste. Eduardo ordered two chicken tacos, which were made in the same manner. They each ordered a beer.

They sat on a park bench in the shade of several palm trees. The sound of a water fountain in the center of the park was relaxing. On the far side children played on playground equipment. The temperature was perfect.

"What do you have me eating Eduardo," asked Christopher.

"Your taco, as you can see contains onions and tomato. The green herb is cilantro. It has an unusual taste which is popular throughout Latin America. The green paste is guacamole, made from mashed avocado, mixed with onion, tomato, cilantro, garlic, salt and lemon juice. Pretty tasty, isn't it?"

179

Walking up the gangplank of the *Sharnbrook*, Eduardo said "I hear they have some great bands in Havana and some interesting floor shows. Care to venture out tonight for a late supper and some fun? I was told that most of the night life was in the theatre district not too far from the market."

"What time shall I be ready to go," said Christopher. I could do with some fun."

"Let's meet on deck at 10:00 p.m.," responded Eduardo. I'm going to take a nap."

That evening the two men found themselves in a night club called "La Rambla," named after the night life area of Barcelona. Christopher was having trouble reading the menu, and Eduardo described the food for him:

"Carne asada is a steak with vegetables; Carne guisada is a beef stew; Quesadilla is a tortilla upon which they add meat, cheese, tomato, peppers, cilantro and onion. Another tortilla is added on top and placed in the oven; Frijoles negros y arroz is black beans and rice, a Cuban favorite; Langosta is lobster; Camerones fritos is fried shrimp; Pesce frito con papas fritas is fish and chips. I am sure you can figure out "hamburguesas." See anything you like?"

Christopher's lobster tails were served with copious amounts of melted butter and limes. The home-made bread was piping hot. The bread with melted butter was fantastic. Eduardo's steak was crisp on the outside and pink in the middle. It was served with a sweet potato slathered in melted butter, salt and pepper.

While they were eating the band started. The musicians included a pianist, two trumpeters, one trombone player, string bass, alto and tenor saxophone and a xylophone. The percussion section dominated the group with a drum set, bongo, congo and timbales. Depending upon the tune, the musicians also played a cow bell, wood block, gourd, tambourine and castanets. The sound was like something that neither man had ever heard before. The music had a fast beat that had a pulsating rhythm. Both men found themselves patting their feet under the table when eating.

At the intermission they both ordered flan for dessert. This club had an international floor show.

They were entertained by singers, dancers, magicians, dog acts, a stripper and a comedian who Christopher could not understand. As their coffee was being poured the stage lights dimmed. A platform was brought to the center of the stage. An attractive negro woman in a silk robe stepped on stage and disrobed, exposing her completely naked young body. Her breasts were erect. Then a man, wearing a top hat and spats led a donkey onstage. He introduced the donkey to the audience. The woman got onto the platform. She lifted her legs onto stantions that held her legs up and apart, fully exposing her genital area to the audience. The man in the top hat led the donkey to the platform. As the donkey had been trained to do, he mounted the woman and inserted his penis into her vagina. He continued to have intercourse with her until his orgasm.

When the curtain came down the house lights came up and within minutes their waiter had presented their bills. It was time to clear the restaurant for the late show.

The following morning the meeting went well. The Admiral and the General were greatly impressed with the

181

letter from the king and ordered their supply officer to fill Eduardo's order. The Supply Officer said that he only had 22 horses and would have to order some more beds and mattresses from Madrid. He promised to fill the remainder of the order by having the goods ready for shipment within the week. The admiral and the general both promised to have the transfer orders for the ships, their crew, the marines, and the requested officers issued that day.

"The two ships beside the *Destiny* can be ready for their voyage tomorrow," said the admiral. The marines and the goods can be shipped out next week. Will that be satisfactory?

"Admiral, I appreciate your assistance. My next report will be very favorable. Tell the Commodore to expect me as a passenger. I need to get back to New Orleans.

That evening Eduardo and Christopher closed down the bar at the Havana Officer's Club. They were both sad about the separation. Over the last two months they had become steadfast friends. Christopher also liked Galvez and felt that he was being treated very well by him. They agreed to keep in touch with letters. Christopher said he would try to be the captain on the next ship to New Orleans.

CHAPTER 51

Capt. Butler leaves Havana

Aboard the *Sharnbrook*

May 5, 1777

Christopher left Havana with a full hold of Cuban cargo. After Eduardo departed for New Orleans, Christopher had met with an English speaking warehouse agent. He went on a shopping spree at the agent's warehouse. It had taken three days to load his purchases. His hold was full of cargo.

With such a large cargo, he would have to make a stop in Charleston to drop off part of the goods and pick up what was heading north together with the mail.

Christopher had often thought of his lovely wife, Sara. As the wife of a mariner, she was accustomed to his long absences. Before he left Havana, he went to a jewelry store to pick out a present for her. He selected a beautiful two carat emerald ring.

As he sailed past Morro Castle, he wondered if he would ever see Eduardo again. He planned on

a trip to Philadelphia to meet with his brother. They had to devise a fleet schedule that incorporated regular trips to Havana and New Orleans.

CHAPTER 52

New Orleans Presidio

May 18, 1777

What an abrupt change had occurred in Eduardo's life over the past six weeks. His routine at sea had been relaxed compared to his busy life at the presidio. Galvez had asked him to get the garrison looking like professional soldiers. He ordered that they be drilled every morning after calisthenics. In the shipment that came with him, there was a case of 30 rifles. Those had been given to Platoon A. They were so much more accurate than muskets. Platoon A's primary afternoon duties became rifle practice. Hopefully, there will be more rifles delivered soon.

For the time being he was conducting an inspection every Friday afternoon. The garrison failed inspection the first two times for multiple reasons. The barracks on those initial inspections were dirty. Their bunks were messy. Their boots were unshined and their uniforms were disheveled.

On both weekends he denied the garrison liberty. On the third week he assigned Marine Sgt. Robert Sanchez as acting sergeant major. Within three weeks the entire garrison appeared to be military.

Eduardo's next major concern was building up a militia without arousing suspicion of the several British spies who lived in New Orleans. He called a meeting of his officers. They spent hours deliberating a plan to recruit quietly but could not arrive at a workable plan. Each officer was requested to put on their respective thinking caps and come back with a plan at next week's regular meeting.

Eduardo welcomed the weekend. He needed some time to relax. On Saturday evening he planned on going to the weekly dinner party. He had arranged to dine with Governor Galvez and his fiancé, Felicite. When Eduardo arrived at the officer's club there was an attractive young woman seated with Bernardo and Felicite.

"Colonel Lopez, allow me to present Miss Antoinette La Salle of Paris, France. She was Felicite's classmate. Miss La Salle, this is my Chief of Staff, Colonel Eduardo Lopez, a boyhood friend from my hometown, Marcharaviaya, Spain.

Eduardo's world was thrown out of kilter. This woman was beautiful. Here silken auburn hair had blonde highlights. Her light green eyes accented her beautiful face. It had been so long since he had a romantic attachment, he was afraid that he might scare her away. He was as nervous as a long tailed cat in a room full of rocking chairs.

"Please call me Toni," she asked, as he sat beside her.

Edwardo recovered his senses. "Toni, how is it that you find yourself in this backwater hole in the middle of nowhere," asked Eduardo?

"Colonel, my father is in the liquor and wine business. He is an old acquaintance of Felicite's father. Our fathers have entered into a partnership to distill and market what you folks call "moonshine" and sell it in Europe. They also plan to market "Cajun beer," and "Louisiana rum.

185

"For a Spaniard, you speak French like a native speaker. Where did you study," she asked?

"My mother is French, so I grew up speaking it. Do you speak Spanish," he inquired?

"Yes, I learned Spanish and English in school. Do you speak any other languages?

"English, German and Italian. I have some ability in Portuguese and Dutch.

"Well, Colonel. It seems that we shan't be at a loss for words," she said as she laughed. Simultaneously, she gently laid her hand on his forearm and looked into his eyes.

When the music began Eduardo asked Toni to dance. He was mesmerized. Her perfume was like an aphrodisiac. Her body pressing next to his was exciting. The feel of her breasts against his body caused him to have an erection. When he looked into her eyes he was lost.

Before calling it an evening the four agreed to go sailing on Lake Ponchetran the following day. The ladies were to provide the picnic lunch and the guys were to bring the beer and wine. The love game was afoot!

CHAPTER 53

Christopher arrives home

Edenton, Chowan County, NC

May 21, 1777

The *Sharnbrook* eased into Albermarle Sound, sheltered by the North Carolina Banks. Within a few hours he would be reunited with his wife, Sara. He hoped that he would get to visit with his children and grandchildren this visit. A stiff wind hurried his ship to his home in Edenton – a hometown he had shared with both corrupt governor Eden and Blackbeard. Edenton was in Chowan County, N.C., which was on the Virginia border.

The stiff wind also brought with it a thunderstorm. As they docked in Edenton it was pouring rain.

"First, I am going to see my wife. Set the watch. When the rain abates, you can begin unloading. Give the crew liberty."

Because of the electrical storm he had to agree to pay the carriage driver double his normal fare. Both of them were soaked when they arrived at the Butler home. Sara almost peed on herself when she opened the door to find Christopher standing there. First, she threw her arms up in the air. Almost immediately, she wrapped both her arms around him and squeezed as hard as she could, while at the same time giving him a long kiss. Their dog "Blue" a black and white mixed breed was overjoyed to see his master. He jumped up on Chris until Chris stooped down to pet him. The dog got the name because he had one brown and one blue eye.

187

"Let's get you into some dry clothes," said Sara. While you are changing clothes, I'm going to get your dirty clothes out of your sea bag.

A few minutes later, Chris sat down in his favorite chair in the living room. Just as he reached for the local newspaper, Sara rushed into the room. "I found this gift wrapped present in your sea bag. Is it for me," she asked? Her face was filled with excitement.

"Yes, darling. Just a little something I picked up for you in Havana."

"Havana – why were you in Havana? I thought you were going to New Orleans.

"First things first sweetie. Go ahead and open your gift."

"Christopher Butler, did you rob a bank? If this is a real emerald, there is no way we can afford it. What is going on?

"Darling, why don't you fix us a cup of tea and I will tell you all about it. Our lives have changed for the better."

CHAPTER 54

New Orleans Courtship

Summer 1777

Eduardo's life had been filled with school and work; he had had little time to contemplate developing female companionship. Toni was the first woman to pique his interest. Late spring and summer were like living in a dream for him.

He was with her almost every day. They enjoyed dining and dancing together at the Officers Club, and dining at Lake Ponchetran, in the French Quarters and occasionally at her father's mansion.

Their days were spent on long carriage rides, picnics, lawn games, sailing on Lake Ponchetran, swimming, going to church and shopping. They spent a good part of one weekend at a Cajun Music Festival in the suburb of Poydras. Their evenings were spent playing cards and parlor games. Toni was an excellent Whist player, which was George Washington's favorite card game. Eduardo enjoyed the times at night when they sat together, looking at the moon and talking about their hopes and plans. These talks were frequently interrupted with long passionate kisses and light petting.

By mid-July they were engaged to be married.

Simultaneously with his active courtship, his duties kept Eduardo busy. His officers had been meeting regularly to devise a recruiting plan for the militia. The plan they agreed upon was fairly simple:

1. Current militia will camp near villages one weekend per month, to allow locals to witness them drilling and at target practice.

2. Current militia to sponsor sharp shooting contests and award medals.

3. Current militia to sponsor sharp shooting contests for kids.

4. At each village, post printed flyers seeking militia members.

5. Place ads in all local newspapers seeking volunteers.

It was agreed that the militia would be required to spend one weekend each month in New Orleans or a designated village. The militia would be assigned to tents. Eduardo ordered additional rifles for the new militiamen, replacing their outdated muskets.

With all the new marines and soldiers, Eduardo supervised the construction of a new Army barracks, marine barracks, cannoneer's barracks, an NCO Club and an expansion of both the Officers Club and the BOQ. With so many ships, it was also necessary to add a new pier.

To improve morale Eduardo ordered a welcome reception for the officers of the two new ships, the Marine detachment and the new Army Company, as well as a few other new officers. To welcome the new army, navy and marine enlisted men he ordered a picnic with beer. To entertain the enlisted men at the picnic the garrison band was joined by several solo artists and singers from town. Other entertainment included a magician, native American show, a juggler, and a comedian.

He established a weekly dinner dance at the officer's club on Saturday nights and started a Friday night sing along at the NCO club, inviting young ladies from town to participate. Friday evenings was the time for young officers to meet single ladies with a reception offering free drinks for the ladies. Every Sunday afternoon, there was a free concert by the garrison band, which was sometimes joined by musicians from town. The fort was opened to the public for the concert. Town vendors were allowed inside and offered food and beer. A weekend market opened each weekend just outside the gates of the presidio.

Many young soldiers, sailors and marines spent much of their spare time at Madam O'Mally's

House of Pleasure. Her prostitutes were French, Spanish, American, Mexican, Choctaw Indian, Cajun, Negro and Creole. Each week, the Presidio doctor treated the soldiers for syphilis and gonorrhea.

The picnic for enlisted went so well, Eduardo arranged a picnic for officers, enlisted and government employees.

CHAPTER 55

New Orleans, Louisiana

Shipments up the Mississippi & Ohio Rivers

Before July 1777

Another shipment of military supplies arrived in New Orleans. Governor General Galvez shipped another 2,000 barrels of gunpowder, lead and clothing up the Mississippi River to assist the Americans.

HRM Carlos, III, King of Spain made a secret loan to the Americans of 1,000,000 Livres.

Benjamin Franklin, American representative in France, arranged for the secret transport from Spain to the colonies of 215 bronze cannons, 4,000 tents, 13,000 grenades, 30,000 muskets, 30,000 bayonets, 30,000 uniforms, 50,000 musket balls and 300,000 pounds of gunpowder.

CHAPTER 56

Edenton, N.C.

July 30, 1777

Chris stood on the dock looking up at his huge home under construction. It was a two story with a covered porch on the front and both sides. At 4,500 square feet it was double the size of their current home.

What a busy month it had been for him since he returned from Cuba. He had been negotiating with a ship agent in Philadelphia about the purchase of three new ships, while trying to ensure that most of the crews were willing to continue working for him.

He spent as much time as possible with Sara. Within a few days of his arrival, he took her shopping for dresses, blouses, skirts, hats, shoes, cosmetics, perfumes, fancy soaps and unmentionables. The next night he took her to the best restaurant in town for a champagne dinner. On Sunday, after church, they went to lunch with some old friends.

He was now drawing the salary of a Spanish Captain in addition to his income from shipping, warehousing, and his stores. He had decided that two of the three new ships would be placed in two ports where he had not done business before, but which looked inviting: Washington, D.C. and Savannah. The third he would home port in Philadelphia for the time being. In the back of his mind, he thought that one day New Orleans might generate enough business to justify home porting a ship there.

Starting business in Washington and Savannah meant that he had to get an agent in each port and arrange for warehouse storage until he had enough business to justify buying or building his own warehouse. Opening a gift shop would follow after business was flowing.

With 11 ships he now needed his own ship repair facility. His own ships would keep the facility busy. The profit from repairing vessels for other owners would only lower his overhead. It seemed reasonable to think that Philadelphia was the perfect spot for a repair facility because it was convenient to ships from all his ports, and because Philadelphia was the largest city on the east coast, with more ships based or making port there than anywhere else on the coast. He also felt that since he spent so much money on sails, he should open a sailmaker shop next to the repair shop in Philadelphia.

He wrote to Gardoqui to advise that he was prepared, if necessary, to send his ships to Bilbao to pick up cargo and deliver it to New Orleans.

CHAPTER 57

Louisiana Bayeux

New Spain

August 1, 1777 -

"Private Martinez" - "Aqui"

"Private LaSalle" - "Oui"

"Private Running Wolf" - "Ugh"

"Private Dorfmann" - "Ya"

"Private Jones" - "Here boss"

-

As Sergeant Dominguez called the roll, Colonel Eduardo Lopez thought to himself that he was in command of an international militia. Many of the Frenchmen were living here when the area was under French control. Other Frenchies were recently removed from Arcadia, who call themselves Cajuns. Who would have thought there were so many Germans in the swamp? A large number of Canary Islanders joined the Military. They had volunteered to colonize New Spain. The first Canary Islanders arrived in San Antonio. Several runaway slaves joined the group, hoping to earn their freedom.

Eduardo pondered his present position. Although New Orleans was one of the nicest cities in the new world, since arriving he had spent much of his time in the boon docks seeking militia recruits. This was no garden of Eden. For at least 10 months each year the temperature was scorching, which with the muggy humidity made life uncomfortable. The stinky smell of horse manure permeated the city during the warm months. Only the wealthy and farmers could live outside the city. The tiny mosquitoes could give you malaria, broke bone fever or several other ailments. The battalion first sergeant reported that "some of the mosquitoes were so large they were attacking the sparrows." Horse flies constantly buzzed around your face. Chiggers were a constant nuisance. Poisonous snakes were in the grass, in the water and in the trees. The log you were about to sit on turned out to be an alligator.

"Some 710 men answered Colonel," reported the sergeant. "There are 23 missing, but I think most of them were across the river trying to put out the fire of a local man's barn."

"Very good sergeant. Captain Rodriguez will march the unit back to the presidio. These men smell like a zoo. When you get back to the fort, each man is to shower with soap and put on clean clothes. I have arranged for a bar-b-que for the militia to celebrate their completion of training. The garrison will be joining you to celebrate that some of their current duties will now be handled by the Militia. The menu will include paella like from home, with local shrimp and seafood and bar-b-que beef and cabra and all the beer and wine they can drink. They deserve this because they have all worked so hard. I'll double the guard because I don't want any of our drunks to cause problems in town. I have a special treat for the non-coms. The French bakery has made up a large box of French pastries for your pleasure. Finally, Governor Galvez has declared that tomorrow will be a holiday. He knew that most would have a hangover and be worthless anyway. The governor and I will both make an appearance and drink a toast to the men."

CHAPTER 58

Madrid, Spain

September 1, 1777

By September 1777 Spain had already furnished
1,870,000 Livres to the Americans. Much of

this was contributed through the dummy corporation
Rodrique Hortalez and Company, in Paris, for which
France mistakenly received 100% credit.

CHAPTER 59

Battle of Saratoga

Saratoga, New York

October 17, 1777

The Massachusetts Militia, 1,300 strong surrounded British General Burgoyne's English troops on three sides. Some additional 1,100 men of General John Stark's New Hampshire Militia completed the total surrounding of the English. The British could not get out to obtain food or supplies. The Americans then captured all of the British small boats.

After being bombarded by the Americans from four sides, with no cover available, General Burgoyne surrendered. This was a major victory for the Americans – they took about 5,000 prisoners, along with the weapons, ammunition, and military stores.

. . .

Patrick Henry, while Governor of Virginia, wrote two letters to General Galvez thanking Spain

for its help and requesting more supplies. Henry suggested that the two Floridas which Spain lost to England, should revert back to Spain.

CHAPTER 60

Galvez Wedding

New Orleans, LA

November 1, 1777

The wedding of Governor General Bernardo De Galvez and Felicite Saint-Maxent was the most elaborate wedding in the history of New Orleans. The ceremony was conducted by the priest of the Catholic Church. The church was filled with more flowers than normally are found in a florist shop. The choir loft was filled with 30 robed singers. A young Creole girl sang two solos to the tune of the new piano. Felicite's father insisted that the church be illuminated by 1,000 candles. Everybody who was anybody in New Orleans was in attendance. Carriages and coaches were lined up from the church to River Road and up the road about ¼ mile. Courtesy of Mr. Saint-Maxent, each of those drivers was delivered a cup of champagne.

The reception was held at the home of the bride's father. It was a gorgeous day, so the tables with the food were outside under a tarpaulin. The garrison band was stationed under the shade of a large oak tree, from where they entertained the outside guests. Inside, there was much champagne drinking and the cutting of the wedding cake to the gentle sounds of a string quartet.

Again, there was a long line of coaches and carriages down the Saint-Maxent driveway to the road and down the road aways. Like at the wedding, each driver received a cup of champagne.

The couple honeymooned at a cottage on Lake Ponchetran. Eduardo took command while Bernardo honeymooned.

CHAPTER 61

France Declares War on England

Paris, France

February 6, 1778

The "Treaty of Alliance between France and the United States was executed. King Louis XVI of France declared war on England on February 6, 1778.

Because the Borbon Family Compact signed in 1776 by King Louis XVI and King Carlos III provided that if either county was at war, the other country would lend them military aid.

Now England was at war with France and Spain. England just didn't know yet that they faced Spain as well as an adversary.

Captain Butler continued shipping money and military goods from Philadelphia to New Orleans, making stops in Havana in each direction. While his cargo was being unloaded in Havana, he was introduced to French Admiral Henri Hector d'Estaing at the Havana Officer's Club. Fortunately, this officer also spoke English. They had lunch together.

Chris explained his relationship with Eduardo; his contract with Gardoqui, and his agreement with Galvez. Admiral d'Estaing chuckled when he learned that Galvez had commissioned Chis a Captain in the Spanish navy.

"Captain Butler, now that France is at war with England, it will be much more difficult for us to get supplies from France to our outposts in Haiti, Santo Domingo,

Dominica, Grenada, Guadeloupe, Marie-Galante, Martinique, St. Barthélemy, St. Croix, St. Kitts, St. Lucia, St. Martin, St. Vincent and Tobago. If you would be willing to enter into an agreement with me similar to that you have with our Spanish allies, I will pay you 150% of what you are receiving from Spain. What do you think," he asked?

"Admiral, to enter into such an agreement with you, here's what I would need from you:

A letter from you with your personal seal:

1. that introduces me as your personal representative,

2. Advising that I have been retained by the French government to carry mail, supplies and passengers,

3. Instructing all who encounter me to treat me as if I were a Captain in the French Navy,

4. Naming me as an agent of the French Government,

5. Granting me freedom of the port for each French Port you direct me to, thereby allowing me to purchase and sell goods at the civilian markets; and to have an agent purchase and warehouse those goods.

6. Authorizing me to use the Officer's Club and BOQ,

7. Authorizing and instructing the supply officer at each French Port to pay my invoice in gold upon delivery,

8. Making a deposit of 1,000 French Francs,

9. Providing me with an English-speaking French lieutenant as a permanent member of my crew effective on the date I begin loading your cargo. This is my protection against some French warship that might stop my ship or some harbormaster who causes me trouble. You will continue paying the French officer's salary and

benefits. As an incentive, I will pay him a small salary also, and

10. Providing me with a squad of French Marines on each voyage to provide security for my ship.

"This sounds agreeable. Will your schedule allow you to accompany my ship back to Port-au-

Prince, Haiti? I have some important cargo that must get to Santo Domingo, Dominican Republic. I can give you your retainer today if you will accompany me back to my ship. My Judge Advocate General will draft our formal agreement, which we can sign in Port-au-Prince.

"As we say in France, *bienvenue*. Shall we retire to my ship? _____

"Before leaving port, Chris used part of that 1,000 French Francs to purchase a *French-English Dictionary,* a *French Primer, and a bag full of candy*.

CHAPTER 62

Ft. Nelson, Kentucky County, Virginia

General George Rogers Clark receives Spanish supplies.

1778-1779

American General George Rogers Clark obtained a
considerable amount of his military supplies from General
Galvez in New Orleans. These supplies were used in his
victories over the British in Kaskaskia and Cahokia,
Illinois and Vincennes, Indiana.

. . .

In January 1778, Patrick Henry wrote another letter to
General Galvez, thanking Spain for its help and
requesting more supplies.

CHAPTER 63

Fort Pitt

March 1778

U.S. Captain James Willing left Ft. Pitt with an expedition of 30 men, bound for New Orleans to obtain military supplies for the war. As they traveled, they plundered the British settlements along the Ohio and Mississippi Rivers.

General Galvez welcomed them to New Orleans and assisted them in auctioning off their British plunder. Galvez also provided them with Spanish war materials for their return to Fort Pitt.

CHAPTER 64

Spain Declared War on England.

June 21, 1779

Spain declared war on England on June 21, 1779. The Spanish flags Eduardo's ships had been using to deceive the English was no longer useful.

Chris received a letter dated June 30, 1779, from Gardoqui. Senor Gardoqui informed him that the owners of their three leased ships refused to allow their ships to carry goods into a war zone. Gardoqui requested that Butler provide three ships for supply trips from Bilbao, Spain to America and New Orleans. He offered to double the price for each voyage. Realizing that part of Butler's profits came from the sale of goods acquired from other ports, he offered a bonus for non-stop runs from Bilbao to NOLA. One provision was that he must stop in Havana coming and going. Gardoqui offered to act as Butler's agent in Bilbao to provide cargo for return voyages. The letter ended with "If you are willing to accept this agreement, please arrive at our dock in Bilbao as soon as possible. You may claim your retainer of 1,000 Reales at our bank in Philadelphia, by signing a receipt.

That evening Chris and Sara had a long talk. The North Atlantic would be filled with English war ships trying to interdict shipments to the Americas. About one-third of Americans were loyalists, who would report their own mother. If caught, he or one of his captains could be imprisoned and his ship and cargo confiscated.

To accept this proposal was dangerous and much could be lost. But with the cash involved, after a year or two, he and Sara would be rich enough that they could retire. Chris said, "Our country is at war, and we have a moral duty to do everything in our power to ensure that we win."

The next morning, he started packing for his trip across the big pond.

CHAPTER 65

Battles in Central America

1779-1782

José de Gálvez y Gallardo, 1st Marquess of Sonora, Bernardo's uncle, worked to rebuild Guatemala City after the earthquake of 1773. He was the brother of His Excellency, Jose de Galvez, Viceroy of New Spain, and the father of His Excellency, Bernardo de Galvez, Governor General of Louisiana. Matias established a mint and built the cathedral. In 1779, when Spain declared war against Great Britain, it was up to him to plan for the defense of the colony against British incursions. His army defeated the redcoats at San Fernando de Omoa, and captured several British positions in Belize in 1779.

Both England and Spain had been preparing for war for some time. King Carlos, III set the defense of Guatemala as one of his highest priorities in the Americas, after the regaining of British West Florida.

The British sought control over all of Central America, and their initial goal was the capture of San Fernando de Omoa, a fortress that Matías de Gálvez, the Captain General of Guatemala, called "the key and outer wall of the kingdom." It was the largest defensive fortification in Central America, and one of the Guatemala's principal ports.

The British arrived on September 27, 1779, with three ships and 500 men, but were forced to withdraw by the

Spaniards. The British returned with a force of more than 1,200 men and twelve ships in early October.

The British established some batteries to fire on the fort and supported them with cannon fire from three ships. On the night of the 20 October, a small number of British attackers climbed into the fort and opened one of the gates. After a brief exchange of small arms fire, the Spanish commander surrendered. The British gained control of Omoa. The English also captured two Spanish ships, anchored in the harbor, that held more than three million Spanish dollars of silver.

Gálvez immediately began planning a counterattack. On the 25 November his forces began besieging the fort, with exchanges of cannon fire. After four days of siege, the British commander, whose troops were decimated by tropical diseases, withdrew his men from the fort and evacuated them that same day.

The British continued to make attacks on the Central American coast but were never successful in their goal of dividing the Spanish colonies and gaining access to the Pacific Ocean.

CHAPTER 66

Proclamation of HRM Carlos, III, King of Spain

Madrid, Spain

August 29, 1779

On August 29, 1779, King Carlos, III issued a proclamation stating that the main purpose of Spanish troops in America was to drive the British out of the Gulf of Mexico and the Mississippi River Valley.

The king required that all males, including Indians, over 18 in New Spain to become a member of the Militia in their respective area.

CHAPTER 67

Battle of Manchac

Manchac, West Florida

September 7, 1779

Galvez' spies had informed him that the English army in Pensacola had been building up their army in Mobile, Manchac, Baton Rouge and Natchez. For two years Galvez had been building up both his garrison and the Louisiana Militia. The moment had arrived that King Carlos had warned him about. He was ready.

He and Eduardo departed New Orleans on the morning of September 7, 1779, with 667 men which included 170 veteran Spanish soldiers, 330 recruits from Mexico and the Canary Islanders, and an international militia from Germany, America, Cuba, and Puerto Rico. Although most of them walked along the shore, they were accompanied by four boats on the river under Eduardo's command. These Spanish troops were the first foreign troops to fight for American Independence on what is now American soil.

Galvez must have been a very persuasive person. As they marched the 90 miles, he and his officers recruited about 600 men from the German and Acadian coasts together with 160 Native Americans, mostly Choctaws. Along the way on this two week march, two men were attacked by alligators. There were several snake bites, which ended up killing two more. They had no tents to shelter them from the elements. Many men dropped out because of the harsh conditions. When Galvez arrived at Ft. Bute in Manchac he led a force of 1,427 men.

When Galvez confronted Ft. Bute, the British were not aware that Spain had declared war on England. After a brief skirmish, The English surrendered. Galvez took 20 prisoners, with all their arms, ammunition and two cannons.

Galvez detached a platoon from Company A as a garrison for Fort Bute, which was now a Spanish outpost.

CHAPTER 68

Battle of Baton Rouge

Baton Rouge, West Florida

September 20-21, 1779

It had taken the Spanish warriors two weeks to trudge through the swamps from Manchac to the outskirts of Baton Rouge. Galvez and Eduardo recruited a large number of new militiamen on the way, but also had almost as many drop out. The heat and humidity were oppressive, and insects were constantly attacking. There was the constant threat of alligators and poisonous snakes.

Baton Rouge was protected by Fort New Richmond. Dense woods covered all the land some 2530 yards behind the fort. The area in front of the fort was clear. Galvez and Eduardo came up with a plan.

The Spanish forces were to be divided into two groups. The group led by Eduardo was to go into the woods behind the fort and make as much noise as possible. The idea was to deceive the British into thinking that the entire army was in the wooded area. Eduardo had his men chopping down trees and making noise. That night, he had them build three times as many campfires as were actually needed. All during the day riflemen from the woods shot into the fort and drew constant return fire from the fort. Two cannons had been placed just inside the woods, sheltered by large trees and partially concealed by Spanish Moss and native plants. Cannon fire from the woods continued all night, so that nobody slept.

The British commander ordered that the two cannons guarding the main gate be moved to the rear of the fort and double their defense against the Spaniards.

During the day and night Galvez had his group digging trenches leading to the main gate. Their activities were concealed by a large fence. When the trench nearest the main gate of the fort was completed about 10:00 a.m., Galvez had a cannon rolled to the end of the trench. With one cannon shot the main gate was shattered. Immediately, Galvez' group stormed the gate, entered the fort and after a few hours battle, captured it. Galvez took 375 English prisoners, a dozen cannons, arms, ammunition and supplies.

Galvez detached the remaining two platoons of Company A to garrison Fort New Richmond. The cannons were left in place but the small arms and much of the ammunition was loaded onto wagons to be returned to the New Orleans armory.

As part of the surrender agreement, Galvez insisted that the English Commander also surrender the English Fort at Natchez. The English Lt. Colonel in charge of Fort New Richmond wrote a letter to the Officer in Charge of the Natchez Fort, who was under his command, which ordered him to surrender.

A week later a Spanish junior officer, under white flag of truce, presented the letter to the Officer in Charge of the Natchez detachment. He immediately surrendered his sword together with his 80 soldiers, their arms, ammunition and supplies and two cannon. Their weapons and supplies were loaded onto wagons and the prisoners were marched back to New Orleans.

Galvez did not feel that the post at Natchez would benefit the Spanish at this time, so the facility was left vacant.

CHAPTER 69

Hurricane hits New Orleans

Cattle drown. Grains fields flooded.

September 30, 1779

With very little advance warning a violent hurricane hit New Orleans. Large trees were unearthed; homes were lifted from their foundations and blown away; ships in the harbor were found several miles inland; fields were flooded, and livestock drowned. When the storm subsided, New Orleans looked like a war zone.

To assess their predicament, Bernardo and Eduardo took a carriage ride through the city. The entire city was devastated. One street was blocked by the roof of a building. Herds of bloated cows from the army herd floated in what had been corn fields.

"Bernie, it is going to take us weeks to clean up the presidio. Our troops will need to help the civilian population. It seems like our most serious and immediate problem is food. We have about 1,800 military personnel and 500 English prisoners to feed. All our cattle have drowned, and our flooded fields means that we won't have vegetables.

"Lalo, we are going to put your nautical training to good use. Congratulations. You are now the Commodore of the New Orleans Spanish fishing fleet. Four of our 8 ships will be rigged to fish. Each of them will be escorted by a war ship in the event they run into an English war ship. Have two of them rigged to bottom fish for shrimp, oysters, lobster, etc. and the others to go after fish.

Rigging those ships to become fishmen will take some time. I suggest that you purchase fishing poles and put the garrison at work fishing from the dock and small boats. "In the meantime, I have a plan to get us some beef."

CHAPTER 70

Galvez sends to Texas for Long horn cattle.

October 5-21, 1779

Galvez remembered well the long horn cattle from his duties in west Texas. He wrote a letter to Spanish Texas Governor Domingo Cabello explaining his predicament and requesting the sale of 15,000 head of Texas longhorns, and hay to feed them. He asked Francisco Garcia to be his emissary, and when he got to Texas to be sure to remind Governor Cabello that an army travels on its stomach.

Upon receipt of General Galvez' letter, Governor Cabello traveled to San Antonio, the heart of longhorn country. He knew that each of the missions along the San Antonio River had cattle ranches and that there were many private ranchers who also had large herds.

Galvez' idea worked. Between the fall of 1779 and the summer of 1782 between 9.000 and 15,000 head of Texas longhorn cattle were trailed from San Antonio to New Orleans. Their arrival was delayed a few days because the steers had to be trailed north to avoid the Comanche territory that lay between the two cities.

In addition to the cattle, the Texans sent several hundred horses and enough bulls to perpetuate the herd, as well as thousands of pounds of hay, corn, and other grains to feed the animals. These herds were driven by Spanish soldiers, militiamen, native Americans and vaqueros from the San Antonio ranches providing the livestock. Many of the herd drivers remained in New Orleans to fight with Galvez.

CHAPTER 71

Thomas Jefferson writes Galvez

Charlottesville, VA

November 8, 1779

Thomas Jefferson wrote a letter to General Galvez expressing his thanks for Spain's assistance to the United States during its quest for freedom.

CHAPTER 72

Marriage of Eduardo Lopez and Antonette La Salle

New Orleans, Louisiana

December 23, 1779

The war and the hurricane interfered with Toni's plans for a big wedding. A somber mood pervaded all of New Orleans. The newspapers had warned of a possible British attack. The English had enough soldiers in Pensacola to wipe out the Crescent City, not to mention the red coats at Mobile, which were closer. The graves were still fresh from those who died in or as a result of the hurricane. The survivors all went through periods of hunger, and many people starved to death. Life savings had to be used to build back homes and businesses. Alligators and poisonous snakes sought dry ground, that put them in contact with the humans, often resulting in injury or death.

No, it was not the time for a fancy wedding in New Orleans. For all these reasons the couple decided to have a small wedding in the church chapel with just family and close friends in attendance. Bernardo was Lalo's best man and Felicite served as Toni's matron of honor.

As the newly married couple exited the chapel, they walked under cross swords of the garrison's

officers. After the couple's reception at the Officer's Club, they left in a coach for Lake

Ponchetran for their honeymoon.

221

CHAPTER 73

The Donativo

Madrid, Spain

1780

By 1780 Spain had been supporting the Americans for four years. King Carlos was experiencing financial problems operating his empire. King Carlos issued an order requesting a one-time voluntary donation of two Pesos per Spaniard and one Peso per Indian in each provincial site in Spain's new world empire, to defray the expense of the war with England.

The "request' for a Donativo was viewed as a crown order, followed by a high level of participation...

CHAPTER 74

Battle of Mobile

Mobile, West Florida

January 11 – 9 March, 1780

By the time the Texas cattle started arriving in New Orleans the garrison was sick of seafood. In celebration, Galvez ordered that each man was to have a steak dinner. The fleet was ordered to dismantle the fishing nets and resume their normal duties. The daily routine was back to normal.

In King Carlos' proclamation, he had said that the Spanish purpose in North America was to rid

The Mississippi River Valley and the gulf coast of the English. Galvez had already ejected the English from the Mississippi River valley. England had two fortified area on the gulf. One was at Mobile, and the large British facility with three fortresses was at their western hemisphere stronghold in Pensacola.

Fort Charlotte was vitally important because of all the cattle and feed in the area. It was also an excellent fallback position in the event they were unable to take Fort George in Pensacola.

Fort George and its two satellite forts were obtained by the British from France in 1763 by the Treaty of Paris, which ended the French and Indian War. Both these military complexes were a threat to New Orleans.

Since before Christmas Galvez had been working on his plan. On January 2, 1780 he had written to Havana to

223

request additional troops for an attack on Fort Charlotte, which guarded the entrance to Mobile Bay.

On January 11, 1780, Galvez' strike force left New Orleans for Mobile. His flag was on the *Galveston*, a British ship captured on Lake Ponchetran and renamed in his honor. Eduardo was in command of the old pirate ship. His fleet had grown to 12 ships, which were transporting 754 men. It took them a week to traverse the winding Mississippi River to its mouth in the Gulf of Mexico. Two days later they rendezvoused with the American ship *West Florida*, under the command of Captain William Pickles, with 58 onboard.

On January 20th the officers and men toasted King Carlos, III, on his birthday.

As this battle convoy made its way northeast to Mobile it was hit by a strong electrical storm.

This storm scattered the fleet, causing Galvez to worry that his plans were going to be destroyed.

However, they fleet was soon reassembled, and within another three days they arrived at Mobile.

His initial attack of Fort Charlotte on February14th was disappointing. Two of his ships ran aground on sand bars in the channel. He blamed this on the poor intelligence of the harbor. His ship *Volante* was so damaged by English cannon fire that it was useless. Eduardo ordered that the crew establish a gun battery at Mobile Point[10] with the guns from the *Volante* to guard the entrance into the bay by English ships, leaving the Captain of the *Volante* in command. Moving 12 cannon from a ship and creating a gun battery took three days. Each night Eduardo had sent

---

[10] Site of present day Fort Morgan.

small boats into the bay to take soundings in hopes of finding the channel. On the evening of February 19th, Eduardo was having dinner with Galvez on the *Galveston.* "Bernie, we have found the channel," he said!

Shortly after sunup on February 20, 1780 the cavalry arrived. On the southeastern horizon appeared a Spanish task force of 24 ships, including two cargo ships carrying food, ammunition and supplies. The transport carried over 1,400 soldiers increasing the total Spanish forces offshore to about 2,400. An English deserter had informed Galvez' intelligence officer that the English fort was manned by only about 300 men.

The Havana troops and their cannons were landed about 10 miles from Fort Charlotte near the Dog River on February 25th. They marched to a point north of the fort where they spent the next few days establishing batteries of cannon to the northeast and northwest of the fort. With cannon fire from the bay, they had surrounded the fort.

Beginning on March 1, 1780 the fort was bombarded from three sides. The shelling lasted for almost two weeks. On March 13, 1780 cannon fire demolished the entrance to the fort and a section of its walls. The following day the British commander surrendered. The Spanish took 281 prisoners, 20 cannons, arms, ammunition and supplies.

In Galvez' plan to capture Pensacola, he knew that he must defend his rear. That meant that he must secure Mobile Bay. "Lalo, I am leaving you in charge of Ft. Charlotte with about 500 men to protect our backside. Choose the units you want and let me know. I must travel to Havana to make plans for the attack on Pensacola. The remained of our troops will return to New Orleans, while we wait on decisions that must be made in Madrid."

225

Because of this important victory, Galvez was promoted to Field Marshall and placed into command of all Spanish operations in America. His promotion to Field Marshall did not reach him until June. He then promoted Eduardo to Brigadier General in command of all Spanish forces in North America.

CHAPTER 75

John Adams visits Gardoqui

Bilbao, Spain

January 15-20, 1780

John Adams visited Bilbao, Spain and met with Diego Gardoqui of Joseph Gardoqui and Sons. In one of two letters sent by him from his inn in Bilbao, John Adams wrote the following:

We have had the pleasure of finding Mr. Gardoqui and sons friends willing to collaborate with us in all respects.

Joseph Gardoqui y Hijos of Bilbao, Spain sent 120,000 Reales to the United States in pieces of eight cash and payment amounting to 50,000 Reales on other orders. These coins were used to support the U.S. public debt and give rise to its own currency, the dollar.

CHAPTER 76

Meeting of Spanish Officers

Ft. Charlotte

Mobile, British West Florida

March 11, 1780

"Gentlemen, we have been detached here to be a rear guard for General Galvez' expedition. We must be on guard for an attack by the English. They may attack with ground forces from Pensacola, or we might be attacked from the sea. Either way, we must prepare ourselves," said General Eduardo.

"First, the crew of the *Volante*, other than its gun crews must be rescued from Point Mobile. Six of the *Volante's* guns and gun crews are to be stationed on the southeastern tip end of Dauphin Island. This will allow us to defend the entrance into the bay from both sides. We must supply both sets of gun crews with tents, tarpaulins to cover the cannon and their living areas, food, water and supplies. The junior officers left in command of these small detachments should ensure that gun emplacements are dug and that a palisade is constructed to protect them from enemy fire. To each gun crew should be assigned a flag signalman, so they can communicate with one another.

"A platoon of marines is assigned to the bay entrance to protect these naval gunmen, with half going to either side of the bay entrance. The crew and the marines will assist in salvaging anything of value off the *Volante*. An inventory of salvaged goods is to be provided to me as soon as possible.

"I am establishing an outpost on the other side of the bay with 8 cannons so that if an English ship threatens Fort Charlotte, it will be subject to crossfire. It will also serve to warn us of an enemy attack from the west. It is to be garrisoned by the New Orleans Negro Military Company and C company, along with the sailors from the *Volante*. The cannon will be operated by the cannoneer company. You will also be assigned a signalman. Latrines must be dug at all three outposts.

"We have two fast Caravels at our disposal. One will remain in the bay. It will be responsible for patrolling the bay, delivering messages from the fort and exchanging signals from all three outposts. It will also make runs to deliver food, water and supplies. The other Caravel will patrol the area surrounding the outer entrance to the bay to warn us of the approach of English ships. "Our dry rations will be supplemented with game and fish, as I have delegated some of our sharpshooters as hunters, and all those available can drown some worms to feed us fish." On the third day the bodies of two of his hunters were found. Both had been scalped by Indian allies of the English.

CHAPTER 77

English Siege of Charleston

Charleston, South Carolina

March 29 – May 12, 1780

The English navy laid siege on Charleston, South Carolina, between March 29 and May 12, 1780, blocking the entrance into the harbor.

Captain Butler's ship was forced to make deliveries to the port of Georgetown to the north. This delay not only caused him a loss of three days, but it also prevented him from delivering the cargo onboard destined for Charleston or receiving and loading the cargo his agent had for him to pick up.

For the first time Chris realized how the war could touch him and his livelihood. He began to have second thoughts about running to Spain.

His next stop was in his new port of Savanna. Then he was off to Port-au-Prince, Haiti.

CHAPTER 78

Cadiz, Spain

Soldiers depart for America.

April 1780

The Spanish fleet sailed from Cadiz, Spain to America to reinforce the army of General Bernardo de Galvez. These soldiers were transported to Havana to support General Galvez' attack on Pensacola.

CHAPTER 79

Battle of Fort San Carlos

St. Louis, MO

May 28, 1780

"Those British Bastards! We will pay them for this attack!" Those were the angry words of Captain Don Fernando de Leyba, Lieutenant Governor of the Spanish Province of North Louisiana, and commandant of Fort San Carlos[11]. He was Galvez' Deputy Governor General.

On May 26, 1780, about 300 English soldiers and about 1,500 of their Indian warriors attacked Fort San Carlos, which was named for King Carlos.

Fort San Carlos was a Spanish outpost on the Mississippi River at the present site of St. Louis, Missouri. It was inhabited by about 900 people, including many French trappers and their families and merchants, with only about 300 capable of firing a weapon. Captain de Leyba had constructed a tower and placed two cannons on top. When the English attacked de Leyba fired the cannon and the Indians scattered, causing the English soldiers to retreat.

The attack was part of the British master plan in effect to sweep down the Mississippi River attacking Spanish forts on the west side and American settlements on the east. When they reached New Orleans, they were to be joined by British troops to be landed up the Mississippi River and on the shores of Lake Ponchetran.

---

[11] Now known as St. Louis, MO.

This defeat halted their plans.

CHAPTER 80

Morro Castle

Havana, Cuba

May 1780

"Your excellencies," said Bernardo, "I have traveled here to discuss with you capture of Fort George and its two satellite forts in Pensacola. As you know it is probably the strongest fort in the Western Hemisphere outside of where we sit. The ships and men from here that were involved in the capture of Mobile were exceedingly helpful. We will need a force at least twice that size to capture Pensacola. We must write to Madrid to obtain the transfer of more ships and men for this armada. The king has ordered that we clear the English from the Gulf, and Pensacola is the last blight on our chart."

After two days of discussions the officers agreed to request the following from Navy Headquarters in Madrid:

> 3,000 soldiers
>
> 35 troop transports
>
> 25 warships
>
> 300 cannons
>
> 10,000 pounds of gunpowder
>
> 5,000 cannon balls
>
> 25,000 bullets
>
> 15,000 musket balls
>
> 1,500 tents

600 tarpaulins

The dispatch making this request was placed on a fast ship to Spain. The *Galveston* also made sail back to New Orleans, with General Galvez embarked.

CHAPTER 81

Spanish fleet capture 55 English ships

August 9, 1780

The Spanish fleet under the command of Admiral Luis de Cordova y Cordova encountered an English convoy of 63 ships headed to Boston with replacement troops, arms and ammunition to counter the insurrection in America. After a brief sea battle, 8 of the British warships guarding the convoy, abandoned the battle, allowing the Spanish fleet to capture 55 English naval vessels, 3,144 men of the English 90th Regiment of Foot, and about 1.5 million Pounds of goods. This was the largest wartime capture of enemy ships in world history.

Of the 55 ships captured seven were warships. All 55 ships were placed into the Spanish fleet. Lloyds of London sustained its worst financial loss in history.

CHAPTER 82

Gardoqui & Sons

Bilbao, Spain

September 3, 1780

"Joseph," said Diego, "we just received a letter from North Spain Shipping Company. They are putting us on notice that they will not allow their ships leased to us to make delivers to North America, the Gulf of Mexico or the Caribbean. They point out that there is a "war clause" in their lease."

"We're going to be forced to hire embargo runners and be prepared to pay them a premium for risking their ships and their lives. I think I can persuade Captain Butler to come to Spain for our cargo. If we use him, we can speed up delivery by shipping the goods from Bilbao to Cadiz.

This will save him several days coming and as many on his return trip."

"I'll start looking around for wagons, teams and drivers. Then, I'll line up an available warehouse on the Cadiz waterfront. I'll leave the arm twisting of Captain Butler to you, Diego."

CHAPTER 83

King's Mountain

King's Mountain, North Carolina

October 7, 1780

Up until the fall of 1780 the English had been having their way with American Forces. That was when a reversal of luck began for the Americans. English Major Patrick Ferguson was in command of a regiment of 1,200 loyalists on top of King's Mountain, which was the North Carolina – South Carolina line in the western part of the state. Ferguson had a reputation as a "butcher" in Carolina and was hated by all.

At the time the western part of North Carolina was filled with backwoodsmen, who had to be crack shots with their long barreled rifles, or they couldn't survive. Ferguson had warned them that if they didn't stop attacking the crown that he would invade their territory, destroy their settlements and hang their leaders. Now he was here in their territory to fulfill his threat.

The North Carolinians were still in contact with a number of former neighbors who had moved across the mountains to Tennessee territory against the king's orders. A runner was sent to Tennessee requesting military assistance.

The leaders of the patriot opposition included Colonel Isaac Shelby of Virginia, Colonel John Sevier of Tennessee, Colonel Benjamin Cleveland and Colonel Frederick Hambright, both of North Carolina.

Some 900 mounted "Over The Mountain Men" of the 1,400 assembled were divided into 8 elements which were evenly spaced around the mountain. At the appointed time the 1,400 attacked at the same time working their way up to the top. Their marksmanship was the difference. Ferguson refused to surrender and was shot dead. Over 1,000 Tories were killed, wounded or taken prisoner.

It was a great victory for the Americans.

CHAPTER 84

Pensacola hurricane

Spanish fleet destroyed.

Oct. 16, 1780

Galvez' prayers had been answered by the Spanish Navy Department. He received a note from Havana that the ships, men and equipment requested were all scheduled to arrive in Havana about October 1, 1780. On September 15, the *Galveston* departed New Orleans with Galvez and his battle staff embarked. They arrived in Havana on September 26, 1780. Galvez conferred with the Havana flag officers about the plan of attack for the next several days and developed the nucleus of a plan.

The convoy arrived from Spain a day early, and the following day there was a meeting of all senior officers who were to play a part in the invasion.

On October 16, 1780, Galvez led his armada out of Havana harbor headed toward Pensacola. This task force included 7 gunships, 5 frigates, 3 smaller warships, and 49 transports. Aboard this fleet were 164 officers and 3,829 enlisted men.

In 1780 there was no way to accurately predict the weather. A strong hurricane hit the task force decimating it. About half of his ships and men were lost at sea. Many of the other half of the men and ships were cast ashore from Texas to Cuba. Miraculously, Galvez and the *Galveston* were unscathed. From the men and ships salvaged, he felt it necessary to reinforce Eduardo's garrison in Mobile to prepare for a possible attack from

Pensacola. He reassigned two additional warships and another 500 men to reinforce Mobile, while he worked on a new plan.

Galvez returned to Havana to start all over again. He was very depressed.

CHAPTER 85

Mobile garrison defeats attack

January 1781

The British at Pensacola were irritated. They had read in the *London Times* that Galvez had lost 2,000 men in the hurricane who were on their way to attack Pensacola. They had lost Manchac, Baton Rouge, Natchez and Mobile, and had been defeated at Ft. San Carlos. They were out for blood.

British Fortress Commander Colonel John Campbell, sent over 700 men, including several hundred members of the Choctaw, Creek and Chickasaw Indians to attack Fort Charlotte at Mobile. The British forces attacked at dawn. With the additional 500 men General Galvez had dispatched to Mobile Eduardo won and easy victory.

The Pensacola soldiers and their Indian allies retreated to the east and did not ever again attempt to take Fort Charlotte.

On January 20th the victorious officers and men toasted King Carlos, III on his birthday. This toast was rendered by Spaniards all over the world.

CHAPTER 86

American Victory

Cowpens, South Carolina.

January 17, 1781

General Cornwallis continued to pacify the Carolinas. The American forces were now under the command of General Nathan Greene. The English were commanded by Lt. Colonel Bannister Tarleton. A patriot spy had sent Tarleton and his men to 96, South Carolina to corner the Americans. When Tarleton got to 96 and found no American soldiers, he raced his men to Cowpens.

When the British arrived at Cowpens they were malnourished and exhausted. Rather than wait until his men had had food and water and time to rest, Tarleton ordered them into battle. The Americans were dug in, and divided into three groups, two of which gave way, allowing the third to demolish the British on the field.

Tarleton's force of 1,100 British troops were outnumbered by 1,800 American troops under Morgan. Morgan's forces suffered casualties of only 25 killed and 124 wounded. Tarleton's force was almost completely eliminated with 90% of his men killed or captured. About 200 British troops escaped.

General Cornwallis was almost in a panic. He was having to explain to the Admiralty how the mightiest army in the world had been defeated by backwoods sodbusters at Kings Mountain and Cowpens, following the losses up the Mississippi and the defeat at Mobile.

243

CHAPTER 87

Pensacola Siege

13 Feb – 9 Mar. 1781

Galvez promoted to Captain General

"Dammit Calvo! Order your fleet into the Bay," Galvez shouted at no one in particular! Captain

Calvo de Irazabal was in command of the Spanish fleet from Havana. Calvo had the entire Spanish fleet jammed up at the entrance to Pensacola Bay. There was a narrow entrance between Santa Rosa Island and Perdido Key, both of which had British cannon bombarding the Spanish fleet. Calvo's ship, the 64 cannon *San Ramon* had grounded in its attempt to transit the straits.

By flag message Irazabal ordered his fleet to hold fast, citing the danger that British guns on both Santa Rosa Island and Perdido Key seemed to have range to the bay entrance.

"Imbecile!" said Galvez when he received this message. Galvez went back to his cabin to come up with a plan.

After an hour there was a knock on his cabin door. "Enter," said Galvez.

"Chief Galvan, I have a job for you. As soon as its dark I want you to take a long boat with two men and a sounding line[12]. I want you to find and mark a channel into the bay.

---

[12] A sounding line is a rope with a weight on the end. Knots are placed in the rope every six feet to measure the dept of the water in fathoms.

"Aye, Governor, we'll find it," said Chief Galvan.

And find the channel they did, after working past midnight.

At dawn he hoisted a flag that said "Follow Me" as he eased the *Galveston* through the channel, past the incredulous Calvo watching from the quarterdeck of his ship, into the bay. Three of his New Orleans based ships followed. Calvo, with a red face dripping with sweat reluctantly ordered the remainder of the Havana fleet to follow Galvez.

"Captain Menchaca, take your marines and clear Santa Rosa Island and Perdido Key of English gunners. Your men will man those guns to guard against British ships entering the harbor." "Aye, sir," Captain Menchaca responded. With a sharp salute, he turned and left the cabin.

Galvez' thoughts turned to the upcoming battle:

An attack on Fort George was really an attack on three forts. Red Cliff Fort was located seven miles southwest of Fort George. Fort Half Moon was about five miles east of Fort George. All three fortresses were earthen works upon which palisades had been built. The three forts, two redoubts with cannons, and batteries on Santa Rosa Island and Perdido Key were manned by about 2,000 English soldiers and 500 native Americans. Galvez' forces included about 3,500 when he attacked on March 9, 1781. These included 500 men returned by Eduardo in Mobile and 1,400 soldiers from New Orleans. This was to be a long siege.

Galvez had directed that all his ships form a line in the bay facing the fortresses and commence shelling the forts.

Many of the English guns could not be lowered enough to fire on the ships.

On April 12, while directing naval gunfire, Galvez was shot in the left arm. He was helped to his cabin, where the doctor joined them. The doctor examined the wound and said "You are lucky general. The musket ball went clear through your arm. No surgery is required. I will have you a new man in no time," exclaimed the doctor. Galvez was treated and his arm was placed in a sling. With his sword in his right hand, he continued to direct gunfire from the deck of his ship.

For the next week nobody was able to sleep. The sound of cannon fire and explosions as well as small arms fire, raged on day and night. The soldiers on both sides felt like zombies from lack of sleep.

A week later additional help arrived – 1,600 reinforcements from Havana, and 725 French soldiers who arrived on four French frigates. By the end of April Galvez was in command of about 7,800 combatants. Also, by that time his troops had completed the stationing and preparing cannon emplacements.

Galvez at the Battle of Pensacola 1

The 7,800 men were significant. George Washington's Continental Army consisted of only about 6,000 men, which also was about the number of British soldiers at Yorktown, when General Cornwallis surrendered.

On May 8, 1781, a Spanish artillery shell hit the powder magazine at England's Fort Crescent Redoubt. The initial explosion set off a series of explosions that destroyed the entire redoubt.

Some 57 English soldiers were instantaneously killed and hundreds more were wounded. Spanish forces immediately occupied the redoubt, installing Spanish cannons. This redoubt was within range of both other British forts. After two days of shelling from this redoubt, the British surrendered.

That day Bernardo Galvez took 1,113 prisoners and paroled about 300 English soldiers to Georgia, upon their oath not to rejoin the British army. The British sustained over 200 dead, and an unknown number of wounded. Spanish casualties totaled 74 dead, with 198 wounded.

Significantly, in the surrender document, England granted all of East and West Florida to Spain – which was one of King Carlos' goals. In addition, Galvez captured 153 cannons, cannon balls and ammunition, thousands of muskets, and military supplies. As icing on the cake the English also forfeited to the Spanish the 18-gun HMS *Port Royal*, a sloop.

After the surrender document was executed, Galvez had all the British prisoners sent to Havana.

He spent the next several weeks repairing and strengthening the three forts. One of the former British batteries was moved closer to the bay. The two batteries on Santa Rosa Island and Perdido Key were reinforced.

When all the construction was completed, Galvez ordered two of the battalions from Havana to garrison the three forts, two redoubts, and two outposts. He dispatched three ships, including the *Port Royal* to remain to protect the bay. The Executive Officer of the *Galveston* was named skipper of the *Port Royal* and given authority to pick his crew from the other ships in the bay. Lt. Colonel Esteban Rincon was designated as Commander of Pensacola area military command, including Ft. George, Red Cliff Fort, Fort Half Moon, the two redoubts and the two batteries at the entrance to the harbor. Junior officers were designated to command each post.

. . .

"I knew he could carry it off," said King Carlos to the Marquis de Grimaldi, his Prime Minister. "Galvez has kicked the English out of the Mississippi River Valley and the Gulf Coast of America. Now our American Friends won't have to worry about a new front in the west or the south. The British are on the run and one of our goals has been obtained. We now have regained control of East and West Florida."

"Also," the king continued, "we have another hero to recognize. General Eduardo Lopez obtained a decisive victory against the British at Mobile. I am promoting General Galvez to Lieutenant General, and General Lopez is to be elevated to Major General. Also, General

Galvez is to be awarded two titles: 'Count of Galvez,' and 'Viscount of Galveztown.' Since he restored Spain to ownership of East and West Florida, henceforth he shall be Governor of Louisiana, East and West Florida,"

"Your majesty, I will have the appropriate orders cut immediately.

About 1,600 Spanish reinforcements from Havana arrived in Pensacola.

CHAPTER 88

Captain Butler loads Spanish Goods

Philadelphia, Pennsylvania

June 3, 1781

Chris sat in his brightly paneled captain's quarters. He was excited about going back to New Orleans. Gardoqui's ship Captain had alerted him that since the war seemed to be about over, there might be no more shipments. He looked forward to meeting and spending time with Bernardo and Eduardo's new brides. The three ships he recently purchased had been merged into his fleet, with new warehouses in Washington, D.C. and Savanna, Georgia. There was talk that Washington might become the nation's capital. The third new ship had been dispatched last year to Bilbao, Spain to pick up cargo.

He and Sara had moved into their new home which she had completely furnished. When he left the week before, Sara was still hanging pictures and repositioning nick knacks. She was a happy wife, even though she knew that it could be months before she saw Chris again.

The ship was noisy while the cargo was being loaded. He had gone shopping that morning. First, he purchased three kinds of candy for Eduardo. He purchased a pocketknife for Bernardo that had several attachments including a corkscrew. For Bernardo and Eduardo, he purchased newspapers from every city. For the two new brides he purchased perfume and linen handkerchiefs.

For Admiral d'Estaing he selected a fine case of French wine.

That afternoon a representative of the French Consulate delivered several small packages and a diplomatic pouch to be delivered to Admiral d'Estaing in Port Au Prince.

There was a knock on the cabin door.

"Come in," replied Chris.

"Captain, we have completed loading. Shall I notify the crew that we sail on the tide," asked First?

"We sail at 8 bells. Ready the crew," answered Chris.

CHAPTER 89

New Orleans, Louisiana

June 12, 1781

Galvez received his promotion to Lt. General (three stars[13]) , and Eduardo got his promotion to Major General (two stars) at the same time. Both received high medals for bravery. Along with the package containing the promotions and medals for he and Bernardo, was an envelope from King Carlos to Eduardo. It read as follows:

May 15, 1781

Dear General Lopez,

From your promotion and the award of another medal to you, I am confident that you are aware of the high regard in which I hold you. I must now call upon you to uproot yourself for what could be a journey they may well take a year or more of you being away from your family.

The colony of Louisiana is almost bankrupt. Spain has loaned over 1,000,000 Reales[14] to the Americans. Unfortunately, the Americans currently have no funds to repay us. Yet, our creditors are demanding payment.

My solution is to use the gold and silver from Mexico and Peru and the goods from the Orient to make those payments. Because of the war it appears that our

---

[13] At this time in history, in most armies in the world a three star general was the highest rank obtainable. George Washington was a three star general. [14] A Real is a Spanish Piece of Eight.

deliveries have been slowed considerably. It is urgent that our supplies of gold and silver be expedited. It is also necessary to explore the handling of our oriental goods from the Philippines. I need you to come up with a plan to expedite the transfer of these goods.

Enclosed you will find a letter of introduction from me with my royal seal which says that you are acting as my personal representative and advising all who encounter you to treat your requests like an order from me. That should give you all the clout you need to accomplish this mission.

You are hereby ordered to make your way from New Orleans to Vera Cruz, Mexico. There you will travel overland to Acapulco, Mexico. You will be a passenger on the

Caca Fuego, one of our huge treasure ships, from Acapulco, Mexico to Manila,

Philippines. You will remain in the Philippines long enough to make any changes that would allow the goods to arrive in Spain sooner. Once your duties are completed in the Philippines, you are to travel to Lima, Peru, where you will investigate the entire process from work in the mines until shipment to improve our procedures. When your duties are completed there, you will return to Acapulco, from where you will follow the cargo on donkey trails to Taxco, Mexico, where much of the Mexican silver is mined. Again, you are to remain in Taxco until your report and recommendations are concluded.

From Taxco you are ordered to Mexico City, where you are to analyze our procedures at the mint. Is there a faster way to mint coins? You are to secure enough

253

bullion to pay our debts in Louisiana and follow this fortune to New Orleans, via Vera Cruz.

You are authorized to take with you an aide in the rank of Colonel, an assistant in the rank of Lieutenant and a Sergeant as an orderly. Governor Galvez has been authorized to advance you10,000 Livres to cover payroll for you and your staff and any expenses.

To assist you I am sending in a separate package, copies of the financial records of our operations in Mexico, the Philippines and Peru.

HRM Carlos de Borbon, III Catholic King of Spain

When Toni read the letter from the king that night, she cried. "You just got back from months away fighting up the Mississippi and in Mobile. Now, you are leaving for a year, maybe." she said as a tear rolled down her cheek.

Eduardo walked across the room and gave her a big hug. "Toni, darling, when you married me, you knew I was a soldier. I am going to miss your smile, your laugh and your kisses, but when the king calls, I must go. This is a great honor. Look at this second letter. How many people in Spain can say they were ever the "personal representative" of the King?

That night the couple made mad, passionate love.

"Lt. Colonel Garcia, are you interested in some paid travel," asked General Lopez with a crooked smile?

"Where are you taking me this time, General," Garcia asked?

"Fernando, this is a deluxe trip, which must remain secret, but I can offer, Mexico with its lush beaches, the wide expanse of the Pacific Ocean and the Philippines, the gateway to the Orient. To that I add the land of the Incas. All that and you will still be fed and paid."

"But sir, it sounds like we could be away for the better part of a year."

"In fact, Fernando, we may be gone for more than a year. I need you. I know you, and I trust you. If you say yes, you will magically convert yourself from Lt. Colonel to Colonel. Does that help," asked Eduardo?

"Sir, you knew that I would have followed you without the promotion – but thanks. When do we leave and what do you need me to do before we leave?"

"Fernando, this time there will be four on our staff. I leave it up to you to select an assistant and an orderly. The assistant can be a lieutenant and the orderly a sergeant. We have to wait on a ship that can be directed to Vera Cruz. When I discover our departure date you will be the first to know. As soon as you have designated our assistant and our orderly you may go on leave. You and your wife might enjoy some time on Lake Ponchetran.

The following day Eduardo shared his news with Bernardo.

"Lalo, I'm going to miss your ass around here. You've become a fixture. You've been a busy guy around here and now you plan to leave me in the lurch just because our king ordered you to," he said laughingly. "You and Toni need some time together, so I am granting you leave starting tomorrow. While you are away, Felicite and I will take care of Toni.

255

"I also received a letter from King Carlos. He has instructed me to provide you with enough money to pay the salaries of you and your staff, plus an additional 10,000 Livres to cover any expenses you might incur. I will have a locked chest of coins for you before you leave," said Bernardo.

"Check with me before you leave the post."

Two weeks later Galvez received a message from Havana, informing him that Capt. Butler was in Havana and was expected to depart on June 25th on his way to New Orleans.

CHAPTER 90

Captain Butler Arrives

New Orleans, Louisiana

July 3, 1781

Bernardo and Eduardo were both on the dock waving as Christopher's crew tied up the *Sharnbrook* to the New Orleans pier.

"Permission to come aboard, sir," shouted Bernardo as he topped the gangway.

"Permission granted," answered Christopher as he extended his right hand. As they shook hands each man grabbed the upper arm of the other. Eduardo followed close behind and followed the same greeting.

"Your Excellencies, allow me to present Lieutenant Francois DeVille, my French Liaison officer. Admiral d'Estaing assigned him to me when he made me a Captain in the French Navy and engaged me to deliver cargo, mail and passengers to other French possessions in the Caribbean. He will be assigned to me until my final French Port.

Lt. DeVille was ecstatic to be with two French speakers. Although he was fluent in English, he preferred to speak in his native tongue. "I know you gentlemen wish to speak privately, so I will excuse myself. It was a pleasure to meet you," he said as he took off his hat and bowed.

"Lieutenant, General Lopez and I and our wives are treating Captain Butler to dinner tonight at New Orleans finest restaurant, *Chez Maurice*. You will be expected to join us. We will send a carriage for you and Captain Butler at 7:00."

"It will be my honor to join you General," he replied.

"Please, let's have a celebratory drink in my cabin," said Christopher. "First, begin the unloading process," ordered Christopher. "Aye, aye, sir," responded the first mate.

The three men were excited to be rejoined after such a long time.

"Chris, why is this French Lieutenant on board now," Eduardo asked?

"When I leave here, I am scheduled to make calls at a dozen French ports in the Windwards and Leeward's[14] before I return to Port-A-Prince. Since I speak only a few words of French, I figured that I needed a competent French Speaking officer to run interference for me – *N'est pas*?"

Bernardo spoke briefly of their victories in the Mississippi River Valley and their triumphs at Mobile and Pensacola. From their respective promotions and the new medals on their chests it was self-evident that they were heroes.

Chris told of his meeting with Admiral d'Estaing; being made Captain in the French Navy; being contracted to carry mail, cargo and passengers for the French; building a new home; buying three ships; opening two new ports; and making runs from Spain to Boston and Philadelphia.

Chez Maurice was established by the French in 1760 and was New Orleans oldest, finest, and most expensive

---

[14] The Windward and Leeward islands of the Caribbean.

restaurant. It was in the French Quarter across the park from where the Cabildo was being constructed and to the right of the church. The candlelight from five crystal chandeliers was reflected by the smoky mirrors on all four walls. The main dining room was lush with tropical plants and statuary. From the adjacent cocktail lounge diners could hear the soft melodies of a pianist.

When Christopher and Francois arrived, they were escorted to a large table for eight in a partially private area. The table was near two French doors opening onto a patio. The sweet smell of magnolia blossoms wafted into the dining area, along with a cool breeze to temper the heat. Already seated were Bernardo and Felicite, Eduardo and Toni, and Lieutenant Colonel Fernando Garcia and his wife, Esmeralda. Champagne glasses were filled all around except at their place settings. Their glasses were filled before they could put their napkins on their laps. Introductions were made all around. Soft piano music flowed into the restaurant.

"Chris," said Bernardo, "since you spent so much time on the *Sharnbrook* with Fernando, we asked him and his wife to join us. This restaurant is operated by a couple, David and Justine Dantone. My favorite dish is Crabmeat Justine. What most restaurants call Oysters Bienville, they have renamed Oysters Galvez. Everything on their menu is good.

That evening champagne and conversation both flowed. Everyone laughed when Chris presented Eduardo with his large bag of candy. Bernardo loved his knife and Felicite and Toni both got up from the table and each of them gave Chris a hug in appreciation for their perfume and linen handkerchiefs. Just before they finished dinner they

259

toasted the King of Spain, The King of France and George Washington.

Bernardo tapped his glass with his knife to get everyone's attention. "As most of you know, Eduardo and I have been friends since childhood. All of a sudden, this guy Christopher comes into our lives. He becomes our steadfast friend. In a few days Lalo and Chris will depart for Vera Cruz. Lalo will be gone for a year or more. Although Chris may return briefly for a few days in a month or so, who knows when we will see him again. I propose that we form a group and agree to the following:

1. That we keep in touch by mail.

2. That we exchange newspapers from our travels.

3. That we get together annually with our families.

4. That we encourage our children to keep in touch with each other."

Lalo said, "I'll second that, but I want to amend your motion to require each of you to keep me in Candy," he said laughingly. The others laughed agreeably.

"What shall we call our group," asked Toni?

"Since all the men are senior officers, I propose we call ourselves 'The Warriors'," proposed Felicite.

"All in favor say aye," said Bernardo.

"Aye," said each of them and "The Warriors" came into existence.

"We are agreed then to get together when Lalo returns from his adventure.

"Chris," said Bernardo, "Please come to my office tomorrow at 10:00. We have some business to discuss."

"See you then, General."

. . .

The following morning, they all felt a bit hung over. The delicious coffee with chicory helped decidedly. Chris loved the little pastries with powdered sugar. "What do you call these pastries," Chris asked? "We call then *beignets*," answered Bernardo.

"Gentlemen, I brought you the latest news of the outside world. Here are some old newspapers which I hope you enjoy.

"Chris, please read this," asked Eduardo, "It's a letter to me from King Carlos."

"So, I guess you want my ship to deliver you to Vera Cruz. Is that it," he asked?

"Chris, as you can see, this is an urgent matter. With the war, we can't spare one of our war ships to transport Lalo and his entourage.

"Admiral d'Estaing will be upset with a delay of a month or more, and my wife, Sara will be disappointed."

"Chris, I made you a Spanish Captain before he made you a French Captain, so your loyalties should be to me before d'Estaing." The conversation drug on for about ten minutes.

"Alright, when do we leave," asked Chris.

"You are not going anywhere dressed like that," exclaimed Bernardo. "You are out of uniform, Admiral," said Bernardo with a huge smile on his face. "I am promoting you to Rear Admiral (two stars). Here are

261

your stars and your shoulder boards and a pennant with two stars to fly on your ship. Chris was so shocked, he sat back down. For a moment he had a blank stare on his face, which changed to a belly laugh. "Me, an admiral. Who would have ever suspected?"

"Also, I have prepared a new Letter of Introduction for you indicating that you are the personal representative of the Governor General of Louisiana, West Florida and East Florida, and that you are to have freedom of the port wherever you go. Since this is a special journey, you will be paid 150% of your normal fee. You are to return here for mail and cargo as soon as possible. Then you may attend to our French friends.

Eduardo spent the afternoon in the supply room securing blank ledgers, journals, logbooks,

paper, pens, ink, sealing wax, envelopes and salt for use by his staff.

CHAPTER 91

The *Sharnbrook* Departs

New Orleans, Louisiana

July 9, 1781

"Haul in the gangway," ordered Christopher.

"Single up all lines."

"Let go forward line."

"Let go aft line."

"Let go amidships."

"You've got the con, First. Set your course for Vera Cruz."

"Aye, aye sir," responded the first mate.

The *Sharnbrook* eased into the channel and headed downstream towards the Gulf. Eduardo had enjoyed breakfast with Bernardo that morning. Bernardo presented Eduardo with the chest full of gold and silver coins, three locks and three keys. "Please sign this receipt," requested Bernardo. After breakfast the two men rode in a carriage to the pier, were Sgt. Blanco and a seaman delivered it to Eduardo's quarters.

Eduardo always wore his sword when traveling by coach, carriage or on horseback. None of the officers were wearing their swords because swords are worn only to prepare for battle, for repelling boarders and for ceremonial purposes.

Felicite, Toni and Esmeralda stood together on the pier waving goodbye to their husbands. Chris joined Eduardo and Fernando at the port side railing, waving goodbye to their wives and Felicite. Bernardo had sent the garrison band to serenade their departure. A few vendors circulated among the crowd that had come to see them off. It was a festive departure.

At dinner that evening in the captain's quarters there was a new face. Navy Lt. Javier "Javi" Ramirez had been selected by Colonel Garcia to serve as assistant to General Lopez and himself.

Others around the table included Rear Admiral Christopher "Chris" Butler, Major General Eduardo "Lalo" Lopez, Colonel Fernando "Nando" Garcia, his Aide De Camp, and Lt Francis DeVille, Chris's French Liaison Officer.

"Lt. DeVille," instructed Eduardo, "you will take command of the French rifle squad onboard ensuring that they have exercise every day and that they are kept busy and out of the way of the deck crew. Lt. Ramirez, you will supervise Sgt. Blanco. Have him report to you in the morning and evening for assignments.

Chris stood up and tapped on the table. "Dear fellow officers, I want to welcome you to my ship. I hope this will be a pleasant journey for you all. The British have not been active in the western Gulf, so we should have a relatively quiet journey. Of course, there are always pirates.

After dinner Eduardo met with his staff in his quarters. He gave Colonel Garcia the large package with five years of financial records of Mexico, the Philippines and Peru. He asked them to analyze the records and let him know if it appears there has been embezzlement. They were instructed to make charts. He asked to establish a work schedule of 10:00 a.m. to noon and 2:00 p.m. to 4:00 p.m., except when they were in port. The officers found a way for Sgt. Blanco to help.

The officers and crew enjoyed a week of strong winds in the sails until one day all the sails luffed. They became becalmed. Not a hint of wind. The ocean was as smooth as glass. After about an hour Chris ordered two longboats into the water to tow the ship hopefully into a wind.

The longboats didn't actually tow the ship into the wind.[15] The longboat allowed the ship to be kedged or warped ahead. The ship's anchor and cable were placed in the longboat. It would be rowed a distance from the ship where they would drop the anchor. The crew onboard would then man the ship's capstans to haul the ship forward to the point where the anchor was dropped. This procedure would be repeated as many times as needed to find wind. Multiple ship's boats could also be manned to physically tow the ship.

After about 12 hours the *Sharnbrook* was towed into the wind. The longboat crew came back onboard, and life returned to normal for the remainder of the voyage.

That evening Eduardo had Sgt. Blanco prepare his weekly bath. Although most officers at this time bathed only once per week, Eduardo had felt more comfortable bathing twice a week. It was so much trouble. One had to bring a large wooden tub in from the outside and make multiple trips to the well or water cask to get enough water for bathing. Onboard ship it was too time

---

[15] When the ocean was deeper than the length of the anchor chair, the longboat would actually pull the ship into the wind.

265

consuming and drinking water was a precious commodity. On days when he didn't bathe, he used a soapy wet washcloth to wash off his entire body.

Many men of his day still shaved their heads to avoid lice. This required them to wear wigs. Eduardo washed his long hair weekly.

As he stood in front of his mirrow shaving, he thought to himself: "I hate shaving. It is a waste of time. For years he had been promising himself that when he retired, he would stop shaving and grow a long beard.

There were no toothbrushes, and many people had rotting teeth. There were only a few dentists in those days, and they mostly pulled bad teeth. Eduardo used a wet sponge to clean his teeth daily.

After a bowel movement, he would clean his nether regions with pages of the *Farmer's Almanac*.

CHAPTER 92

Vera Cruz, Mexico

July 29, 1781

As they entered the Vera Cruz harbor they passed the harbor island, San Juan de Ulnia, upon which was built the strong colonial fortress and prison. It was built to fight off pirates who in the past had frequently raided the city. Vera Cruz was founded in 1519 by the explorer, Hernando Cortez. It is Mexico's main port in the Gulf of Mexico which also enjoys a large fishing fleet. European diseases devastated the indigenous population so drastically in the 17th century, that the Spanish government imported between 500,000 and 1,000,000 African slaves to tend the sugar cane, bamboo and coconut plantations. Immediately, the Black people intermarried with the natives. Their children were referred to as Mestizos. Some Spaniards married the Africans, and their children were Mulattos. Over the years there was so much interracial marriage that Vera Cruz, like Havana, was known as a Creole city.

The port of Vera Cruz was sheltered by a large, curved peninsula, high atop which sat San Juan Castle, the military headquarters. The naval base was in the lee of the peninsula. Three ships were already tied up at the navy pier. Of the two on adjacent piers, one was a cargo ship, sitting deep in the water, and the other was a two masted Spanish Navy sloop. The third ship was berthed in front of the Naval Headquarters. The harbormaster signaled to the *Sharnbrook* to dock at pier three.

After the *Sharnbrook* was tied up at pier three, Lt. DeVille assumed the duties of Officer of the Deck. He ordered the lowering of the gang plank. Almost immediately, a Spanish Colonel walked up the gang plank briskly.

"Permission to come aboard," the Spanish Colonel requested?

"Permission granted, sir," he said as he saluted smartly. What is your business," asked the Officer of the Deck?

"I request to speak to the captain of this ship."

"First," he said to the first mate, "please show the Colonel to the Captain's quarters." Have a good day, sir," He said as he saluted again.

"Come in," said Christopher, in response to a knock on his cabin door. He and Eduardo were having a business discussion.

"Good afternoon, Captain. Please pardon the intrusion. My name is Colonel Antonio de Guzman. I am the adjutant at the military fortress in Cartagena, Columbia.

"Welcome aboard, Colonel. I am Rear Admiral Butler, and this is Major General Lopez. How may we help you," Chris asked?

"The two ships berthed on piers one and two are under my command. The cargo ship is here awaiting the arrival of the next treasure ship back to Spain. The warship is here as an escort.

It carries a precious cargo of emeralds worth a king's fortune. Also, its holds are filled with coffee, tea, spices, palm oil and sugar. Unfortunately, the treasure ship was damaged in a storm and still sits in the repair facility in

268

Havana. I am in hopes that your ship can take my cargo and allow me and my two ships to return to Columbia.

"Colonel, I don't see a problem, so long as you assign your escort ship to me from here to Havana. Do you have a copy of your manifest with you," asked Christopher?

"No, I do not a have a copy, but I will have it delivered when I return to my ship. The escort will be assigned to you Admiral. When do you plan on departing Vera Cruz?

"Once we start unloading our cargo, it should take about two days to unload and clear the pier.

If your ship's hold is full, it could take four or five days to transfer your cargo to my ship. I am here at the pleasure of General Lopez, so my departure date will depend on his schedule."

"Admiral, when would be a good time to get together to discuss details," asked Colonel Guzman?

"Colonel, the General and I have some business to tend to for the next few days. Please allow me to get back to you."

"Very well sir. Sir, without being impertinent, please help me understand: This is an American ship flying a Spanish flag, with an American Captain and Crew; this American Captain is a Rear Admiral in the Spanish Navy; your Officer of the Deck is a French Lieutenant; and there is a squad of French Marines onboard. What is going on," he asked?

"Let me set your mind at ease Colonel. Here, read this letter and you will understand," said Eduardo as he passed the king's letter to the Colonel.

After reading the king's letter Colonel Guzman said, "But general, that still doesn't explain the presence of the French."

"Well Colonel," said Christopher, "I also carry freight, mail and passengers for the French. Admiral d'Estaing was so pleased with my services that he appointed me a Captain in the French Navy. Since I am not a French speaker, he attached Lt. DeVille as my French Liaison Officer so long as I am carrying cargo to French ports. The squad of marines was assigned for protection of French cargo, some of which is to be unloaded here. Does that explain things to your satisfaction," he asked?

"Yes Admiral. I feel I can safely turn over my cargo and return to my duties. May I be excused," asked the Colonel?

CHAPTER 93

Spaniards loan money to France

Havana, Cuba

July 30, 1781

A French fleet delivered 6,000 French soldiers at Newport, Rhode Island in July 1780. These troops were under the command of Count Rochambeau. They were disbursed to three different camping sites. For the next year they enjoyed themselves. They mixed and mingled with the local populations. Many of them married local girls and deserted.

Starting in early 1781 the French had no money to pay their troops. Their soldiers were owed three months' salary. The French troops were threatening to desert if they were not paid. Admiral de Grass went to the Caribbean in an attempt to raise money to pay his troops but was unsuccessful. He sent a note to Governor General Galvez in New Orleans, requesting a loan.

Galvez immediately took his ship the *Galveston* to Havana. Within 48 hours of his arrival in Havana, he had raised over 500,000 Livres from loans by local Havana businessmen and the officer corps. Galvez delivered the bullion to Admiral De Grass in Port-Au-Prince. De Grass was able to get the money to his troops in Virginia before they deserted. From this sum, the

French loaned money to the Americans to pay their soldiers some back due pay.

CHAPTER 94

Governor's Mansion

New Orleans, Louisiana

August 1, 1781

"May I pour you another cup of tea, Toni," asked Felicite?

"Yes, please Felicite, and if you don't mind, I would love another one of those tasty little sandwiches.

"How about you, Esmerelda? More tea," Felicite asked?

"Yes, thank you," Esmerelda replied. "And I'll also take another of those delicious little sandwiches."

"Me too – tea and sandwich," said Lynette Ramirez, wife of Eduardo's new assistant, Lt. Javier Ramirez.

"I'm glad you ladies could join me today for tea. Since your husbands are together and will be away for a year or more, I thought it was fitting that we spend more time together. I propose that we get together once a week – for lunch, brunch, tea or dinner. What do you ladies think," Felicite asked?

Toni said "I think that is a great idea. Esmerelda, Lynette, and I are here alone, thousands of miles from Europe with no family. We appreciate your hosting us today, but in the future, I suggest that we take turns hosting or that we get together for dinner at the Officer's Club or at one of the nice restaurants in the quarter."

The ladies all agreed to get together socially on a regular basis. They then turned the conversation to local gossip.

Before the tea was over Felicite, with a plain face told the ladies "It appears that next spring I am going to need some new furniture and new clothes."

Blank stares. The other three ladies looked at her with incredulity. They all thought "Why is she telling us about new furniture and clothing?

"Felicite continued "General Galvez and I will need a new baby bed, bassinet and rocking chair, and we'll need clothes for our new baby." Felicite clapped her hands together and laughed as she spun her body around. The ladies all congratulated her, and they talked of babies for another hour.

CHAPTER 95

Vera Cruz, Mexico

August 2, 1781

The Vera Cruz Naval Base was commanded by Captain Alonzo Palmero. The military commander for the area, and Palmero's boss, was Brigadier General Hugo Montemayor, whose office was in the castle overlooking the harbor. Each received a note from Eduardo, which read as follows:

August 2, 1781

You are cordially invited to dinner aboard the Sharnbrook, pier 3, Vera Cruz Naval Base at 7:00 p.m.

Signed

Eduardo Lopez, Major. General, Personal Representative of HRM Carlos de Borbon, King of Spain

Christopher Butler, Rear Admiral, Spanish Navy

Why does a flag officer want to see me? What is this about him being a personal representative of the king? Am I about to be charged with a crime? Am I about to be relieved of command? These were just some of the questions that these two senior officers were asking themselves as they rode toward the ship.

Captain Palmero was walking up the gangway when General Montemayor's coach stopped at the bottom of the gangway. Eduardo greeted each officer as they boarded and welcomed them aboard. He escorted them to the

Captain's cabin. That evening the junior officers ate ashore. Both guests were a little shocked to find an American as a Spanish Rear Admiral, but neither said a word. An air of mystery hovered over the cabin.

"I propose a toast to you General Montemayor and to you Captain Palmero. *Salud*. Now, I would appreciate it if you would join me at the table.

"I am a representative of the king. I am traveling with an entourage of three others. In a few days I will be leaving for an overland trip to Mexico City, and sometime in the future will be returning. At present I have no requests for either of you, but in the future, I may ask for your assistance. I wanted to pay you each the courtesy of introducing myself and Admiral Butler.

General, please read this letter, then pass it to Captain Palmero.

Each man read the letter after which both had a blank stare on his face. "Is something about to happen General," Captain Palmero asked?

"No, I am simply in this part of the world as the king's representative. Nobody is about to be relieved, and no criminal charges are about to be filed, so neither of you have anything to worry about. Now, let's eat. I'm starved."

"General Montemayor, it would be of great assistance if your office could arrange hotel accommodations for my officers for the next few nights, and for a coach and escort to Mexico City. In the interim, it would be a pleasure for me and my staff to tour each of your facilities.

While the *Sharnbrook* was being offloaded and onloaded, Eduardo and his staff toured the navy base and the castle.

275

They were wined and dined in the Officers Clubs. They met with the mayor who not only gave them a tour of the city but also hosted them to a fine dinner at Vera Cruz' best restaurant.

At the restaurant, the waiter asked Lt. Ramirez if he would like some "*Pico de Gayo*" on his enchilada. "What's *Pico de Gayo*," he asked? "Sir, it's a spicy relish with chopped tomatoes, bell pepper, onion, cilantro and Jalepeno, with a squeeze of lemon. In Spanish it means beak of the rooster because the pepper is about the same shape as a rooster's beak.

"Gracias, now all I need is a dictionary to learn about *cilantro* and *jalapeño*. Go ahead, I'll try it," he said.

. . .

Over the next few days Eduardo, Fernando and Lt. Javier Ramirez all wrote letters to their wives and shopped for gifts. Eduardo bought a colorful fiesta dress and an ivory and silver Rosary for Toni. Fernando purchased a silver bracelet for his wife, while Javier picked out a gold charm for his new bride. Christopher purchased candy for Eduardo and a case of Tequila and a newspaper for Bernardo. For Sara, he found a beautiful gold necklace so she would know how much he adored her. Eduardo found time to go to confession at the small church near the navy base. Before he blew out the candle on his last night in Vera Cruz, he finished reports to both Bernardo and King Carlos.

. . .

It was a joyous occasion. It was a sad occasion. Eduardo and Christopher had become fast friends, who enjoyed each other's company. Eduardo's travels were taking him west to far distant lands, while Christopher's life was to the east. Would their paths ever cross again? Each of these men faced unknown dangers.

Their farewell dinner was at *Casa Morales*, Vera Cruz' finest restaurant. They were joined by

Fernando, Lt. Ramirez and Lt. DeVille. They all chose the restaurant's signature dish of Roast

Suckling Pig with vegetables. The festivities were enhanced by the music of a group of Mariachis who played for tips. For dessert they selected chocolate flan with port wine. Eduardo and Chris talked until the wee hours of the morning.

CHAPTER 96

Coach from Vera Cruz to Mexico City

August 6, 1781

General Montemayor had not only arranged for a coach for the four men to Mexico City; he assigned a cavalry platoon to escort them. The commanding officer of the platoon was Lt. Emanuel Garza, who grew up in Las Palmas, Grand Canary Island. He was assisted by Sub Lieutenant Jaime Pachecko of Barcelona, assistant platoon commander. This was to be a long and arduous 280 mile journey crossing the Sierra Madre Mountains.

"Good morning, General. Allow me to introduce myself. I am Lt. Garza. My platoon will escort you and your entourage to Mexico City. This is Sub Lieutenant Pachecko, my assistant."

"Good morning, Lieutenant. This is Lt. Colonel Garcia, my aide; Lt. Ramirez, my assistant; and Sgt. Blanco, my orderly. What can you tell me of our journey?"

"Sir, there are two possible routes. Our intelligence tells us that part of the southern road has been washed out due to heavy rains. With your permission, we will be traveling the northern route. Going through the mountains it will take us about two weeks to get to Mexico City, if we can average 20 miles per day."

"Some nights there will be an inn where you spend the night, but most evenings we will be camping out. Supply has loaded tents and camping supplies on the covered wagon that will accompany our Caravan. That wagon will also carry food and water. Our food will be supplemented by games. Much of our journey will be at high altitudes. We will pass several snow-capped mountains. Mexico City is at 7,800 feet altitude. Many people suffer from shortness of breath when they exercise. One reason the general assigned my platoon to protect you is because there are a large number of highwaymen along both routes."

"General, here is a map of central Mexico for you. I have marked your copy with my proposed route. You will see that from here we travel north-west through Jalapa, La Joya and Las Vigas. The stretch between Las Vigas and Perote is our most treacherous, as we cross the Sierra Madre

Mountains. From Perote you will see the beautiful snow-capped peak of Orizaba on the way to El Pinal which sits on a bluff of the Anahuac Plateau which looks back to the Sierra Madre Mountains on the horizon.

"The next town is Puebla. It is a good size city with a lovely hotel. It would be my recommendation that you spend a few nights there to rest up, stretch your legs, wash your clothes, eat some good food and enjoy sleeping in a bed. On this road there is only one other town before arriving in Mexico City, and another range of mountains to cross." "Thank you for the map, Lieutenant. We shall depart in about five minutes."

Brigadier General Montemayor and his aide were there to see Eduardo off on his journey. Eduardo stepped over to him and shook his hand and thanked him for his cooperation in arranging the coach and support. As he turned to walk to the coach, Christopher appeared in his peripheral vision. Both men had red eyes from their alcohol consumption the night before – or was it from the sadness of their parting? They talked privately for a few

279

minutes and then they hugged, which was something rarely seen in Latin America at the time.

Christopher stood there watching Eduardo's coach until it passed from view. He used a handkerchief to wipe the tears from his eyes.

CHAPTER 97

Aboard the *Sharnbrook*

Vera Cruz, Mexico

August 7, 1781

Christopher had invited Colonel Guzman and the two officers from the escort ship to have lunch. It was necessary to meet them and have them understand their duties. The steward was serving wine.

"Admiral, please allow me to present Navy Lieutenant Ricardo Jiménez, captain of the *Solitude*, Sub Lieutenant Andre Costas, his executive officer," said Colonel Guzman.

"Gentlemen, this is my first mate, who we affectionally call "First" and Lieutenant DeVille, my French Liaison Officer.

"Colonel Guzman, here is the order from General Lopez assigning the *Solitude* and its crew to Admiral Butler. Should you wish to write Havana requesting that it be replaced, I will be happy to deliver your request personally.

"We have a long journey in front of us. We depart with the morning tide. Our first stop will be New Orleans, where we will be in port for a few days. Afterwards our itinerary takes us to Havana, Port-Au-Prince, and several of the French islands in the Windwards and Leeward's. Our first stop on the other side of the big pond will be Grand Canary Island and then, Cadiz Spain. Crossing the Atlantic via the southern route we are less likely to run into an English war ship. At each port we will unload cargo and mail, make necessary repairs, and load outgoing mail and cargo. Your men will have ample opportunity for liberty."

"Lieutenant Jiménez, it will be your job to keep up with the *Sharnbrook*. Messages can be sent by signal flag, or you can be rowed over by longboat.

While eating lunch, the men got to know each other better. Colonel Guzman reported that he had arranged passage back to Cartagena on a cargo ship from Tampico.

"Gentlemen, we sail with the morning tide. I bid you fair winds and following seas," said Christopher as he raised his glass in toast.

CHAPTER 98

La Hacienda Hotel

Puebla, Mexico

August 15, 1781

Eduardo reread his letter to Toni before sealing it:

My dearest darling, the seas were calm for our passage from New Orleans to Vera Cruz. Chris and I solidified our friendship on the voyage. Chris must be living right because he was engaged to transport a valuable cargo to Spain and provided a warship to escort him all the way to Spain.

The base commander at Vera Cruz assigned a cavalry platoon to escort us to Mexico City. There are only a few towns in this wild area. As a result, we have had to camp out most nights. Even at these high altitudes the sun bears down hard during the afternoon, and it is freezing cold at night. The cots are so uncomfortable that I awake each morning with a backache. Fernando and Javier remain in good spirits. Even Sgt. Blanco is managing without complaint. The roads are poor with many large holes. As a result, my rear end is sore from being thrown around in the coach.

We arrived in the lovely town of Puebla two days ago. It has been heavenly sleeping on a wonderful bed. After being cramped up in a coach for over a week, we have enjoyed walking around this pretty village and trying the native cuisine. I ate chicken fajitas for dinner last night. They were delicious. This morning in the dining room of the hotel I ate huevos rancheros with bacon. I think I am going to enjoy the native food.

We depart for Mexico City in the morning. We plan to camp out four of the five nights of this trip. When I arrive in Mexico City, I plan to visit with the Viceroy of New Spain, Jose de Galvez, Marques of Sonora, Bernardo's uncle, as well as the military commander and the manager of the mint. Within a week of my arrival, I hope to depart for Acapulco. I am told that there are no roads over the mountains that will allow coaches, so I am looking at a long horseback ride.

I miss you, my darling. One day this war will be over, and we can spend our lives together.

All my love,

Lalo

P.S. Please tell Bernardo that after I have met with the officials in Mexico City, I will be sending updated reports to both him and King Carlos.

CHAPTER 99

Officers Club

New Orleans, Louisiana

August 18, 1781

"Ladies," said Felicite, "I have letters and gifts for each of you from your husbands. Admiral Butler arrived last night from Vera Cruz. Bernardo asks that each of you join us for dinner tonight at the Officer Club. Chris will be there to bring us up to date on their voyage and give you an update on Vera Cruz. He will be bring with him three junior officers: Lt. Francois DeVille, Chris's French Liaison Officer, and Spanish Navy Lieutenant Ricardo Jiménez, commander of his escort ship and his executive officer. All three of these young men are single. They will be bored to death listening to us talk. I suggest that we each find a single young lady to accompany us tonight. With four young ladies, it will not appear that we are trying to match them up."

"That sounds like a good plan to me," said Toni.

. . .

General George Washington drank a toast to the kings of France and Spain at the Philadelphia home of Robert Morris.

CHAPTER 100

Ayotla, Mexico

August 19, 1781

The column was besieged by torrential rains for three days after leaving Puebla. Some of the roads were so washed out that they had to stop so that boulders could be removed from the road. At one such place a wheel on the cook wagon had come off. While the wheel was being repaired, one of the Cavalrymen was bitten by a coral snake. A sergeant acted as a medic for this platoon. The medic treated the snake bite victim by cutting open the wounds and sucking out the venom. His wound was treated with antiseptic, bandaged, and the soldier placed in the mess wagon, with his horse tethered to the wagon.

Just before they arrived in Ayotla an earthquake hit the area, severely damaging the road. Fernando was left with a large bruise on his left shoulder and Eduardo received a deep cut on his forehead. The medic put antiseptic and a bandage on his cut. "General, when we get to the capital tomorrow, you need to see a doctor and get some stitches in that cut." The platoon worked all day making repairs to the road. Thankfully, the rain had stopped before the quake struck.

"General, my orders were to escort you to the capital. We should arrive mid-afternoon tomorrow. With your permission, I will return with my unit to Vera Cruz the following day. It has been a pleasure to meet you and to provide security for you and your group."

"Lieutenant, I have already had Lt. Ramirez draft a letter of commendation for you and Sub Lieutenant Costas for the professional manner in which you have escorted my entourage. It will go out in the next mail bag to Vera Cruz. I wish you well in the future."

"Thank you, sir," he said as he saluted, turned and walked away.

CHAPTER 101

New Orleans, Louisiana

August 21, 1781

The garrison band was playing, and a crowd had gathered on the pier to see the *Sharnbrook* leave port. It was hot and muggy and storm clouds were rising from the southwest. Chris was hoping he could outrun the impending storm. General Galvez arrived in his carriage and walked over to Chris, who was standing near the gangway.

"Chris, here is my current report to the king. I have informed him that not only has the

Sharnbrook supplied us, but that two of your other ships have made five deliveries to us from Spain. Please give my regards to Sara. Tell her I hope that we can meet some day. She sounds like a wonderful woman. I hope your voyage will be a safe one. We all pray for you every night when we say our Rosary.

"Bernardo, I am not a very religious man. Religion is very personal to me. I believe in Christ.

You and Eduardo and your wives are in my nightly prayers."

"Before you depart, I want to share some good news with you. The reports I am getting from up north are that the Americans have the British on the run. Hundreds of loyalists have become patriots. This war may be over soon. Have you given any thought to what changes in your life you will have to make when the war is over? I suspect that the Spanish Admiralty will resume using war ships to transport the cargo that we need here in New Orleans and the Gulf. I assume that the French will react the same way."

"With long days at sea there is plenty of time to think. When the war is over the shipping business with Great Britain and the continent will explode. Tobacco and cotton alone will be enough to maintain weekly shipments. Americans will begin importing goods from the Gulf and Caribbean. At some point in the not too distant future, I may modify some of my ships or purchase new ones that cater to passengers. People will be traveling from New York, Boston, etc. just to visit New Orleans and enjoy its food, music and shopping. As Shakespeare said, I am getting long in the tooth. I want to spend more time at home. Although I don't plan on retiring anytime soon, I plan to hire a captain to take my place and perhaps make him a partner.

. . .

As he watched the *Sharnbrook* and its escort navigate down the Mississippi toward the gulf, Galvez thought to himself: "Who would have thought that an Anglo would end up as one of my best friends?"

CHAPTER 102

National Palace

Mexico City, Mexico

August 25, 1781

On the office door was written the following:

His Excellency Senor Don Jose De Galvez

Marques De Sonora

Viceroy of New Spain

"His excellency, the Viceroy will see you now," said the secretary.

"Come forward General. Please take a seat. My nephew, Bernardo sent me a letter to expect you. I can remember when you and he were boys playing in our little village. I've known your parents all my life. It is wonderful having you here. I understand that you are carrying a letter from his majesty. May I see it now?"

"Yes, your excellency, here it is," as he passed the letter to the Viceroy.

"This is a great honor the king has bestowed upon you. Can you fill me in on why you are here in my bailiwick?

"Your excellency, I am terribly sorry, but the king has forbidden me from discussing my orders with anyone except your nephew, who has been assisting me from New Orleans."

"I understand. Let's have lunch and you can tell me about Bernardo." The Royal Palace dining room was elegant.

He was amazed at Mexico City. It was larger than any other town in the Americas. The five story Royal Palace was beautiful. He was so impressed with the Cathedral on the north side of the enormous plaza he stopped to pray before entering the palace. Eduardo and the Viceroy enjoyed a long lunch talking about Bernardo and New Orleans. Although Eduardo could not divulge the purpose of his travels, he could and did confer with Viceroy Galvez about his itinerary.

The Viceroy reported to Eduardo that the road to Cuernavaca was good enough for his coach, but from there to Acapulco the poor quality of roads and/or nonexistence of roads required travel by horse.

"Let me give you one piece of advice, for which I'll wager you will thank me 100 times. You will die in your wool uniform. There are some excellent tailors in Mexico City."

The Viceroy reached into his desk drawer and pulled out a note with the name and address of the Viceroy's tailor.

"Have a cotton suit made," he said as he handed Eduardo the note. "And get at least three batiste cotton uniform shirts. You'll need them because you will be sweating every day. I also recommend that you purchase at least three pair of cotton hosiery. For your off duty hours, you are going to need about three pair of cotton trousers, a pair of sandals, about three guayaberas, one of which should be a long sleeved white shirt, and a straw hat."

"You must be exhausted from your travels. My executive assistant will hire a guide and a coach for you and your team. There is much to see in and around Mexico City."

. . .

For the next three days they went sightseeing. The first day was spent traveling to the

Teotihuacan Pyramids. Teotihuacan is located in the State of Mexico, 25 miles northeast of Mexico City. The pyramids were built 1500-2000 years ago and covered 8 square miles. At that time, it was the largest city in the Americas, boasting a population of about 125,000. Their guide was very knowledgeable and regaled them with many facts about the civilization that inhabited these marvelous structures. Their lunch of tacos and jicama with beer was very satisfying.

At a newsstand that afternoon he found a three month old newspaper from Madrid, a newspaper from Philadelphia that was a month more recent and the current Mexico City newspaper. The Madrid and Philadelphia newspapers may contain old news, but it is the most recent news of the area available.

The following day their guide kept them closer to home. The first stop was the enormous cathedral. It was still under construction with scaffolding all around it. It looked as majestic as many back home. The guide told them the important information about the paintings and statuary in the church. In the rear of the church, they stopped at a statute of the Madonna which was as black as night.

"Was this statute carved from ebony," Eduardo asked? "No, Senor. The statute was originally carved from light colored wood. Supposedly, a priest of this church some 25 years ago was murdered by a thief in this vestibule. Witnesses saw the statue crying black tears, which were absorbed by the statue. The crying continued until it was entirely black."

Next, they visited the public market, which they strolled through for an hour or so. Eduardo purchased thee cotton guayaberas: a long sleeved white, and short sleeve navy blue and light yellow guayaberas. He also purchased a pair of sandals, three pair of thin cotton hosiery, and a straw hat with a colorful floral hatband. His favorite purchase was the beautiful hand carved walking cane with a rapier embedded inside it. A bootmaker measured him for a pair of waterproof boots. "I will add ¾ of an inch to the heels. It will make you look taller and more powerful," said the bootmaker.

They came upon an outside restaurant and decided to have lunch there. Both started with cold Mexican *cerveza*. While they were enjoying their beer a Mariachi band began serenading the restaurant customers. Three trumpeters, two violins, two guitars, two bass guitars and a drummer made lots of music. Eduardo ordered chicken *quesadillas*, with melted cheese, onions and peppers. Fernando selected super *fajita nachos*, which were served on a sizzling platter with *pico de gayo*, *guacamole* and peppers. Javi tried the puffy beef tacos and Sgt. Blanco ate *carne guisada*, which resembled beef stew. A basket of warm tortillas was served. When the musicians approached their table, Eduardo gave them a tip.

No sooner had the mariachi's left than a new musical group appeared. Six young men wearing black capes and flat top hats with a wide brim began to serenade the crowd. The waiter told us they were "*estudiantes*" who play to pay for their college education. They played four guitars, a mandolin and a bass guitar. Their selections were all ballads and love songs. Eduardo also tipped the student group.

293

Eduardo went directly from the restaurant to Viceroy Galvez' tailor, where he was measured for a cotton uniform, three cotton uniform shirts, two pair of cotton trousers, navy and white.

That evening the four men attended an open air concert by the Mexico City Symphony in the Zocalo.

On the third and last day of sightseeing, they rode about 15 miles south of Mexico City for a day at the *Xochimilcan* floating gardens. It was a lovely sunny day. Hundreds of brightly decorated passenger boats floated on the miles of tree lined canals in the gardens. A festive mood prevailed. The men were entertained by musicians on a floating boat. If you offered them a tip, they would marry their boat with yours while your songs were being played. Food vendors would pull their boats up alongside their boat to offer food, beer and wine. Other nautical vendors offered souvenirs, drinks, flowers, etc.

That evening Eduardo and his staff, including Sgt. Blanco attended the open air concert of the

Army Regimental band. "Gentlemen, I hope you enjoyed this concert because it will be the last cultural event available to us for many months. Our work starts tomorrow. We are going to the mint. Our first job is to audit the mint. We do that by acquiring copies of every financial statement, receipt, journals, ledgers, logs, etc.

. . .

At 9:00 a.m. Eduardo and his staff arrived at the Mint. The Mint Director, Senor Mario Martinez received them immediately. After the usual courtesies, Eduardo showed Martinez the letter from the king.

"First, Senor Martinez, I would appreciate it if you would give me and my staff a tour. I would like to start at the place where the raw silver ore is received, then follow it through crushing, grinding, smelting, refining, pressing, minting and preparing for shipment."

"Gentlemen, the ore is dumped into a cart similar to this where it is weighed."

"Where are the records kept of the deliveries with their respective weights," asked Eduardo? The director walked over to the attendant's desk and showed him the logbook. LT Ramirez was taking copious notes.

At each point of the tour, Eduardo asked about the location of the records of each part of the refining and minting process. At each point LT Ramirez noted what records were created and where those records were kept.

When the tour was over, Eduardo said "Senor Martinez, as much as I hate to interrupt the flow of silver, I must ask that you have every member of your administrative staff to stop what they are doing. My staff has brought with them blank ledgers, journals and logs as well as reams of paper. Your job is to have every scrap of paper in your office over the last five years copied and sorted by department. Naturally, that includes bank statements, Profit and Loss Statements, Balance Sheets and documents created here at the mint. I will need those copies three days before I leave the city. If necessary, you can require mandatory overtime at 150% of their normal salary, which I am authorizing. LT Ramirez and Sgt. Blanco will stay at the mint to supervise your employees. They will order food to be delivered to the mint this evening and until this project is completed. Please go now and make the announcement to your staff.

Please return promptly, as we have other matters to discuss."

Eduardo went to the reception room and asked LT Ramirez to bring in his notepad.

When Martinez returned, he looked distressed. "Am I being accused of a crime? Why are we being investigated," he asked.

"Whoa senor. This is a routine audit. Nobody is asserting that there has been any misfeasance or malfeasance. The king merely wishes to better understand the whole process of silver production from the mine to the mint to the treasure ship.

"I have no training in geology, mining, refining or minting silver," said Eduardo. "From your perspective, I would like to hear in chronological order everything you know about the process. Please start with mining the ore. LT Ramirez will take notes so I may refer to them later. How much are the miners paid per day? How many hours per day do they work? How many days per week do they work? How many shifts per day are worked? This is the kind of information I need."

Over the next two hours director Martinez described the process. Periodically, he was interrupted by Eduardo, with questions like "How many pounds of ore are mined per day? What is the average number of miners working per day? How much are the miners paid per day? How much did the donkey's cost? How many donkeys are used for each transport? What is the cost per ton of the ore when it arrives at the mint? What kind of security is used at the mine; at the processing plant; at the mint; and during transport from the mint to the treasure ship in Vera Cruz?"

296

"My final question to you is what, if any coordination is there between the mint and the treasure ship about deliveries of bouillon?

"None, sir. Why do you ask?"

"Director, it appears that at times the bouillon sits in a relatively unsecure warehouse in Vera Cruz for a month or more. There is a daily mail run between Mexico City and Vera Cruz. Are you provided with the arrival and departure schedule of the treasure ships?

"No, general."

"Director, I'm sure that you must have some suggestions about how to make the mint more effective. Please put those in writing for me. I'm afraid I must use your office for an extended period of time. Please alert the following employees that I need to interview them here and have them stand by. I need to talk to the following:

Refining Manager

Refining Foreman

Mint Manager

Mint Assistant Manager

Mint Foreman

Mint Bookkeeper

Mint Assistant Bookkeeper

Mint Transportation Coordinator

Chief Administrative Officer

Chief Financial Officer

"The mint employees were kept until 10:00 p.m. that night. Colonel Garcia and Sgt. Blanco stood at the door

297

to ensure that no records were removed from the building. Eduardo's interviews lasted two additional days. In the meantime, Colonel Garcia and Sgt. Blanco circulated through the administrative employees cataloging each journal completed and comparing them page by page. Their mere presence spurred the employees to complete these assigned tasks as quickly as possible and get back to their assigned tasks. It took Sgt. Garcia less than a day to copy the logs in the ore processing area.

By 3:00 p.m. on the third day, Eduardo called a meeting of all administrative employees. "Ladies and gentlemen, I wanted to let you know that the mint has undergone a routine audit. There is no alleged impropriety. I want to express my great appreciation for your overtime work this past three days. To make up for your inconvenience, I am releasing you early today and declaring tomorrow a holiday."

That evening Eduardo took his coach to the palace, where Viceroy Galvez had invited him for dinner. Jose Galvez obtained a law degree from the University of Alcala. Galvez correct title was "inspector general for the viceroyalty of New Spain", which was shortened to "Viceroy." New Spain was all of Mexico and from the Gulf shores to the arctic snows. He was the highest ranking Spaniard in North America.

The Viceroy's first wife died the year after they married. He then married Lucía Romet y Pichelín, a French woman, who was well connected at the French royal court. Her family secured a job for him as the legal adviser at the French embassy in Madrid. This high visibility position allowed him to later secure a job as personal secretary to Jerónimo Grimaldi, Prime Minister to the new king Carlos de Borbon, III. In 1762, he became the attorney of Prince Carlos, IV. In 1765, he was appointed inspector general for the viceroyalty of New Spain.

"General, I am so impressed with your French. You speak with no accent. How so," enquired Madam Galvez?

"My mother was French, so French was my second language. The school from which I graduated refined my French. I am sure my headmaster would appreciate your compliment," Eduardo replied. And Madam, your Spanish is likewise pristine without accent. How is that" asked Eduardo?

"I attended a private finishing school in Leon, where I learned both Spanish and English. France and Spain have been aligned against England for centuries, so it seemed those were the most important languages to learn."

Most of the evening was spent with the Viceroy discussing events in Marcharaviaya, Spain when Eduardo was a young boy. He talked of his times with Bernardo's father, Matias de Galvez, who two years before was promoted from General in the Army to Captain General of Guatemala, a position that he still held.

...

Eduardo's last day in Mexico City was spent at the military warehouse within the Presidio. Once the treasures from the Philippines were received from Acapulco, they were inventoried; repackaged and shipped to Vera Cruz. He and his staff were given a tour by the warehouse manager. Eduardo was provided with the Bills of Lading from Manila, treasure ship manifests, warehouse receipts, inventories and shipping receipts. Eduardo was pleased to see that there was a large metal safe in which was

299

stored gold, silver, pearls and precious stones and other high value items. They discussed the number of guards and their security procedures. Eduardo was provided with information about all others with the safe combination. Finally, he asked the manager for any suggestions he might have to smooth or reduce the cost of his operation.

After dinner all the officers penned letters to their wives. Eduardo spent most of his letter describing the vibrant city, their sightseeing and the concert in the plaza. He told her how much he missed and loved her. Their letters were all dropped into the mail before they departed Mexico City.

. . .

"Thank you for meeting me for breakfast Eduardo," said Viceroy Galvez. I wanted to introduce you to Lt. Tomas Chavez. He commands the cavalry platoon I have assigned to escort you to

Acapulco. Lieutenant, please brief General Lopez on the journey."

"General, we have a coach for your comfort to our first town of Cuernavaca, which is about 35 miles away. We should reach Cuernavaca in two days. After Cuernavaca you and your staff will have to travel by horse. The road beyond all the way to Acapulco is too narrow for coaches or wagons. In some areas it is nothing more than a narrow trail, where each rider must dismount and lead his horse. All our food, water and supplies will be carried by pack mules."

"My second in command is sub lieutenant Ramon Gonzales. My platoon consists of three squads of 9 men each. Additionally, a native guide, who supervises the 18-20 native donkey handlers, two cooks and a medic have been attached to my command for our journey. With your permission, the first squad, with our guide and medic, will be led by me at the front of the column, followed by your coach. The second squad will follow your coach, after which comes the mule train of about 18-20 donkeys, with their native handlers who are supervised by our native guide. The third squad, along with the two cooks, led by Sub Lieutenant Gonzales will bring up the rear."

"We will stop every two hours to rest, answer nature's call or to eat. Normally, we dismount each afternoon for about ½ hour and lead our mounts to give them a break. We normally start making camp about 4:00 p.m. We don't want to run out of daylight while we are setting up tents, building a fire and preparing dinner. My men take turns on camp setup and dismantling, feeding and tending to the horses and donkeys, guard duty, latrine duty and kitchen duty. Does that meet with your approval, Sir?"

"Lieutenant, it appears that you have thought of every contingency. I approve of your plan. Please ask my staff to board the coach and give your men a head's up. I will be ready to depart in five minutes."

"Eduardo, with that letter from the king you should have no problems. Just in case, I have prepared a similar letter for you to use as needed. I wish you well and look forward to seeing you again after your odyssey. *Vaya con Dios*," said the Viceroy.

At 8:00 a.m. the military column moved out.

CHAPTER 103

Morro Castle

Havana, Cuba

September 2, 1781

"So, Galvez made you a Rear Admiral. Will you outrank me the next time we meet," asked Admiral d'Estaing, his belly going up and down as he laughed? "What is your itinerary? "I am headed to Cadiz, Spain, where I will unload my cargo and load a shipment from Gardoqui, headed back in this direction, which they are shipping by land from Bilbao. What do you have for me," asked Christopher?

"Well, "Admiral," I need you to deliver and pick up mail and cargo on the islands of Guadalupe,

Marie Galant, Martinique, Saint Martin, and Saint Barthelemy to be delivered in Le Havre, France.

These islands are so close together that from Guadalupe, you can just about swim to Marie Galant. Using the southern route across the Atlantic you can avoid the English fleet and make a stop in the Canary Islands for food and water.

"The only problem is that my cargo hold is almost full," replied Chris. If you have any large crates, we'll have to secure them on the quarterdeck. I can put the mail and small packages in my cabin."

Chris said, "I'll make you a deal. If you will buy me dinner tonight, I will give you the case of Tequila in your reception room."

"*Si, como no,*" d'Estaing replied with a happy look on his face.

CHAPTER 104

Palace of Cortez/La Posada Restaurant

Cuernavaca, Mexico

September 3, 1781

Eduardo thought to himself, "This is a beautiful place. Budding trees, fragrant vines, blooming flowers and waterfalls everywhere." He and his entourage checked in to the Palace of Cortez for sleeping accommodations for the night. This two story fortress was originally built by Hernando Cortez in 1526. At an altitude of 5,000 feet this city was always at a delightful temperature of between 70-79 degrees Fahrenheit year round.

Lt. Chavez had recommended La Posada Restaurant as the best in town.

"Lieutenant, you and Sub Gonzales meet me and my staff at La Posada at 6:00 p.m. I'll notify the coach driver. I'm picking up the tab for everybody. This will be the last decent meal we get for weeks.

. . .

As they entered through the gates, La Posada at first looked like a circular garden rather than a restaurant. In fact, it was a garden surrounded by tables and chairs in private covered dining areas. The garden was filled with beautiful blooming plants and palms, the fronds of which tickled the soft breeze. A sweet smell permeated the air. Candles burned on each table and at strategic places in this circular dining area. A brightly colored macaw was hanging in a large cage between their dining area and that of their neighbor. Nearby was a talkative parrot. Eduardo was surprised when he saw two beautiful peacocks strutting through the garden, spreading and unspreading their magnificently colored tail feathers.

Fernando said, "If the food is half as good as the atmosphere, we are in for a treat." "Colonel, responded Lt. Chavez, "I've eating here before, and I don't think you will be disappointed – and the service is usually pretty fast."

They all enjoyed their meal, the wine and the lime pie for dessert.

Sgt. Blanco was always uncomfortable around officers. He had less than a high school diploma and grew up poor as dirt. Half the time he didn't understand what they were talking about. He preferred to spend his time with fellow non-coms. This assignment, however, had its perks. Up until tomorrow, it had been a lot more comfortable traveling in the coach, rather than on horseback. He usually got out of any dirty details and often got to eat with the officers, who enjoyed wine with dinner and had a far better menu than offered at the NCO club. All the officers he had encountered on this assignment had treated him very cordially. Another plus was he was getting to see parts of the world that would have never been available to him.

"General, I will have saddled mounts for you, your staff, our medic and the two cooks waiting in front of Cortez Palace at 7:00 a.m. tomorrow. I have taken the liberty of providing pistols, swords and sword sheaths for each officer and water canteens for each rider. Your pistol belts with bullets are hanging on your saddle horns. It is about 200 miles from here to Acapulco, but we can't continue to make 20 miles per day because of narrow winding trails which are sometimes dangerous. To cross the mountains that separate the two cities, our horses and the donkeys will have to spend much of the time with strenuous climbing. Going down a steep incline is just as difficult for our four legged friends as climbing. As a result, the animals wear out quicker each day. I'm estimating that we will arrive in Acapulco in about 16-18 days. A lot will depend on our weather, as muddy trails can be extremely dangerous. We have tools in the event we have to clear a landslide. Any questions, general?"

"Lieutenant, it appears that you have the situation well under control. Tomorrow, I would like for the column to take a short side trip to Xochicalco to view the ancient pyramids. I have read about the 1,500 year old Temple of the Feathered Serpent. I understand that there is a breathtaking view of Cuernavaca from the hilltop."

"General, I will make it happen. Good night, sir."

"Sleep well," replied Eduardo.

Eduardo took a stroll around the plaza, admiring the cathedral which was built in 1529. He

entered the church, dipped his fingers in holy water, made the sign of the cross, and walked to the confessional.

CHAPTER 105

Battle of the Capes

Off Chesapeake Bay

September 5, 1781

   The Battle of the Capes was a sea battle at the mouth of
Chesapeake Bay which took place on September 5, 1781,
during the American Revolutionary War. The British fleet
of 19 ships of the line, commanded by Rear Admiral Sir
Thomas Graves was destined for Yorktown, Virginia to
resupply the British Army led by General Cornwallis. A
French fleet of 24 ships of the line, led by Rear Admiral
François Joseph Paul, the Comte de Grasse had arrived
before the British fleet.

Admiral De Grasse's ship was carrying 500,000 Livres
secured by Governor General Bernardo de Galvez as a
loan from the Spanish merchants and Spanish officers
corps in Havana. De Grass arrived in time to pay the
back due salaries of the French soldiers. Many had not
been paid for four months or more and were threatening
to desert. Since arriving in Newport a large number of
French soldiers had deserted, most just to marry an
American girl. The French established a naval blockade
of Chesapeake Bay to prevent entrance by the British.

General Cornwallis' army was surrounded by the
American and the French armies with its back to the sea.
It was running very low on food, water and ammunition.
The French fleet prevented the British from reinforcing
and resupplying Cornwallis or evacuating his
overwhelmed forces. The French navy also bombarded

the British on shore and landed French infantry replacements.

The naval battle lasted only about two hours. With fewer ships the British suffered higher casualties and greater ship damage. At sunset, the British fleet ceased activity and retreated.

Cornwallis, seeing that his condition was hopeless, surrendered on October 19, 1781.

CHAPTER 106

Taxco, Mexico

September 10, 1781

Eduardo's staff spent five days at the three silver mines in Taxco. Each mine manager gave them a tour of their mine and the warehouses used to store the silver ore. The donkeys that carry the silver ore to Mexico City are given a two day rest in Mexico City. They are then loaded with supplies needed by the whole town, such as flour, corn meal, coffee, tea, sugar, spices, beer, wine, liquor, dried beans, clothing, and mail. Their loads on the return trip are much lighter than going to the capital. They are given another two days rest before being loaded for their next trip to the mint. In Taxco, the donkeys are housed in a large stable but can walk or rest in the large corral that connects to the stable.

While Eduardo conducted interviews with the managers, assistant managers, foremen and administrators of each mine, his staff was copying all their records. Eduardo elicited their complaints and suggestions, keeping notes of his conversations. He discovered that except for night watchmen at the mines and warehouses, there was no security.

Taxco was a beautiful mountain town. It was pleasantly cool, with no humidity. It was chilly enough at night to require a blanket. The most important and the most elegant building in town was the baroque Sana Prisca Church, with its beautiful pink stone towers. It was just finished in 1759. Eduardo went inside one afternoon to pray.

The officers all enjoyed a few days out of the saddle and both the men, and the animals needed a rest from the long days over difficult terrain. What the officers enjoyed most were good meals at local restaurants with tables and chairs, as opposed to sitting on the ground and eating off of their laps. One night some strolling mariachis serenaded them in a restaurant.

One the last day Eduardo called a meeting of all the mine officials. He thanked them on behalf of the king for their cooperation. He informed them that he had found no problems with their record keeping. He informed them that what they were doing every day was vitally important to the prosperity of Spain. He noted the lack of security and informed them of his concern that an agent of another country or enemy of the king could destroy all three mines with dynamite. He informed them that he was going to put a letter into the mail that day suggesting to Viceroy Galvez that a company of Spanish soldiers be assigned to garrison the town and provide security for the three mines.

CHAPTER 107

Offshore off Martinique Island

Onboard the *Sharnbrook*

September 23, 1781

The *Sharnbrook* was sitting deep in the water. This was the heaviest load Christopher had ever carried. Every nook and cranny in the holds of his ship was filled with cargo. His cabin was crammed with mail bags and small packages. Large crates had been nailed to the deck, covered with waterproof tarpaulins and lashed to the mast or whatever was available. The idea was to prevent these crates from moving during rough seas.

His transit among the French islands of the Caribbean had been relatively uneventful. His cargo holds were already so full, he had no room to purchase local goods. So, in each port he enjoyed sightseeing or time on the beach with a sweet rum drink. He was wined and dined in each port by whatever French officer was in charge of that island. Many nights after a fine dinner he would find a bar with a good band, where he would listen until the music stopped. He took personal mail for many of them. He brought each of them up to date on his recent travels and the news from each port. In return, the French officials gave Chris their view on what was happening in the Caribbean and in each man's island.

The first port call on the other side of the Atlantic was Grand Canary Island. He estimated that he could be there in a month. He would stop there for food and water and to make any necessary repairs. He would deliver any mail for that island and pick up what they had for Spain or France. From the Canary Islands his plan was to sail to Cadiz, Spain. From Cadiz he would sail to Le Havre and then back to America.

On this trip he had a passenger. Navy Captain Martin de Trentian was going back to Le Havre,

France to take command of a new squadron of big gun fighting ships. Since Admiral d'Estaing had engaged his services, he had been studying French. Now, he will have somebody to practice with.

Captain de Trentian was a bit over six feet tall and weighed about 240 pounds. He was beginning to have a beer belly. His brown hair was beginning to thin on top, which seemed a bit incongruous with his long sideburns. There was a slight separation between his two front teeth.

He was multilingual, speaking French, Spanish and English. He had studied at Oxford, so he spoke perfect English. When he was assigned as the Naval Attaché to the Spanish Consul in Zaragoza, Spain, he had been granted time off to study Spanish at the university. Chris was pleased that he would have some intelligent conversation across the Atlantic. The captain was well read, friendly, and a good conversationalist.

As they zigzagged through the French islands much of their spare time was spent bending their elbows at bars with local bands. Captain de Trentian spoke with the French Marines every day.

"Martin, what was your job in Havana," asked Chris?

"I was the Assistant Commander of a Squadron of Seven Caravels homeported in Havana. I was just promoted. I have been ordered to Le Havre to take command of my own squadron, which includes ten ships."

In their conversations Chris learned that Martin grown up in Caen, France, the capital of Normandy. He had married his childhood sweetheart and they have two children, a boy and a girl. His wife and children were meeting him in Le Havre. As yet, he had no idea how he would spend the 30 days leave he had been granted before he reported for duty.

They were provided splendid weather for their crossing. Their evenings were spent in pleasant conversation and dominos.

CHAPTER 108

Eduardo and Staff arrive.

Acapulco, Mexico

September 20- October 21, 1781

Eduardo arrived in Acapulco on September 20, 1781. They had endured almost daily afternoon tropical showers, but the trail had remained strong enough for them travel over without any problems. Eduardo still had not gotten over the two young boys, about 10 years old, who on their last day of crossing the mountains had rigged a rope across the trail and attempted to rob the column. Lt. Chavez had given them a few coins, spanked their butts with the back of his sword, and sent them on their way.

Acapulco was a small village on an enormous semicircular bay lined with coconut palms. Just behind the village the lush mountains rose several thousand feet. The sun was setting behind golden topped clouds over the ocean and dozens of fishermen had drug their fishing boats onto the beach for the night. Some of the larger boats bobbed at anchor in the harbor. Sea gulls played in the air currents above the shore. The muggy humidity was slowly being replaced by a cool evening breeze.

The town was in two separate parts. The Plaza was northwest of the bay. The Presidio was on the north side of the Plaza. The Presidio was a 2 acre fortress which contained a headquarters,

commander's quarters, guard house, bachelor officers' quarters (BOQ), barracks, recreation hall, armory, mess hall, stables, corral, wagon storage area and warehouse. The mission was on the south side.

Attached to the mission was a small parsonage for the priest and a garden he had planted. The Royal Palace occupied the east. The "Palace" was a small office building with nothing "Royal" about it. The west side of the plaza was home to a small hotel, bar, restaurant and general store. Other small businesses lined the streets leading into the plaza, such as a barber, doctor's clinic, feed and seed store, stable, blacksmith, and a brothel. The civilian population resided in homes surrounding the plaza area and on the roads leading into and out of the town.

The other part of the town was on the water. On the south side of the bay stood the navy base. It was home to the Central Pacific Fleet commanded by Rear Admiral Adonis Contraris, who was senior to the army colonel who commanded the Presidio. Admiral Contraris had two squadrons under his command. The treasure ship squadron consisted of three of the largest and newest ships in the fleet which were constructed to carry cargo. One of them was responsible for transporting gold from Peru. The other two made periodic trips from Manila, Philippines bringing Oriental treasures.

The second squadron consisted of 10 warships of various sizes which were charged with patrolling the central Pacific in search of the enemy. They were on constant alert for an attack by Captain Cook. Reports had been received for months that Captain Cook was active in the Pacific. When Eduardo arrived, there were three warships in port. Also as part of the admiral's command was a

315

company of Marines who acted as guards; a platoon of cannoneers, a hospital group; and a kitchen group.

The Navy Base looked more like a fortress than a naval facility with its 14 foot high walls. Yet, its military look was tempered by the dozen or so vendors hovering near the front gate who catered to the officers and sailors who worked inside. Among the offerings were food, scrimshaw, carved ships, handmade purses, jewelry and clothing. The vendors sat on blankets with their wares displayed in front of them. Some of them sat under awnings to protect them from the tropical sun.

There were guard towers at the four corners of the ramparts surrounding the 15 acre facility, and a guard house at the main gate. The ramparts of the fort were guarded by 12 cannons. A redoubt just inside the gate was defended with three cannons. A new lookout with an eye glass monitoring the sea, came on duty every two hours.

As they entered the main gate, on the right they passed the stables, wagon storage area and blacksmith. To the left were the barracks, mess hall, ball field and enlisted recreation hall. They passed the headquarters buildings for each squadron, fire station, Clinic, BOQ/Officers Club and married officer housing, park, playground and school.

Facing a large parade ground was the Headquarters which overlooked the dock area. A huge Spanish flag fluttered in the breeze. Eduardo and Fernando dismounted and tied their mounts to the hitching post in front of headquarters. They were saluted by a sentry, guarding the front entrance. The petty officer at the reception desk greeted them and stepped into an office adjoining the reception area. Almost instantly appeared a Fragata Captain[16], who escorted them to the Admiral's office.

"The admiral has been expecting you. We are honored by your presence. He will see you now.

Please follow me."

"General Lopez, welcome to Acapulco. I am very pleased to meet you," said Admiral Contreras.

"This is my Chief of Staff, Fragata Captain, Antonio Villarrell."

Admiral Contreras was a handsome 50 year old with a full head of white hair, which was trimmed neatly. He was about 5' 11" and 200 pounds. He spoke without emotion.

"Admiral, this is my aide Colonel Garcia," replied Eduardo. "As you might imagine, we are exhausted from our ride from Cuernavaca. I am sure that all of my officers and men are interested in is a bath and some rest, followed by a clean uniform, a drink and some food.

"Ask Chief Petty Officer Perez to step in," ordered the admiral to the petty officer on the desk. After a few minutes Chief Perez entered. "Chief, the column we have been expecting has arrived from Cuernavaca," informed the admiral. "Direct all the enlisted men to the barracks where they will be assigned bunks and linens; and then advise the Mess Hall Manager to prepare for an extra 50 men for a late dinner tonight. The 20 donkey handlers will pitch tents on the football field, but we will feed them while they are here. Ensure that all horses and donkeys are unsaddled, fed, watered, and rubbed down.

"General Lopez, Captain Villarrell will escort you and your officers to the BOQ, where you will reside in our VIP suite. We have our meals in the Officer's Club

---

[16] Equivalent to a US Navy Commander or Army Lieutenant Colonel.

which is attached to the BOQ lobby. He will instruct the restaurant manager that you will be eating late and to prepare for the additional five officers for the next several days. Today is Sunday. With your permission, I would like to give you and your staff a tour of the base. Would tomorrow morning at 10:00 a.m. be satisfactory," he inquired?

"That would be fine Admiral," he Replied. "Colonel Garcia, please inform our staff and our two Cavalry officers of the base tour tomorrow at 10:00 a.m.

"Excuse me general. With your permission, I would like to conduct a reception in your honor at the Officers Club on Saturday night. All of our officers and their wives will attend. We will also honor your staff and the two cavalry officers who accompanied you. The next treasure ship is not expected for about three weeks."

"Admiral, a reception would be delightful. I'll see you in the morning, but now I'm looking forward to that bath."

Sgt. Blanco carried Eduardo's luggage and briefcase to the VIP suite. He opened the door into a comfortable lounge, with a couch, two end tables with candles, a coffee table and two comfortable lounge chairs with a table between them. There was a coat rack in the corner. Against the middle of the wall was a table filled with bottles of whisky, rum, Tequila and brandy. Also on the table was a keg of beer and glasses. Large, framed paintings of sea battles decorated two walls. Under one of those paintings was a desk with a candle and a chair. On the desk was an ink well, quill, salt and a ream of writing paper.

The bedroom was furnished with a large bed, upon which lay the most recent Acapulco newspaper and last week's base newsletter. Next to the bed was a table with a candle. Also on the bedside table was a handwritten list of all officers assigned to the command, including the officers aboard the 13 ships attached. A chest of drawers hugged one wall under a framed chart of the Pacific Ocean.

The bathroom opened into the bedroom. A huge porcelain bathtub was the center of attraction. On the wall next to the tub hung two large bath towels. On a table next to the wall there was a wash bowl, a pitcher of water, and a bar of soap. On the wall above was a hand towel and a wash- cloth. At the other end of the bathroom was a slop bucket for bodily waste.

"Sgt. Blanco, grab a couple of seamen, get a fire going and boil me some water for a hot bath.

After the 10:00 a.m. tour tomorrow, your main job is to wash and press my filthy uniform. Get yourself checked into the barracks and get some hot food in you at the mess hall. They are expecting a bunch of you to come in late.

Eduardo luxuriated in his hot bath. His body ached from days of riding over difficult terrain. This was his first hot bath since Mexico City. He slowly flexed the muscles in each arm, then both legs. He put the warm washcloth behind his neck and rested his head on the edge of the tub. His eyes closed and his thoughts went to Toni. While he soaked, he snoozed.

He dried off, dressed and was sitting at a table in the Officers Club bar within 15 minutes. When he arrived Colonel Garcia and Lt. Ramirez had already joined up with the two cavalry officers, Lt. Chavez and Sub Gonzales. They had all already ordered but had not been served except for drinks.

After examining the menu for a couple of minutes he ordered grilled swordfish and sweet potatoes. The atmosphere around the table was one of satisfaction – they had completed an exceedingly difficult and dangerous journey. They could rest for several days. The junior officers all waited until General Lopez had finished his meal, before leaving the table.

Upon returning to his quarters, he noticed a copy of the Acapulco weekly newspaper on his desk. The feature story was about the mayor cutting the ribbon for a new seafood restaurant which included information about the menu. Also on the front page was an article about the damage caused in Guadalajara by an earthquake. There was a column for fishermen; a weekly weather forecast; a listing of arrests during the week; a list of cases set for court the following week; a report on the football games played the last week, and an article about a young boy who was caught in an undertow and drowned. A good part of the newspaper consisted of ads for local merchants and the cliff divers.

On the ride from Mexico City, he had made only a few entries into his journal. After his relaxing bath and satisfying dinner, he spent about an hour updating his entries. He blew out he candle and put his head on his pillow. He enjoyed a wonderful night's sleep.

. . .

Even with a cross breeze from two open windows, Eduardo's quarters were hot and muggy when he awoke. After throwing some water on his face, he quickly decided it was time to break out his cotton uniform.

Promptly at 10:00 a.m. on September 21st the Admiral greeted Eduardo, his staff and the two cavalry officers.

From the Admiral's office there was a large wooden porch, which afforded them a view of the entire waterfront. A stairwell led to the dock area.

To the north were two piers. The closest was for pleasure craft owned by officers and men of the base. Tied up to this pier were the Admiral's gig, small row boats, sailing vessels from 8 ft to 25 feet, and a half-dozen fishing boats. A fish cleaning station stood behind the cannon emplacement. Secondly was the pier for the treasure ships, behind which were two warehouses – one for gold from Peru and the other for Oriental goods. Both warehouses were protected with guard houses in front and back; a guard house between them and one on either side.

To the south were three piers to accommodate the 10 war ships. Landward from those piers was a huge storage area containing spare masts and sails, lumber, paint, tools, and miles of lines of assorted sizes; a repair facility, and the armory, containing cannon, cannon balls, mortars, mortar shells, small arms, and gunpowder.

To protect the base from an attack by sea the commander had placed a cannon at the seaside end of each of the five piers, to supplement those on the fortress ramparts. All cannon crews were "at the ready" to respond quickly. Guard houses were placed at the landward end of each pier to limit access to all ships. One of the ten warships was on constant patrol parallel with the base just over the horizon to provide advance warning of an impending attack.

The base had its own water well. It was covered to prevent bird droppings, leaves and trash from contaminating the water. Next to the well had been built an elevated cistern capable of holding 2,500 gallons of water. Each enlisted man took turns hauling up buckets

321

of water, climbing the dozen steps of the cistern and emptying his bucket of water into the cistern.

Also, the navy had built a small lookout post on top of the mountain just behind the base about 3,500 feet high, where two senior enlisted men would take turns scanning the sea with a looking glass. It was a sparsely furnished post with two cots, a table with 2 chairs and a fireplace for cooking. The lookout post was reachable by horse and every two days there was a shift change. The lookouts had to transport their own food and water on a packhorse. A third man would accompany them up the mountain and would lead their horses back to the base. The guards loved his duty because they had two days off when they returned to the base.

The public pier was in the center of the bay. The larger ships of the fishing fleet and private boats were tied up on the pier. In the shade of a mott of palm trees at the end of the pier was a boat rental shack, bait shop, outside bar under a canopy, and vendors who set up under the shade of canopies, offering tacos, carne guisada pies, jicama, etc. Two little boys sat on the pier, their bare feet hanging down. Each had a pole made of cane. It appeared they were having a good time drowning worms.

The temperature was in the mid 90's and it was matched by the humidity. "Thank you, Viceroy Galvez, for suggesting that I purchase a cotton uniform," thought Eduardo.

CHAPTER 109

Naval Base Headquarters

Acapulco, Mexico

September 21, 1781

"Good Morning Admiral. Last night I had the best sleep I have had in three weeks."

"Great, Now, can you tell me the purpose of your visit," asked Admiral Contreras, with a quizzical look on his face?

"Admiral, please read this letter," he said as he tendered the king's letter to him.

"Let's just say that I am looking around this theatre of operations for the king. Perhaps I can come up with suggestions that would benefit our kingdom. Let me say that I am already extremely impressed with your command. Clearly, you have a good handle on security. I am also impressed with all the extra-curricular activities you have available to officers, enlisted and dependents who are thousands of miles from home. These are great for morale." "Admiral, what I require from you are the following:

1. Documentation of dates of arrival and departure of all treasure ships from Manila and copies of their respective manifests.

2. Documentation of dates of arrival and departure of all treasure ships from Lima and copies of their respective manifests.

3.　Which of your warships, if any, escorted any of the Treasure Ships, and if so, the dates of departure of each?

4.　Details of any problems you have had with Treasure ships, their officers and/or their crew.

5.　Copies of all documents pertaining to the transfer of gold to the Mexico City Mint.

6.　Copies of all documents pertaining to the transfer of silver ore to the Mexico City Mint.

7.　Copies of all documents pertaining to the transfer of Oriental goods to Vera Cruz.

8.　Any suggestions you have that might improve the handling of the transfer of goods from Manila or Lima, and the transshipment from Acapulco to Mexico City or Vera Cruz.

9.　Records relating to the security of donkey trains to Mexico City or Vera Crus.

10. Any complaints that may be of concern to you."

"That shouldn't be a problem, general. I can have a good part of those documents ready for your review by tomorrow morning. There is an empty office down the hall which you and your men can use while you are here. I'll have my staff provide office supplies.

"That will be wonderful. By the way, I had breakfast this morning with Lt. Chavez. I took the liberty of ordering him and his platoon to await the arrival of this next ship from Lima, and to escort the cargo on the donkeys to the Mint in Mexico City.

"Since your staff has the day off may I entertain you this afternoon? I would like you and your staff to be my guests to see some spectacular diving exhibitions. If Sgt. Blanco would be willing to sit up front with the driver, we can all go in my coach. If you are willing, I'll pick you up at 4:00 in front of the BOQ?" asked Admiral Contreras.

"Sounds great Admiral. We'll be there at 4:00."

. . .

The coach turned left heading west on the coast road. The road took them through the town. They passed a public park on the right with dozens of food and craft vendors in bamboo huts on the beach with straw roofs. All the trees lining the road and in the park were painted white up to the four foot mark. The beach stopped abruptly. At the water's edge monolithic rock swelled up from the sea several hundred feet high.

After about another ten minutes, the coach pulled off the road and went through a narrow gap in the mountains on a gravel road. The coach was parked in an area with other coaches, carriages and wagons. Then they followed an even narrower foot path until they found themselves on a wide flat spot large enough to accommodate about 50 people. As might be expected vendors were there peddling food and drink. Separating their viewing area from the adjacent mountain was a narrow inlet of water.

Admiral Contreras told them that divers would jump from the mountain into the shallow and narrow inlet which measured 16 feet deep after the wave subsides, and 19 feet it the diver could hit the crest of the wave at its height. Timing of the wave was everything. A representative of the divers passed through the audience to collect a small viewing fee, which the Admiral paid. This dive was also dangerous because the water was not directly beneath the diver. The diver had to jump out so that he landed at least 10 feet from the shore. Otherwise, he would be splattered on the rocky coast.

They craned their necks looking up the mountain to watch three boys dive from 100 feet up. Just before each diver leaped out an individual on the platform threw a shiny coin into the inlet. Each time, the diver came out of the water holding the coin.

The ticket taker came by again to collect another fee if we wanted to watch them dive from 135 feet. To see the diver on his elevated perch, they had to not only bend their necks, but they also had to lean back as far as they could. Wouldn't you know it, they were facing west and had the late afternoon sun in their eyes. Three more divers made breathtaking dives from 135 feet. After the last dive, all the divers climbed up to the viewing area to shake hands and thank the crowd for coming. They were trolling for more tips.

On the return coach ride, Eduardo asked the Admiral to have lunch with him the next day. When he returned to his quarters there was a copy of the Acapulco Navy Base weekly Newspaper, which covered ships in port; testing dates for promotion; an article about "Sailor of the Quarter", Special Services article about things to do; football schedule; NCO and Officers club specials, new books at the library, etc.

That evening Eduardo composed a letter to Viceroy Jose Galvez:

His Excellency Jose Galvez

Viceroy of New Spain Mexico City, Mexico

September 21, 1781

Your Excellency,

I trust you are well and in good spirits. I have not heard from Bernardo since we last talked. We are in Acapulco auditing the records of shipping to and from it and preparing for our journey to Manila.

Admiral Contreras has been very helpful. I am very impressed with him. His security measures are the finest I have ever seen. In this distant outpost the morale of his officers, men and dependents are all very high. Enclosed please find the list of activities for his base. He is very businesslike and well organized. I would highly recommend him for an early promotion.

The two young officers who commanded the platoon that escorted us to Acapulco are also worth special mention. Lt. Thomas Chavez gave me a thorough brief of what to expect on our journey. Several times each day he would ask me if I had any questions, problems or issues. He was polite, efficient and handled his responsibilities timely and with proficiency. Sub Lt. Gonzales also conducted himself in a military manner and was always willing to go out of his way. My entourage was treated well, and we arrived without incident. I have sent a letter of commendation to his commanding officer recommending early promotion for both of them.

While in Mexico City recently, my staff and I conducted an audit of the Royal Mint. We spent three full dames examining and copying all books, records, journals, ledgers, logs, receipts concerning the receipt, processing, refining of silver ore and the minting of silver coins. In a separate container I am forwarding all those copies to you.

327

Utilizing the above mentioned data, we composed charts which are very disturbing. These charts clearly reflected that over the past five years the tonnage of silver ore received has remained constant. In the past two years there has been a severe drop-off in the number and value of silver coins minted. It appears to me that a million Livres or more.

is missing in each of those two years from theft, and that this embezzlement is an ongoing affair.

I would suggest that a secret investigation be commenced immediately in such a manner as not to alert the possible suspects. It would appear to me that your investigator would initially focus on the following:

> *Mint Director and his wife*
>
> *Mint Manager and his wife*
>
> *Mint Foreman and his wife*
>
> *Mint Administrative Officer and his wife.*

I would hope that your investigator would do at least the following:

1. Obtain a valid appraisal on all real estate owned by the employee and his wife, including vacation homes and rental property.

2. Check with all banks in Mexico City and the employee's hometown for bank accounts or safe deposit boxes in his and his wife's name.

3. Have each of the above employees and their wives followed to ascertain if they have a problem with gambling, drugs, mistresses, or prostitution and to monitor their spending.

4. Check with the Mexican Corporation and Partnership office to determine if any suspects are listed as the owner, partner or shareholder in any corporation or partnership. If so, follow up investigating that corporation or partnership.

5. Review the bank accounts of each for large deposits and cost of vacations, automobiles, jewelry or other items of high value.

6. Review their tax returns to see if they are reporting any income from dividends, rental income, etc. and if so, determine the source of that income.

7. Get a spy into the mint as an employee to watch where the coins go after being minted.

8. Put the mint under discrete surveillance 24 hours per day. Follow every truck that leaves the mint to its destination and watch what is unloaded. If silver is being unloaded at a private business or residence, put that building under 24 hour watch and investigate the owner.

9. If by this time you have no clear evidence of the identity of the embezzler, my last suggestion is that an investigation be conducted on the suspects parents and children in Spain.

I understand that the voyage to Manila, which must stop in Guam for food, water, repairs and crew liberty, takes almost three months. The treasure ship from Lima is due about October 12th. We are scheduled to depart Acapulco about October 20th, so I estimate that without incident we should arrive in Manila about mid-January, 1782. My duties will require that I spend several months in Manila and its environs. With scheduled stops on the way to Lima, Peru that journey should take about four months, and after my duties there another three months to

329

Acapulco. Hopefully by then we will have captured our embezzler at the mint. It appears that it will be mid-year in 1782 when I return to Mexico City. I look forward to visiting with you then.

I am enclosing a notice of available activities by naval personnel in Acapulco.

Warm personal regards, I remain your faithful servant

Eduardo Lopez, Maj. General, Army of Spain

SPECIAL SERVICES DEPARTMENT

Acapulco Navy Base Activities for September 1781

Always Available:

1.   Horseback ride to view Acapulco Divers. Every Saturday at 4:00 p.m. Return by 9:00.

2.   Charter fishing boats. Daily at 8:00 a.m.

3.   Charter sail boats. Daily at 8:00 a.m.

4.   Playground opens from Sunup to Sunrise.

5.   Gymnasium – Open daily and weekends from 8:00 a.m. to 10:00 p.m.

6.   Beach – Lifeguard on duty 10:00 a.m. – 6:00 p.m. everyday.

7.   Library – 1:00 p.m. – 10:00 pm M-F; Sat. 9:00 a.m. to 1:00 p.m.; Sunday 1:00 p.m. to 5:00 p.m.

8.   Trail rides – every Sunday from 8:00 a.m. to 4:00 p.m. Bring your lunch.

Monthly Specials:

1. *Sailing lessons – every Saturday and Sunday for six weeks. Class 21 begins 1ˢᵗ Saturday. Register at Enlisted Recreation Hall.*

2. *Horseback Riding lessons - every Saturday and Sunday for six weeks. Class 12 begins 1ˢᵗ Saturday. Register at Enlisted Recreation Hall.*

3. *Star Gazing – Friday evenings after dark (weather permitting) at Pier 1.*

4. *Swimming lessons (age 10-above) – every Saturday on the beach at 10:00*

5. *Supervised weight training*

6. *Sailing race – Sunday, Sep. 2 @ 8:00 a.m.*

7. *Sailing race – Sunday, Sep. 16 @ 8:00 a.m.*

8. *All hands Picnic with Mariachi music from Acapulco. Children's activities. Last Sunday each month from 11:00 a.m.*

9. *Officer's Club weekly dinner dance every Saturday night from 8:00 – midnight.*

10. *Enlisted meet and greet young ladies from the community. Friday evening 6:00 p.m. – 8:00 p.m.*

FOOTBALL LEAGUE SCHEDULE

All home games are played on the Navy football field, beginning at 2:00 p.m.

Sunday, Sep. 2 Army	Civilians Presidio		
Sunday, Sep. 9 Navy Treasure Army	Navy		
Sunday, Sep.	Civilians	Navy	Acapulco Stadium

331

16

Sunday, Sep. 23	*Navy War*	*Army*	*Navy*
Sunday, Sep. 30	*Navy Treasure*	*Civilians*	*Acapulco Stadium*
Sunday, Oct. 7	*Navy Treasure*	*Navy War*	*Navy*
Sunday, Oct. 14	*Navy War*	*Civilians*	*Acapulco Stadium.*

CHAPTER 110

Officers Club

Acapulco Naval Base

September 23, 1781

Eduardo and the admiral both enjoyed the seafood buffet lunch at the club. In casual conversation the admiral informed Eduardo that he gets milk, fruits, vegetables, bread, beef, lamb, goat, and pork from farmers; and that he secured seafood, beer, wine and liquor from local merchants.

Eduardo asked him about the treasure ships, and why they did not have a warship escort. Admiral Contreras told Eduardo that we he first took command, he asked for authority to have each treasure ship escorted but was turned down by higher authority because the three ships were fast and well gunned, and the escorts were needed to patrol the vast Pacific.

"Admiral, based upon my letter from the king I am ordering you to assign one of your warships to each of your three treasure ships so that they are always under escort. If you can justify it to me that you need those three ships replaced, then I will recommend that the three ships I have diverted are restored. Please let me know which ship will be escorting the *Caca Fuego* to Manila as soon as possible, as I need to speak with her captain.

That afternoon he conferred with his staff about their progress in going through the records of the Naval base. As he looked out the window a fourth warship was approaching the pier.

That evening he composed a letter to his wife, Toni:

September 23, 1781

My dearest Darling,

I miss you terribly. It is so terribly depressing to think that it may be another year before I see your beautiful face. The Admiral in command of the military area runs a tight ship so I suspect that our audit will indicate no problems. The admiral took me and my staff outside the city to watch some young boys dive into shallow water from high up the mountain. He is sponsoring a reception at the Navy Officer's Club Saturday evening, for me, my staff, and the two young officers who escorted us here from Mexico City.

Yesterday, I had lunch with the Colonel who commands the Acapulco Presidio. He is honoring me and my staff and the two officers who escorted us at the Army Officers Club the following Saturday at the Presidio Officer's Club. I am beginning to enjoy Mexican food, just as I am leaving Mexico for half a year.

The ship I am taking to Mania is scheduled to arrive here in Acapulco the second week of October. We will probably depart a week or 10 days after that. After two months at sea sailing due west, we should arrive in Guam for a few days to take on food and water, to make any repairs, and to let the crew have some time ashore. I will put my next letter to you in the mail from Guam.

It's another two to three weeks from Guam to Manila. I'll have another letter ready to mail when we arrive in Manila. Please send all mail C/O Admiral Contreras. He will know whether to forward it to me in Manila or Lima or just hold it for my return. My time in Manila will be at least one month but probably more like two to three months. I feel like the work I am doing is important – no - vital to the kingdom. I have already made a startling discovery that greatly benefits Spain.

I purchased a sterling silver necklace for you and am mailing it with this letter, but they may arrive separately.

I love you with all my heart and soul and look forward to the day when I can lay my eyes on your beautiful face.

> *Lalo*

. . .

The following day Eduardo met with the skippers of both the Treasure ship and warship; at which time he showed them both the letter from the king. He informed them both that he was transferring three of the warships to the command of the treasure ship command, with specific warships wed to a particular treasure ship as its permanent escort. Both were informed that if any escort ship was unable to disembark, that the treasure ship commander could requisition a fourth warship until such time as the original escort has been made seaworthy.

Admiral Contreras advised Eduardo that he had designated the *Diligence*, a 28 gun, two masted sloop as the escort for the treasure ship *Caca Fuego*.

Her captain was Corbeta[17] Captain Esteban Francisco, from Barcelona. Spanish was his native tongue, but he was also fluent in Portuguese, his mother's native language. He was 40 years of age, possessed of a good

---

[17] Equivalent to a Lieutenant Commander in the Navy or Major in the Army.

education, was well read, and was an interesting conversationalist. He had carrot red hair, a light complexion and freckles. He was about 5' 10" with a thin build. Both his father and grandfather had served as Captains in the Spanish Navy.

Her XO was Lieutenant Filemon Escobar, from Cadiz, Spain. He speaks only Spanish. A

Mustang who served five years as an enlisted man before being selected for Officer Candidate School. He did not attend college. He graduated from the school of hard knocks. He knows how to do the quick fixes when repairs need to be made in an emergency. He was very reliable 6' 2" 230 pounds, all muscle, and was extremely strong.

Her Gunnery Officer was Lieutenant Henri Dias, of Cordoba, Spain. He had spent part of his childhood living with his father's brother in Dover, England. His father's brother was a gunmaker by trade, so Henri grew up around cannons. He knew everything about cannons. He was fluent in English. He frequently had his gun crews practice gunnery shooting at a target pulled by the escort ship.

The Navigator was Fragata Lieutenant[18] Manuel Sosa, who grew up in Escorial, Spain, where all the ancient kings of Spain are entombed. His father was a history professor at the University of Escorial. He spoke only Spanish, but he could talk your ear off about history and geography. He was an excellent celestial navigator.

Midshipman Emilio Rangel was the senior Midshipman by two months. He served as the Supply officer. His was

---

[18] Equivalent to an Ensign in the Navy or 2nd Lieutenant in the Army.

from Valencia, where his father was a trial lawyer and his mother taught science in the public high school.

Midshipman Pedro Saucedo served as Assistant Gunnery Officer, Assistant Navigator, Laundry Officer, and Assistant Supply Officer. An eager young man whose mother was from Austria. He spoke German fluently in addition to Spanish.

. . .

The following day Eduardo met with Captain Esteban Francisco, skipper of the *Diligence*, together with his XO Lieutenant Filemon Escobar. He showed them both his letter from the king and explained they would henceforth be assigned as permanent escort to the *Caca Fuego*. He informed them that he was hosting a reception for the officers of both ships on the evening of

October 10th at the Officers Club. "We are about to make a long journey together, so it is only fitting that we get to know one another."

"Not later than October 7 you will report to me any repairs needed to your ship before we depart and that you are fully stocked with gunpowder and cannon balls. If any member of your crew is sick or disabled, I need to replace him. Since you don't have a doctor, you may use the doctor assigned to the *Caca Feugo*. Since the manifest of the Caca Fuego doesn't begin to fill her holds, I am ordering that it carry extra cannons, cannon balls and gunpowder. If we get into a battle, we can provide you with a reserve supply to keep your guns firing. The *Caca Feugo* will also be carrying live animals, so your meat ration will be extended considerably."

He also met with his staff. "Fernando, did you find any discrepancies in the Admirals records," asked Eduardo?

337

"General, everything checks out. Mainly we were concerned that the weight of gold delivered to Acapulco checks out with the weight of gold shipped out to the mint. Because there were so many products from Manila, it took a bit longer, but his records mesh perfectly."

That evening he penned a letter to the king. He repeated much of what he had written to Viceroy Galvez about embezzlement at the mint. He provided a detailed report on their audit of the Acapulco Navy Base with his conclusions and recommendations including his recommendation that Admiral Contreras be promoted to Vice Admiral. He reported that he had taken it upon himself to order that each treasure ship be constantly escorted by a warship. He updated his itinerary.

CHAPTER 111

Officer's Club

Acapulco Navy Base

Acapulco, Mexico

Saturday September 29, 1781

The reception at the Officer's Club for all the officers was very nice. Present were eighteen officers from five of the 13 warships, together with Eduardo's staff, the two cavalry officer escorts, the Admiral, his Chief of Staff, doctor, supply officer, chaplain and the COs and XOs of the two ship squadrons.

After the officers finished going through the reception line, the admiral made a toast to General Lopez and his staff. Then Eduardo made a toast to the Admiral and all officers assigned to Acapulco.

The cook had prepared a delicious roast suckling pig, which was on display during the reception. It was served with roasted vegetables. For dessert he had prepared pineapple flavored flan.

The Navy band played soft music during the reception and while the officers enjoyed their dinner.

That evening he wrote short letters to both Bernardo and Christopher to bring them up to date.

He reported the full story about the embezzlement at the mint and excellent records in Acapulco.

. . .

Fernando accompanied Eduardo to church in Acapulco across from the Presidio. The priest invited them to his parsonage for a glass of wine after church. The priest was delighted to meet new Spaniards, even though he loved caring for his native flock.

They tried the Cantina on the plaza for lunch. Surprisingly, this local fare was very tasty.

By mid-afternoon, the two men were relaxing on the beach in two comfortable chairs. Constant waves washed ashore on this beautiful bay. Periodically, pelicans dove into the ocean for a fish. High above the bay a flight of ducks in a "V" formation migrated south. A cool breeze and full stomachs made them drowsy. They both had books in their hands, but it appeared that most of their time was spent talking with one another. When a waiter from a nearby beach bar asked them if they would like a drink, they both order a rum punch. Fishing boats returned to the beach with their daily catch. Before sunset, six rum punches were served to these two men.

Before returning to the BOQ they enjoyed some fried shrimp.

CHAPTER 112

Officer's Club

Acapulco Presidio

Acapulco, Mexico

October 6, 1781

As promised, the Presidio Commander had sponsored a reception at the Presidio Officer's Club. The army club was larger than the navy club even though there were more officers assigned to the navy. The difference was that most of the naval officers were at sea a good deal of the time.

The colonel in effect was a regimental commander. Under his command were two infantry companies, each of which had three platoons which contained 14 officers; a cavalry company with three platoons, containing 10 officers; a company of cannoneers with 10 officers; mess officer, chaplain, doctor, administrative and supply officer.

The reception line punishment lasted longer than the one at the navy base. The commander gave a toast to Eduardo and his staff. In return, Eduardo gave a toast to the colonel and officers of the Presidio.

Eduardo made a short speech in which he spoke on behalf of King Carlos. He thanked them for their service to Spain. He told them of the great activities available at the navy base and suggested that they develop a similar program.

CHAPTER 113

Caca Fuego[20] arrives in Acapulco.

Acapulco, Mexico

Oct. 12, 1781

 Eduardo was alerted by a messenger from the admiral that the *Caca Fuego* had been spotted on the horizon. He and the admiral were both on the pier awaiting its arrival as it neared the base.

The *Caca Fuego* arrived in port mid-morning on October 12, 1781. It was the largest ship Eduardo had ever seen. It was a three masted galleon about 300 feet long and 90 feet wide. It displaced 5,000 tons of water. This four deck monster carried 64 guns on two decks, and carried a crew of 230, which included 135 in gun crews and 30 sharpshooters who manned the top deck and the riggings. It sat deep in the water drawing 30 feet. It carried a cargo of 2,000 tons consisting primarily of silver ore and gold. It was hot and humid. The air was still.

[20] Spanish for "Shit Fire."

Painting of the Caca Fuego 1

As soon as the gangway was extended to the pier the admiral and Eduardo went onboard to meet the Captain. Captain Fidencio Luna was a stout 5' 10" who carried himself with a military bearing. He appeared to be about 50 years old. He had salt and pepper hair which he combed straight back, revealing a widow's peak. His face was clean shaven and weathered. He did not smile much but did have a sense of humor. He was a very senior captain who was all business. Soon, he would be considered by the promotion board for admiral. He tapped his pipe on his boot to empty it, then walked toward the gangway to greet his visitors.

"Good morning, Captain Luna. Allow me to present Maj. General Eduardo Lopez. General, this is Captain Fidencio Luna. Eduardo returned his salute.

"Captain, may we speak in your cabin," asked Eduardo. "And please ask your executive officer to join us."

"General, would you or the admiral care for some coffee? Or perhaps a glass of wine," asked Captain Luna?

"A cup of coffee would be great," answered Eduardo.

As the steward closed the door behind him, Eduardo handed the kings letter to Captain Luna, saying "Captain, please read this letter."

After reading the letter Captain Luna said "I am at your service, General. What are my orders," he inquired?

"Effective immediately your new title is "Commodore" as the Admiral has attached to your command the ship *Diligence*, which has been ordered to constantly escort you. That was my suggestion to further protect our precious cargo.

"Secondly, my staff and I will be passengers on your upcoming voyage to Manila.

"I am not here to investigate any charges or allegations about you, your officers or your ship. The king asked me to visit all our outposts and look around to see if I could recommend any improvements. This is a matter I will discuss with you on our lengthy trip. Before I can make any recommendations, I must first seek to understand the entire process from mining to minting and the transportation involved."

Eduardo continued. "Please provide me with a copy of the ship's Manifest. XO, would you please accompany me while I inspect the cargo? I must make my inspection before you begin your unloading process. I will need you to show me where each cargo item is stored," remarked Eduardo.

"Captain Luna, I would be honored if you and your officers would join me and my staff for dinner on me tomorrow night at the Officer's Club at 7:00. The roast suckling pig is wonderful.

. . .

Unloading of the *Caca Fuego* started after lunch. Fernando and Javi monitored the weighing of the gold, the logging of each cart weighed and its transport to the warehouse and made notes of each step. Next came the silver ore, which was weighed, logged and transported to the warehouse. By 5:00 p.m. the gold and silver had been weighed and stored, so the crew was dismissed for the day.

Unloading commenced at 8:00 a. m. on Saturday. Today, they would next unload the wine, liquor and beer, bolts of Cloth, jewelry, crafts, pottery, Alpaca, Wool, etc. Lt. Colonel Garcia and Lt Ramirez made notation of all weights and descriptions. Admiral Contreras selected the wine, liquor and beer his command would require and signed a chit that he had taken this cargo. He set aside another order for wine, liquor and beer for the Presidio, and prepared a chit for the colonel to sign when his men picked up his order.

That afternoon Eduardo spoke with the manager of the officer's club. "I will have 18 officers tonight for a private dinner party, starting at 7:00 p.m. I would like to have two round tables in as private an area as you can find. The first will seat 9 senior officers; and the second should accommodate 9 junior officers. Here is my seating list. Please have name cards at each place setting. At the table for senior officers, I will be at the head; Admiral Contreras will be on my right and Captain Luna will be on my left. Please have stewards pass appetizers during the cocktail hour between 7:00 p.m.-8:00 p.m. at which time we will sit for dinner. Please ensure that the music starts promptly at 7:00 p.m."

That evening the officers in this private group were wined and dined to the music of an Acapulco band. The cocktail party was elegant. Stewards served fried shrimp, fried oysters, and baked bacon wrapped scallops.

When they sat down, Eduardo made some remarks. He informed the group that he was a representative of the king and was on a fact finding tour. He informed them that their two ships would henceforth travel in tandem. He hosted this dinner party to allow all the offices of the two ships to get to know each other and his staff. He offered a toast to HRM Carlos, III, King of Spain. They all stood and shouted, "To the King!" He then offered a toast to Admiral Contreras and staff – "To the admiral!"

"Gentlemen, I would now like to offer a toast to a safe and uneventful voyage from Acapulco to Manila for the officers and men of the *Caca Fuego* and the *Diligence*."

346

The officers present enthusiastically arose with their glasses held high and shouted, "To a safe voyage!"

The officers of the *Caca Fuego* were particularly glad to eat something other than the food prepared by their ship's cook. They dined on roast suckling pig with a spicy sauce made locally of jalapeño peppers, tomatoes, bell peppers, lemon, onion, garlic and cilantro. Dessert was a bowl of mixed fresh fruit, including watermelon, cantaloupe, honeydew melon, strawberries, blue berries, mangos and pecans with crème.

The officers of *Diligence* were still enjoying the club food after being on patrol for a month. All of those at the junior officer table kept prodding Lt. Ramirez for information about General Lopez and Lt. Colonel Garcia. At the same time, he was quizzing the officers of the *Caca Fuego* about Captain Luna. They ate, they drank, they enjoyed the music, and they finally relaxed. They began to feel at home with their new shipmates – just as planned by Eduardo.

. . .

It was Sunday. Eduardo decided to go to mass at the Chapel on base. He ate a light lunch then spent some time in the base library. He was facing almost three months at sea to reach Manila. He wanted to ensure that he had enough reading material for the journey. Eduardo checked out the following books:

Travel books to Guam, the Philippines, Marshall Islands, Phoenix Islands, Marquesas Islands, Peru, and Galapagos Islands; Spanish Tagalog dictionary; Spanish Tagalog

347

textbook; Biographies of Alexander the Great, Emperor Charlemagne, and William The Conqueror; and the three-volume set of *Encyclopedia Britannica*, published in 1768. He planned on requiring the junior officers to read some of his books on the voyage.

At a small store on the Navy base, he loaded up on Mexican candy.

Back in his quarters he updated his journal.

. . .

At 8:00 a.m. on Monday, some of the crew of the *Caca Fuego* began cleaning out the cargo holds so as not to contaminate any of the cargo to be loaded. Other crew members were swabbing the decks, while still others were cleaning the cabins. This cleaning was scheduled to take the entire day.

Each load was meticulously weighed and identified. Eduardo's crew watched and made copies of each bill of lading. This unloading process took three days.

Eduardo stopped by the supply office to secure writing paper, envelopes, cardboard files, a file storage box, pens, ink, salt, a magnifying glass, a world globe, charts for Guam, Philippines and Peru, an updated copy of Navy Regulations and blank journals.

On Tuesday, the *Caca Fuego* began loading cargo from the warehouse. The mail bags to Guam and Manila were placed in the Captain's cabin. The cargo consisted of rum, vodka, brandy, beer, soda, wine, Cajun moonshine, sorghum, corn meal, Mexican hot sauce, silver and silver flatware, bowls, etc., saddles, bridles, shoes and boots, leather goods, hides, furs, seeds, men's and women's clothing, and machinery.

Because their outgoing cargo was light, they placed straw
in hold #3, and loaded pigs, cows, goats and chickens.
This would allow the crew to have fresh meat well into
their journey. Eduardo had also suggested that since they
had the space, why not carry extra cannon, with cannon
balls and gunpowder. They might come in handy on the
voyage. In the back of his mind, he was thinking that
Manila or Guam might need to reinforce their defenses.

The loads for the donkeys were all completed by late
Wednesday afternoon. At 7:00 p.m. there was a knock on
General Lopez' door.

"Sir," said Lt. Garza, the cavalry platoon leader who
escorted Eduardo from Mexico City, the cargo is ready to
be loaded onto the donkeys. We plan to depart tomorrow
morning. I wanted to discuss with you, our route. The
silver ore and gold both go to the Mexico City Mint. If
you so desire, I can break up my platoon and send the
other goods directly to Vera Cruz.

"That's good thinking Lt. Garza. Although all the other
goods would get to Vera Cruz several days earlier, it
would diminish the protection to our most valuable cargo.
I think it would be better to keep the security detail
together.

"General, it has been a pleasure working with you this
past month. I wish you a safe journey." "Lieutenant, I
should return to Acapulco looking for transportation back
to Vera Cruz in five or six months. Perhaps we will run
into each other along the way. Good luck to you," he said
as Lt. Garza turned and left the room.

As he was dressing the following morning, he looked out
his window to see the donkey train leaving the base on its
journey. He and his staff spent the morning comparing

349

the documentation of goods received from the *Caca Fuego* with the documentation of goods shipped to the mint. There was a minor discrepancy relating to silver ore, but that was an acceptable amount of spillage.

Eduardo walked down the hall to speak with the admiral. He congratulated the admiral on receiving a perfect score on the transfer of the treasure cargo. He told him that he had recommended him for promotion to Vice Admiral to both Viceroy Galvez and King Carlos. "I won't be surprised if you have that third star by the time I return."

"Admiral, the donkey train has departed, and Captain Luna informed me at lunch that he was ready to shove off whenever I was ready. My duties here are complete, so me and my staff will bid you *adieu*, and we will plan on sailing with the morning tide. It has been a pleasure working with you. I look forward to seeing you on my return."

"General, I too have enjoyed out time together. I wish you fair winds, following seas and a safe return."

Back at the BOQ Eduardo knocked on Lt. Ramirez' door. When he opened the door Eduardo said, "Lt. we will be sailing on the morning tide. Please notify Sgt. Blanco, Col. Garcia, and Capt. Francisco, Captain of the *Diligence*, that they should pack up and get on board this afternoon and ask Sgt. Blanco to transfer my luggage to my cabin onboard.

It was a short walk from the BOQ to the pier where the *Caca Fuego* was berthed. As he neared the behemoth, he still could not believe how large she was. He had never seen a ship with 64 guns. In his research he discovered that its speed was only 12 knots. That was why it was so important to have a fast warship as an escort.

As he walked up the gigantic gangway Fragata Captain Borrego, the XO awaited him with a salute.

"Permission to come aboard," he asked?

"Permission granted and welcome aboard General. We are honored to have you onboard. If you follow me, I will show you your VIP Cabin. Our ship has four VIP cabins and can accommodate an additional 30 officers and passengers. Sir, I hope you will be comfortable," said Commander Borrego, as he opened the door. Colonel Garcia will be in the VIP suite to your right as you exit your suite. Dr. Diego and I will be in the two VIP suites on the port side. Your Lt. Ramirez will be in the stateroom next to Colonel Garcia.

Eduardo was very pleased with what he saw. His VIP suit was almost as large as the captain's quarters on Chris's ship. In addition to his bunk, he had an overstuffed easy chair with an ottoman and side table, a table with four chairs, desk and chair, chest of drawers and a built-in bookcase. There was a small area behind a curtain that contained a table with a pan and pitcher of water towels and wash cloths hanging on the war and a chamber pot. In the corner was a clothes rack to hang his uniform. There were two large windows facing the starboard side of the ship. His cabin was adjacent to the Captains.

Captain Luna knocked on his door and asked if his accommodation was satisfactory. "It looks like this is going to be the most comfortable I have ever been at sea," said Eduardo. "I am very pleased. Care to join my officers and me for dinner in town tonight," he asked?

"General, I will be meeting with my officers tonight, so I must decline. We will enjoy many meals together in the next three months," Captain Luna said, laughing.

351

"Would it be possible for you to join me now in my cabin for a few minutes," asked Captain Luna?

"No problem, after you," answered Eduardo.

As Eduardo closed the captain's door behind him the captain handed him a wooden box, the top of which slid off to reveal a very, very expensive bottle of French Armagnac Brandy bottled in 1729.

"General, this bottle of Armagnac is just a small gift to you so that you know how honored I am to have you and your staff as passengers on my ship. If there is anything you desire during this voyage, I will do my best to accommodate you.

"Captain, thank you very much. This is a very generous gift. Don't you think we ought to try it to make sure it's still fit for human consumption," joked Eduardo, as he winked.

"You have a good point there general. We would not want any bad brandy circulating on our ship."

"With your permission general," said the captain, as he reached for the bottle. "I will open the bottle and pour us a couple of drinks so we can run our tests." Without answering, Eduardo watched the captain pour two drinks.

"*Salud*, Capitan."

"*Salud*, General."

. . .

Nando and Javi wanted to have dinner at a restaurant in downtown Acapulco, so they took a coach. They enjoyed their spicy Mexican food and drank too much wine. The highlight of the evening was the cheerful mariachi music. When they arrived back at the ship, Eduardo's orderly had already delivered all his luggage. It took about an hour to unpack. For some reason it made him feel good to get all of his books into the bookcase.

"There is a lot to put into my journal tonight," he thought as he sat at his candle lit desk and

peered out his windows at the lighted warships in the distance.

CHAPTER 114

George Washington Victory

Yorktown, Virginia

Oct. 19, 1781

Following British defeats on the Mississippi, loss of Mobile and Pensacola, and American victories at Kings Mountain and Cowpens, General Cornwallis retreated to Yorktown, on the Virginia Coast. He was surrounded, thereby losing his supply line to Charleston. He was low on ammunition, food and water and hoped to be resupplied and/or rescued by the English Fleet.

By the time Cornwallis' troops were settling into Yorktown, the area offshore was blockaded by the French Fleet.

The uprising of the French troops under Genera Rochambeau who had been threatening to desert were finally paid their salaries for the past three months, courtesy of Spaniards in Havana, whose arms had been twisted by General Bernardo de Galvez to loan 500,000 pieces of eight to the French government.

The Battle of the Capes occurred near the mouth of the Chesapeake Bay on 5 September 1781. The British fleet was led by Rear Admiral Sir Thomas Graves, while the French fleet was commanded by Rear Admiral François Joseph Paul, the Comte de Grasse. The French were able to prevent the Royal Navy from reinforcing or evacuating General Lord Cornwallis from Yorktown, Virginia even though the two fleets were almost evenly matched with men and ships.

With no prospect of rescue and supplies at a minimum, General Cornwallis surrendered. It is interesting to note that General Cornwallis did not participate in the surrender ceremony. He sent a junior officer and feigned sickness to avoid public embarrassment.

. . .

General Cornwallis' surrender was not the end of the war. There were still English soldiers in

New York, Detroit and St. Augustine. Indian allies of the British continued fighting in Ohio and Indiana. It was not until February 4, 1783 that King George of England declared a formal cessation of hostilities.

CHAPTER 115

Onboard *Caca Fuego*

Acapulco to Guam

October 20- January 14, 1781

The *Caca Fuego* fired a cannon salute as it eased out of Acapulco Bay as the sun was rising behind it. The *Diligence*, following close on the port side answered with a cannon salute of its own.

Later, at breakfast, Captain Luna welcomed Eduardo and his two officers to his quarters. The Captain's quarters were extremely spacious. His bed was twice the size of Chris's cot. The dining table was big enough to comfortably seat 20. The revolving floor model world globe had a diameter of a yard. He had a separate chart table with scores of maps and charts, and he had a bar with all manner of libations.

"General, you and your officers are welcome to dine every meal here, but should you need privacy, just inform the cook and you can have meals served in your cabin. Some of my officers prefer to have their breakfasts in private, so feel free to follow suit. You are permitted to request coffee, tea or a snack delivered to your cabin anytime."

"Notice that on the chart table is a chart of the mid-Pacific. Each day at noon, the Navigator will mark our position on the chart and post our progress in the last 24 hours. We will not come close to any islands until we reach Guam in about two months. All hands should keep a keen lookout for English ships. We have had reports that the notorious English Captain Cook[19] is on the prowl somewhere in the Pacific. We must be ready to meet him.

"General, what are your plans for our long journey," asked Captain Luna.

"Captain, I plan to catch up on my reading. I have a three volume encyclopedia to read, three autobiographies and travel books on Guam and the Philippines. I will be working with my staff on our itinerary once we arrive in Manila, and I have some letters to write. Does anybody onboard speak Tagalog?

"I believe the second mate, Domingo Torres is a Tagalog speaker. He is from the island of Mindanao, Philippines."

"I must learn some basic Tagalog before we reach Manila. With your permission I will ask him to work with me during his off-duty hours."

"No problem, general."

"How many languages do you speak," asked Dr. Diego?

Dr. Diego graduated from the Zaragoza University Medical School in Zaragoza, Spain. At age 55, he was a mildly overweight bachelor with large ears, long sideburns and a long thin mustache. Everybody calls him "Doc". He usually had a nice smile on his face. He was from a prominent family in Seville and always acted dignified. He will finish 30 years of military service

---

[19] Unknown to the Spanish, Captain Cook had been killed in Hawaii in February 1779. The
English kept the news of his death quiet because the Spanish had erected presidios all along the California and Mexico Pacific coasts to guard against an attack by him. The English wanted to keep those west coast Spaniards away from the east coast.

357

when they arrive in Manila. Happy that his voyage from Manila will be the first step towards Spain and retirement. His uniform was tailor made and fit perfectly. He planned to volunteer at the Seville Charity Hospital a few days a week.

"In addition to Spanish, I am fluent in English, French and German. I also know a little Dutch and Portuguese," Eduardo responded.

"I can cuss in 5 languages," bragged the Executive Officer.

The XO has dirty teeth and bad breath. He was born to an unwed mother in Madrid. Over the years he worked his way up from cabin boy to XO. At age 49, he has gained weight so that his uniform jacket was pulling at the buttons.

"Commander Borrego, I also hear that you are an excellent chart reader," Eduardo replied with a big grin on his face.

This pleased Commander Borrego, whose comment had been to discount Eduardo's language facility. Captain Luna was pleased that Eduardo had handled the situation so diplomatically.

"Well gentlemen, here's what's in store for us all for the next couple of months. We are now proceeding in a southwesterly direction. When we reach the 18th degree latitude, we will head due west for two months to take advantage of the trade winds. We are scheduled to make a port stop in Agana, Guam for food, water, crew leave and repairs, if any are needed. I'm guessing that we might be in Agana for Christmas. From Agana it is about a 15-20 day run to Manila. Our homeport is actually Subic Bay Naval Base, which is three days by coach to

Manila. That is where we unload our cargo and pick up our outbound cargo.

After a few days, Eduardo fell into a routine. Each clear morning before breakfast he would drink a cup of coffee on deck to examine the sky and sea to assess what kind of day he could look forward to. After each meal he would take a stroll to walk off his meal and get some fresh air. Just before bedtime he would take a final stroll to view the night sky. Almost every time he was on deck there were several crew members fishing. When it was raining, he did not go on deck. Frequently he could hear a harmonica playing in the crew's quarters below forward. Also, at times from that quarter came the sounds of two guitars playing together.

Every Saturday evening the officers of the *Diligence* were invited to dine with the officers of the

Caca Fuego. Since the Diligence was a much faster vessel, it would speed ahead of the *Caca Fuego* several hundred yards. The *Diligence* officers would get in the captain's gig and be rowed over to the *Caca Fuego*. After dinner Fernando and musical crewman would play music until late at night. After dinner the *Diligence* would drop back to receive its officers.

He loaned his biography of Charlemagne to Fernando; the biography of William the Conqueror to Lt. Ramirez; and his biography of Alexander the Great to Sgt. Blanco. He told each of them to swap when they were finished. He hoped that the three men could read all three in two months. He was already starting the "C" section of his encyclopedia.

19 days out of port, the morning greeted the *Caca Fuego* with a red sky. Eduardo had just completed breakfast

and was taking his morning stroll around the deck. Captain Luna walked up to the rail and said, "Looks like we may be in for a storm tonight."

"But Captain, it's a beautiful morning. What makes you think the weather will turn bad," Eduardo asked?

Captain Luna said, "There is an old sailor's rhyme:

Red Sky in the night, sailor's delight.

Red Sky in the morning, sailor take warning."

When Eduardo returned to the deck after lunch the sky was filled with angry gray clouds. The wind had freshened, and the sea was angry. A crewman spotted a water spout a couple of miles due west. The barometer was falling rapidly, and the wind was strengthening. The XO ordered that a jackline be installed on deck for crew to hold on to.

About 3:00 that afternoon, the XO shouted, "heave to", at which time the helmsman turned the wheel hard to port. The ship made an abrupt turn to port, which caused all the sails to luff, and the ship stopped in its own wake. Just as the ship turned a large wave crested against the hull, making a loud crashing sound.

"Take in sails except the foremast," the XO ordered. With that command six seamen began climbing up the shrouds into the riggings. They would lay over the yard and pull up the sails. Then they would climb up to the next yard and repeat the process. With a storm brewing the XO correctly wanted to get the sails down as soon as possible. Leaving sails up doing a storm can cause them to rip and to blow away, taking part of the rigging with them. There was also the danger of capsizing. He left the small sails on the foremast intact, so that the ship could navigate.

"Now furl those sails," the XO ordered. With this order the seamen took lines attached to the sails and tied the sails to the yard to prevent them from blowing loose.

"Make your course 2 9 0," barked the XO.

"Coming starboard to 2 9 0 sir," responded the helmsman. The ships speed decreased from 12 knots to just making headway.

"Batten down all hatches," ordered the XO.

He walked over to the hatch leading to the crew's quarters and shouted down the ladder, "Secure all loose gear below, and lock all portholes shut."

"Lt. Trevino, get a crew to get the anchor secured below decks." "Aye, Aye sir," he responded.

"Commander Valle, I don't want to see any loose cannon or cannonballs on my deck, so you and your gunnery crew should secure them now." "Aye, Aye sir," he replied.

As the waves got bigger the helmsman was thrown by the wheel, which was spinning out of control. The XO shouted down to the crew's quarters, "I need two helmsmen. Take your post." The XO took the wheel and got the *Caca Fuego* back on course.

"Are you OK son," the XO asked the helmsman, who was still on the deck.

"Sir, the wheel hit me on the side of my head. My head hurts and I feel like I could throw up," the helmsman answered.

"You are relieved, report to Dr. Diego," he ordered. The two helmsmen reported to the XO. "This weather will require both of you to steer," he said. "It is important that you hold onto the wheel on both sides, because as you just saw, it can be deadly.

At dinner Captain Luna asked that all officers who weren't required on deck to please stay below deck.

A violent electrical storm hit that evening. Green water crashed over the bow and sprayed the deck. The quarter deck was awash. The ship pitched, rolled and yawed. It was a tempestuous sea. Lightning struck the foremast and split it in two, part of which fell into the ocean with sails, yards and lines attached.

The storm abated just before sunup. Few of the crew had been able to sleep with the noise of the storm and movement of the ship in the tempest. In addition to losing the foremast and its sails, the ship lost part of its riggings and lines.

"Mr. Zerna, how far do you make it to the Sandwich Islands[20]," asked Captain Luna?

"By your leave, sir, I will determine our position and consult the chart."

A few minutes later Lt. Zerna, the navigator, was on the poop deck with his sextant fixing the position of the ship. Then he went back to the captain's cabin to consult the chart.

"Sir, the storm blew us off course, but fortunately it carried us northwest toward the Sandwich Islands. The

---

[20] Currently the Hawaiian Islands.

closest port of any size is Hilo which is 92 nautical miles to the northwest.

"What was our last sighting of the *Diligence*, Mr. Zerna," asked captain Luna.

"Four bells last night sir," Lieutenant Zerna responded.

"Very well Mr. Zerna, lay in a course toward our position at four bells last night. Let's see if we can find her.

After about three hours backtracking, the *Diligence* appeared on the horizon heading toward *Caca Fuego*. Using signal flags Captain Luna informed the *Diligence* that his mast was broken, and they were heading for Hilo for repairs.

"Set our course to Hilo, Mister Zerna. We will either purchase a mast or cut a tree and build one," said Captain Luna with a frustrated tone. "Hawaii is well known for its many varieties of Eucalyptus trees. These hardwood trees grow straight, and some are 300 feet high. They make perfect masts."

"What is your speed, XO," asked the captain.

"We're making 8 knots captain. I think that's all she's got, skipper," responded Commander Borrego.

"We're looking at 8 days. Ask cookie to make up a shopping list for our larder. Ask the bosun if he can rig another sail between the bowsprit and the main mast. Instruct Lieutenants Maldonado and Lopez to inspect this ship from bow to stern on all decks to determine if any repairs are necessary and if any item needs to be replaced. Be sure they check below for leaks.

Eduardo that night began writing a letter to Toni to bring her up to date on his adventure. In the next few days, he

363

also prepared a report of the voyage to King Carlos and sent short notes to both Bernardo and Chris.

He had no travel books on the Sandwich Islands, but there was a section in his encyclopedia about the islands that pointed out some of the sights.

"Captain, perhaps you and I should be thinking about making a ceremonial visit to the king of the big island. Each of these islands has its own king. Captain Cook was on these islands 10 months ago and might still be hanging around. We sure don't need a bunch of natives attacking us while we are trying to repair our ship. We need to come up with a gift for him."

The night before they arrived in the Sandwich Islands, he prepared a letter to Viceroy Jose Galvez. They had gelled on their brief time together and Eduardo wanted to maintain the relationship.

Before he blew out the candle, he studied a few key words in Tagalog.

CHAPTER 116

Las Palmas, Grand Canary Island

Onboard the *Sharnbrook*

October 31 – November 3, 1781

It had been an unremarkable crossing of the Atlantic. This was Chris' first time in the Canaries, which lay 65 miles due west of Spanish Morocco. The sub-tropical island chain contained dozens of islands, but most of the population lived on one of the 8 large islands. These islands produce wine, bananas, oranges, coffee, dates, tomatoes, sugar and tobacco. The islands were not named for the canary bird. They were named after the wild canines that roamed the islands in the early days. Spain conquered the Canaries in the 15th century. The islands became a treasure fleet stop.

The news of Washington's victory at Yorktown had not yet gotten to the Canary Islands.

Chris' passenger Captain Martin De Trentian had tutored him in the French language for an hour a day on the crossing, and a bit of conversation at meals allowed him to practice. Although he didn't always use the correct verb form, he could make himself understood. After dinner, the two men enjoyed playing dominos and talking about their travels around the world.

Chris had been composing a letter to Sara for several weeks. If something interesting happened on the ship he would include a mention of it in his letter. He finished his letter to her on the last night at sea. He wanted his letter to her to go into the mail the moment they arrived on Grand Canary.

He had also been writing to Eduardo and Bernardo to tell them of his exploits and his boredom. In his travels, he had been unable to find any books written in English. He found himself rereading his three volume encyclopedia.

After the mail and cargo for the islands were offloaded, it took only a few hours to load the outgoing mail and cargo. When that was finished, he gave most of the crew shore leave. A repair party had to repair a tear in a sail and replace some line. Another group was to paint a few worn spots on the ship. Those men would get shore leave the following day.

It was a lovely warm day, with a temperature of about 85 degrees, and a soft ocean breeze. Scattered clouds afforded temporary shade. Chris and Martin walked down the dock to a sidewalk bar. They sat and ordered two beers. It was relaxing just sitting there watching the world go by. They were setting targets for local vendors offering food, candy, hand carved wooden figures, leather, and shell objects. An elderly woman with a hunch back offered them a hand knitted tablecloth. Chris thought this would be a good gift for Sara, so he bought it. They walked back to the ship to allow Chris to store the tablecloth in his cabin.

They decided to visit the shopping area of Las Palmas and have dinner there, so Chris notified the cook that they were eating ashore. They took a coach at the end of the pier to the central shopping area. The town was cheerful with all its buildings being painted in bright colors. Many of the dark skinned residents were of Berber stock, the first group to settle these islands. As they strolled down the street the people looked happy. They heard music as they passed several bars and restaurants.

The seafood restaurant they chose for dinner had about half its tables outside in the shade of some enormous trees. As they stepped into the garden dining area they heard "Hello. What's your name?" When they looked to their right, they saw a beautiful red, green and blue talking Parrot. "I'm not Polly. I have a penis," the bird continued.

"Their table offered them a great view of the huge volcano that overlooks the island. The local white wine was a bit sweet, but enjoyable. The wine went perfectly with the fried giant prawns and slaw they had for dinner.

As they were walking off their dinner, Chris heard some music, so the remainder of the evening was spent in a bar listening to music and bending their elbows.

. . .

The next day most of the crew was on shore leave again, so Chris and Martin decided to go to the beach. They packed up towels and blankets. The cook packed a picnic lunch for them and casks of beer and water. Both of them marveled at the beautiful beach. Dense jungle including coconut palms hugged the beach. The sand was the color of eggshells. As they swam out from the beach, they noticed that the water was crystal clear. They could clearly see the conch shells at the bottom some 35 feet down.

After their swim, they dried off and sat on their blankets. From their spot they could see nearby Fuerteventura Island and in the hazy distance to the northeast they could see the island of Lanzarote.

. . .

The next day they departed for Bilboa, Spain to deliver mail and cargo, and pick up needed war supplies for the Americans.

CHAPTER 117

Harbor Dock

Hilo, Hawaii

November 19, 1781

As the *Caca Fuego* limped into the port of Hilo,
Sandwich Islands, dozens of natives in outrigger canoes
rowed out to meet her.

"Signal the *Diligence*. Order her to drop anchor near the
mouth of the harbor to guard against an English ship
entering the harbor. Ask her captain to join me on the
Caca Fuego."

The small harbor was protected by Coconut Island, just a
few miles offshore.

"Close all gun ports. We don't want these natives to think
we are here to bombard them," ordered captain Luna.

The native men and women wore colorful floral leighs as
the only thing above their waists. They shouted and
waived and were glad to see visitors.

"Furl your sails, shouted the XO.

"Secure the bow line."

"Secured the stern line."

"Secure line amidships."

"Double up on all lines."

"Lower the gangway."

A native in a short sleeved floral shirt, and sandals was standing on the pier when the gangway was secured on the pier.

He walked up the gangway and was met by Sub. Lt. de la Garza, the Officer of the Day.

"How may I help you sir," asked the Officer of the day?

"I am a representative of King Kalani'opu'u. I have a message for your captain or the senior officer aboard.

"Well sir, that's two different people, so I will take you to both of them." He took the emissary to the captain's quarters, where Eduardo and the captain were discussing the first move toward getting a new mast.

"King Kalani'ōpu'u, the king of the big island is descended through a long line of kings and queens of this island. He invites the two of you to an audience with him at the palace tonight at sunset, to welcome you and your crew to our island.

Within the hour Captain Francisco joined Eduardo on the *Caca Fuego*.

"Esteban, we are meeting with the king of this island tonight, and you are invited. We could be in this port for several weeks. I need the *Diligence* to remain at anchor guarding the entrance to the harbor, the whole time we are here. You may give your men leave, but I want two cannon crews on alert 24 hours per day, 7 days a week.

. . .

The path to the Royal Palace was lined on both sides with large conch shells. The palace was very unusual looking. The walls were constructed of bamboo with a black

370

volcanic rock wainscoting about three feet high, along which ran a flower box filled with beautiful flowering plants. The supporting columns were from eucalyptus trees. The roof was made of straw. The entire palace was no more than 2,000 square feet.

"Are you English," the king asked them before they were invited to sit?

"No, your majesty," replied Eduardo, "we are Spanish. At the present time we are at war with the English.

We were bound for the Philippines by way of Guam when our foremast was destroyed in a storm at sea. We came to your island in hopes that we could find a mast or cut a tree and build a mast. I am a personal representative of His Royal Majesty, Carlos, III, King of Spain. I have the pleasure to present Captain Fidencio Luna, master if the large ship at your pier, and Captain Esteban Francisco, master of the ship at anchor in your harbor."

The king then related a story about his relationship with Captain Cook:

Kalani'ōpu'u was the king of the island during the times Captain James Cook came to Hawaii.

He went aboard his ship in November 1778. After Cook anchored at Kealakekua Bay in January

1779, Kalani'ōpu'u paid a ceremonial visit in January, 1779 and exchanged gifts. The king gave Cook a feathered cloak, while Cook presented the king with a ceremonial helmet. Cook's ships returned in February to repair storm damage. This time relations were not as good, as a battle ensued when Captain Cook tried to take

371

the king hostage after the theft of an English longboat.
Captain Cook was killed in that battle.

"As a show of hospitality, I will order a luau in your
honor for both your entire crews tomorrow when the sun
sets behind the big mountain. Tell your men to come
hungry because there will be lots of food to eat and rum to
drink."

"Strange bird said Captain Luna. "He knows our ship has
a serious problem but fails to even mention it. Should we
start looking for a mast tomorrow? Shall we go ahead
and cut down a tree tomorrow? What do you think," he
asked Eduardo?

"I think the king less than a year ago had to kill a man he
had been dealing with for several months and he is not yet
sure he wants to help us. Perhaps after we socialize
tomorrow, he will mellow. Tomorrow, I will present him
with my ceremonial sword as a gift from King Carlos.

Perhaps you could take him a bottle of brandy, Fidencio.
We definitely need to get on his good side."

. . .

When the sun sat behind the big mountain the following
day, there was still two more hours of daylight. The men
standing watch on both ships had been broken up so that
all watch standers got to eat and drink at the luau.

It was a sight to see to watch 200 plus crew members
walking from the pier the short distance to the open area
in the center of the native village. There was a low fire,
under which they were cooking the pigs with corn,
potatoes, pineapple, and bananas. A small band
composed of guitarists, ukuleles and drums greeted the
crew with Polynesian music. Bare breasted women with

trays of drinks in coconut shells stood still as their trays rapidly emptied. The crewmen not yet served worked their way over to the bar where the drinks were being prepared and helped themselves.

The crew encircled the fire and sat on straw mats provided by their hosts. A cool breeze was refreshing from the heat of the day. The sweet smell of frangipani wafted through the village. While they ate the musicians accompanied a group of female dancers.

The king proposed a toast to the officers and crews, to which everybody drank. Then Captain Luna proposed a toast to the king. After everybody drank, Captain Luna presented a bottle of fine French Brandy to the king.

"King Kalani'ōpu'u," said Eduardo. "I am a representative of HRM Carlos de Borbon, III. He is the King of Spain, which is much larger than England. On behalf of King Carlos, I want to present this Spanish ceremonial sword to you as a symbol of the friendship between our two countries. I also want to thank you for your hospitality to my officers and men.

Afterwards, two warriors performed an ancient ritual dance with swords. A quartet sang soft island ballads. A children's choir which sang several native songs was followed by some acrobats. For hours the crew was entertained. All the while the rum drinks kept coming. As the luau was ending the king placed his hand on Eduardo's arm. "Tomorrow, we have races in your honor. I will come for you and your two captains' mid-morning."

About 10:00 the following morning the king's barge pulled up next to the *Caca Fuego* ladder. It appeared to be two huge 40 man outrigger canoes upon which a large

373

red and gold platform had been added. The barge was almost 100 feet long with outriggers on both sides. A large red and gold throne sat in the shade of the ornate red and gold canopy, with comfortable chairs on either side. Eyes had been painted on both sides of the bow to ward off evil spirits.

As Eduardo, Captain Luna, and Captain Francisco climbed down the ladder, the king got up to greet them. He shook their hands and motioned for them to have a seat next to the throne. As they sat, the royal barge was rowed away from the ship toward the far side of the bay. Musicians behind the throne began to entertain, while beautiful bare breasted young women served them drinks.

On the other side of the bay, outrigger canoes were already lined up for the race. The first race was for young boys 18 and under racing alone. The race started when an official on the king's barge blew into a giant seashell. In the lull before the next race, they were served oysters on the half shell. The two man canoe race was followed by the four man race. Between each race they were offered fried shrimp, crab claws and other delicacies.

Finally came the most important race of the day. The king's warriors were divided into two groups of 20, each manning a 50 foot long war canoe. Each group rowed to the beat of the drummer coaxing them forward. The natives watching from shore shouted and cheered their canoe to victory.

As the king's barge was being rowed back to the Caca Fuego, the king said to Eduardo, "I like you Spanish." I will help you. This morning villagers cut down a tall eucalyptus tree. My people will help your crew trim it and get it installed."

Creating a mast from a tree is an arduous process. First after felling a tree, one had to trim away all branches. Then the bark had to be removed. Then the tree had to be shaped so that it became smaller at the top. Once the mast had been shaped properly it had to be transported to the pier. This they accomplished by using two horse drawn wagons.

The crew had to build a crane that would lift off the damaged mast and haul up the new mast and drop it into place. That meant felling two additional trees: one tall tree to use as the upright and a smaller tree to serve as the arm of the crane. The crane took a week to construct.

While all that was going on, other crew onboard had to cut away the mast from the keel and stabilize it until it was removed. The most difficult part of the equation was getting the base of the mast aligned with deck opening.

During the two weeks it took to replace the mast, Eduardo and his staff did some sightseeing. They spent one afternoon swimming at the black sand beach. The black sand was the result of black volcanic rocks being slammed against one another for eons.

A native with a wagon took them up to the top of the snowcapped volcano so they could peer into the caldera. From the top of the volcano, they could see the isle of Maui. On the way back to the ship they rode along the "Chain of Craters Road," and stopped to investigate a volcano cave. These caves or lava tubes were created by the flow of liquid magma. They continued along the coast road which was about 2,000 feet high. From that altitude they had an excellent view of the rocky coast below. It was a very windy day with huge offshore waves crashing onto the craggy coast. They continued down Banyan Tree Drive on the way back to the ship.

One evening canoes took them around the island to see the bright red magma pouring down the side of the mountain, brightly illuminating the entire area. A tall column of steam rose from the sea where the magma entered the water. One day they took a picnic lunch to beautiful and breathtaking Rainbow Falls.

The next day the king sent a messenger to Eduardo asking that he and his staff come to the palace. Upon their arrival they were served a drink.

"General, I discovered that while your ship was being repaired that you and your group have been looking around my island. Since you are interested in our history, I wanted to make sure that you didn't miss an important aspect of our history.

For many centuries Hawaiians lived under harsh laws that were strictly enforced. Many offences were punishable by death. Violating a sacred "kapu"[21] meant automatic death. Fellow villagers would chase an offender and kill him.

Hawaiian law provided that if a taboo breaker could reach a Puuhonua or place of refuge they could be absolved of their infraction by a priest in a purification ceremony. Once he obtained absolution from the priest, his fellow villagers accepted that he had been purified and he was forgiven by all.

The king told them that Puuhonua on his island was the most famous and best-preserved of Hawaii's ancient places of refuge. It was built just behind the Royal Palace. There they viewed a massive L-shaped wall, built from

---

[21] taboo

thousands of lava rocks, which separated the king's palace from the refuge. Inside this 1,000-foot-long wall were fine examples of temples and dozens of hand carved wooden statutes of gods. Many of the large statues were displayed with a gigantic erect penis, while other statues contained large breasts. The refuge covered almost 200 acres.

Finally, the day came when the new mast was ready for sails and rigging. The captain had a case of whisky delivered to the palace. Most ships at that time carried spare sails and riggings. It took another four days to make the *Caca Fuego* ready for sea.

During this time the king had loads of fruits, nuts and vegetables and several pigs delivered to the ship. The crew filled the freshwater casks.

CHAPTER 118

Bilbao, Spain

Aboard the *Sharnbrook*

November 24 – Nov. 29, 1781

As the *Sharnbrook* was tying up to the pier in Bilbao Diego Gardoqui was on the dock waiting to greet Christopher. They had met briefly in Philadelphia in 1777 when Gardoqui arranged passage for Eduardo and his staff to New Orleans on the *Sharnbrook*.

"Admiral Butler, I am so happy to see you. This is a wonderful thing you are doing – coming all the way across the Atlantic to pick up supplies."

"Allow me to present Captain Martin De Trentian. Captain De Trentian is a passenger en route to Le Havre to take command of a squadron of ships. And please call me Chris. With General Washington forcing Cornwall to surrender last month, this may be my first and last visit to your fair city."

"But senior admiral, there will always be a demand for our delicious Jerez and Port wines, olives, olive oil, cured ham, and cheese. Some of the best guitars in the world are made in Spain. We produce fine silks and leather goods. People from all over the world seek the best swords in the world that are made in Toledo, Spain. We here at Gardoqui would be glad to represent you in Bilbao."

"While you are in Bilbao you will both be my house guests. Please pack up what you need, and I will send a carriage for you at 6:00 p.m.

Promptly at 6:00 p.m. the two men were picked up by a carriage with the colorful arms of the

Gardoqui emblazoned on the door. They drove up into the hills overlooking the city to the Mungi Community. They approached a large estate gate with a guard. The property was bordered by an eight foot stone wall. Chris estimated the size of the property at 50 acres. The Gardoqui home was originally built as a castle. From its front porch one could see the city below, the river connecting the port with the sea, and the Bay of Biscay.

"*Beinvenidos, amigos. Mi casa es su casa,*" said Gardoqui as he opened the massive front door. Servants retrieved their luggage and followed them into the home.

"Francisco will show you to your quarters. Please join us downstairs at 7:00 for cocktails."

The stone stairway was 10 feet wide and curved upward. Along the wall were ancient tapestries and gold leaf framed portraits of many ancestors. A set of Toledo crossed swords hung on the wall over the landing.

Christopher's room was a spacious apartment including a sitting room, a dressing room, his bedroom and a private room for bathing and the chamber pot. One window overlooked the town, river and beach below, while the other overlooked a beautiful garden with a large fountain in the center. The servant who carried Chris's luggage upstairs was now unpacking. The cold stone floor was covered with beautiful oriental rugs. Like the staircase, the walls were covered with ancient tapestries and ancestral paintings.

379

At 7:00 p.m. the two men entered the study where drinks were being served. The most notable thing in the study was the massive stone fireplace with a roaring fire. Above the fireplace were the arms of the Gardoqui family. The walls were covered with bookcases filled with many leather backed antique books.

"Diego," said Chris, "with this beautiful old castle and your arms there must be a story about your family."

At that moment Diego's wife entered the room. She was a tall, slender, attractive brunette with hazel colored eyes. She was dressed in a long navy blue dress that included a choker at the neck. Around her neck she wore a simple gold necklace which supported an antique Spanish gold coin.

"*Mi Amor*, this is our friend Rear Admiral Christopher Butler from the United States and his passenger Captain Martin De Trentian bound for Le Havre. Gentlemen, this is my lovely wife, Esmeralda."

Diego motioned for them all to sit on the two couches that faced each other in front of the fireplace. Their drinks and some snack trays were placed on the large square coffee table that separated them. The heat from the fire felt good as the old castle was struggling to keep out the cold air, and not doing a very good job of it.

"Esmeralda, just before you entered the room Chris asked me about our old castle and our arms. With your permission I will bore him with our family history."

"First of all, this part of Spain is Basque country. Our ancestors spoke a language somewhere between Spanish and French. This has been a volatile region at war over the centuries. Between 1490-1492 my ancestors were advisors to King Ferdinand and Queen Isabella, who helped rid Spain of the Moors. The Basque region of Spain was the only part of Spain that was never occupied by the Moors. When Philip, I, became King of Spain in 1506 my ancestors were still close to the crown. King Philip made my ancestor the Count of Gardoqui, granted the arms above the fireplace, and granted my ancestor this castle and 10,000 hectares of land. At the same time, he made my ancestor "Purveyor to the King," and we have been in the wholesale business ever since."

The dining room was magnificent. The dining room table that could seat 18 was centered between two huge fireplaces. Over the two ends of the table were two large crystal chandeliers, which magnified the light of the 50 candles of each. Large mirrors along the walls reflected the candles and the light from the fireplaces. The four people had a delicious meal and convivial conversation during dinner.

"Gentlemen," said Esmerelda "if you will excuse me, I will go upstairs and get our two sons ready for bed."

"Let's have our coffee and cigars in the sitting room," suggested Diego.

The sitting room had a more feminine touch. The furniture was covered in light colored fabrics. Instead of portraits of long gone ancestors, this room boasted colorful paintings of flower colored fields. The carpets on the stone floor were bright pastel colors.

As they found comfortable spots near the fireplace Diego passed around Cuban cigars while a servant poured coffee. "Jose, lets also offer our guests some of our famous port wine."

Just as the servant was leaving the room, Esmeralda came in with their two sons dressed in matching flannel pajamas. Gentlemen, these are our sons, Diego, Jr., age 11 and Miguel, age 8. Joseph and Miguel, these are two very important people. Rear Admiral Christopher Butler from America and Captain Martin De Trentian of France. The two young boys each stepped forward and shook hands with each guest. "It is a pleasure to meet you, sir," each said as they greeted their guests.

"Esmeralda, you and Diego must be very proud. You have two fine looking young men with good manners," said Chris.

As Esmeralda and the boys were leaving Jose returned with a decanter of port wine and three glasses. Jose sat the tray on the table, then poured each man a drink and sat it in front of each man.

"Will there be anything further, my lord," asked Jose.

"No, thank you Jose. You may be excused."

Diego felt that he had been ignoring Captain De Trentian, so he asked him a series of questions about his schooling, his military career, his family and his new job.

"Chris, the war is about over. This will probably be the last shipment of pure military supplies we will be sending to the United States. I want you to consider entering into an agreement with

Gardoqui and sons to make regular pick-up of cargo here in Bilbao, and deliver it to the U.S., Mexico and the Caribbean. Spain has some wonderful products that are just not available elsewhere. We would be willing to enter into an exclusive agreement with you, which for the first year would guarantee a minimum profit to you. We would require that you dedicate three of your ships to our transatlantic business."

"Diego, that sounds like a good deal, with one exception. I will be deadheading for six weeks across the Atlantic in an empty ship. I must have a market for my goods from the Americas so I can arrive loaded with a paying customer ready to take delivery.

"Chris, if you will limit your arriving cargo to items on our approved list, we will buy your goods and guarantee you a profit."

"When can you give me that list," asked Chris?

"You will have it tomorrow," replied Diego.

. . .

The next morning breakfast was served in the family dining room with both boys present. As they were finishing up Diego asked, "Have either of you ever been hunting for wild boar?

Both men responded in the negative.

"You won't be able to say that tomorrow. Today, I am taking you to hunt boar. Follow me," instructed Diego. He led them down a hallway to the armory. The armory was about 20 feet by 20 feet with a large table in the center of the room where weapons were cleaned and repaired. The walls were decorated with weapons dating back 300 years or more. Gun racks held muskets and rifles. Pistols were mounted on the wall. There were large containers of gun powder. One wall was nothing but knives and swords of all kinds. They selected their rifles and ammunition and followed Diego to the front door.

In the luggage area of the carriage that was to deliver them to the hunting area, was a picnic basket of food and casks of beer and water. The carriage departed in the

383

direction away from town. The road wound around the hill into a lush valley. A small creek flowed near the road. There was a large muddy area next to the creek.

"This is the spot," said Diego. "These animals normally are active only at night. They all carry a virus in their hide that makes them itch. They have discovered that if they wallow in the mud, the itch goes away. That mud is their favorite place to be. They have been seen here during the day several times recently."

The carriage was separated from the muddy area by a stand of trees. The three men whispered to one another for about an hour, when they saw a boar approaching the creek from the other side.

Before Chris could get his rifle up to aim, Captain De Trentian had already pulled the trigger and the boar dropped dead in its tracks. Diego's servant field gutted the boar and tied it to the back of the carriage.

CHAPTER 119

Le Havre, France

Aboard the *Sharnbrook*

November 29 – December 2, 1781

As the *Sharnbrook* eased into the English Channel he felt awkward. Just a month ago we had been fighting the English, but they had not yet signed a treaty. He worried that some English hot shot might fire his cannon at the *Sharnbrook.*

When Captain Martin De Trentian disembarked in Le Havre, his wife was on the pier to meet him. Marie De Trentian was about 5' 3" and a strawberry blonde. Although she was beginning to show her age, she still had dimples in her cheeks and a sparkle in her blue eyes.

"I want to see your quarters," she said to Martin.

"Chris, it is OK for me to show my quarters to my wife," De Trentian asked?

"Sure, but first you have to introduce me to your bride," responded Chris. After the introductions, the couple went through the hatch on the quarterdeck to Captain Martin's quarters.

"Monsieur Butler, Martin and I would like for you to be our guest for dinner tonight. I have so many questions about your journey. May we call for you at 7:00 p.m.," she asked?

"I would be delighted to join you for some good restaurant food. See you at 7:00."

385

After his passenger had departed Chris involved himself in unloading the cargo and the mail.

"First, I want you to supervise the unloading procedure. I am going to talk with an agent.

"Chris tried to find an English speaking agent because his French was so limited. As he walked down the road to the pier, he saw a huge sign which read:

> *Maurice Talmond*
>
> *Agent – Entrepot*
>
> *Parlez Francais, Anglais et Espanol.*

Chris entered the office and asked to speak to Monsieur Talmond. Chris explained that he owned 11 ships and that he had just contracted with a Spanish firm to dedicate three of his ships for transportation to the Americas from Boston to Havana and Vera Cruz. He asked if they had any goods ready for shipment. To his delight he discovered the agent had a warehouse full of champagne, wine, brandy, cognac, beer, hard liquor, cheese, perfume, beauty products, and women's lingerie.

As Chris walked back toward his ship, he was so happy he wanted to dance and sing. Just a few days ago he had agreed to dedicate three of his ships to trade between Spain and the Americas. Now, through this new agent he would have his ships filled to the brim with each return shipment. He was thinking to himself that he might be able to add a few more ships if business continued to improve.

The next day he purchased an expensive bottle of French perfume and a negligée as Christmas presents for Sara. He also purchased French newspapers for Bernardo and Eduardo.

CHAPTER 120

Departing Hilo, Hawaii

Aboard the *Caca Fuego*

December 8, 1781

As the *Caca Fuego* slipped away from the Hilo pier the king and villagers turned out to see them off. The village band played while the villagers serenaded the crew. While all members of the crew had worked hard replacing the mast, they all had enjoyed liberty with plenty of food and drink and beautiful beaches to cool their tired bodies. They were all refreshed. Many had experienced sexual encounters with native women, whose husbands had no problems with their spouse making love to another man. The native culture was one of free love.

The *Diligence* waited until the larger ship had passed it by before it followed. As the *Caca Fuego* exited the harbor, she fired a 3 gun salute to honor the king. *Diligence* followed with its own salute.

"Mr. Zerna, make your course 2 8 8," ordered Captain Luna.

"Aye, Aye sir. Coming right to course 2 8 8," responded the navigator.

"Well General, at least we no longer have to worry about Captain Cook," said Captain Luna.

"Let's just hope we don't encounter another storm," replied Eduardo.

The officers and crew fell back into their daily routine.

CHAPTER 121

San Miguel, Azores Islands

Aboard the *Sharnbrook*

December 14, 1781

The *Sharnbrook* stopped in the Azores for food, water and crew rest. It was a clear sunny day, but the temperature was about 50 degrees and cool.

Chris sat in a warm bar listening to a pianist sing a love song. He thought of Sara and how he would miss being with her for Christmas. Sometimes the life of a mariner sucked. Being away from your family at Christmas was one of those times.

He had deliveries to make in Philadelphia before getting home to Edenton, so he guessed he wouldn't see Sara until after New Year's.

As mariners do, he worried about the tumultuous Atlantic during the winter. Before leaving port, he would have all hands check the riggings and make sure that everything was lashed to the deck securely. He would personally inspect the cargo holds to ensure that the cargo didn't get loose in a storm.

CHAPTER 122

Theft Aboard the *Caca Fuego*

At Sea

December 17, 1781

"Captain, seaman Juan Ramos stole a silver coin from seaman Joaquin Urrutia," reported the bosun.

"Assembled the witnesses and report to my cabin at 1300 hours with the accused for Captain's Mast," ordered Captain Luna.

At the hearing Captain Luna Swore in all the witnesses. One seaman testified that he had seen seaman Ramos at seaman Urrutia's bunk. Seaman Urrutia testified that the coin was his, and that when he confronted seaman Ramos, he had the coin in his pocket. The accused admitted his guilt and asked for forgiveness. The captain ordered that the accused be required to run the gauntlet at 1700 hours.

Eduardo sat through the trial. He had never before witnessed punishment being administered. He spent an hour or so reviewing the navy regulations of the Spanish Navy. He learned that the punishments were designed to fit the crime.

This was a long voyage. Generally, the longer the voyage the more trouble for the crew to get into and the more punishments must be administered. The law of the sea had developed over the centuries. Non corporal punishments included half rations and time in the brig. In order of severity, the corporal punishments available were:

Punishments at sea:

1. Starting:

The boatswain or bosun's mate always carried a knotted rope, small whip, or cane called a

"rattan," to hit an offending seaman. Sometimes, three canes were tied together and called the

"three sisters." For some unremembered reason, these frequent beatings were referred to as a "Starting.

2. Gagging:

 This punishment was used rarely when a sailor was disrespectful to an officer or committed other minor offenses. His hands and legs were bound. An object would be put in his mouth and tied behind his head. Some sailors died from suffocation.

3. Flogging:

Almost any crime could end with this torture. The day before the lashes were to be administered, the sailor to be punished was placed in irons on the deck and was required to make the cat- of- nine-tails with waxed and knotted ends that would cut into his flesh.

The crew was required to assemble on the quarter deck to witness the punishment. He was tied to the mast bareback. The Bosun's mate rendered the lashes. By 1750, flogging was restricted to 12 lashes by most maritime countries. Sometimes, a captain could get round the 12-lash rule by charging a man with multiple offenses, incurring 12 lashes each. Before this, a sentence could have been issued with hundreds of strikes.

The pain didn't end there. Current medical treatment for torn skin was to have salt and/or vinegar rubbed into the wounds, which caused more pain.

Flogging Around the Fleet:

This was when the ship was in the harbor with other ships. After the offending crewman had been lashed to the mast of a small ship and flogged on his ship, when there was a collection of ships nearby in a harbor.

The small boat was then taken to the next ship where that vessel's mate administered more lashes. This procedure continued through all the ships in the harbor, thus the term "flogging around the fleet. Sometimes, the boat was accompanied by a drummer boy in another small vessel to add formality to the punishment.

4. Cobbed and Firked:

Cooks who lost food, allowed food to spoil, and messed up a meal had their own unique punishment. Instead of a cat-of-nine-tails, the cook was flogged on the buttocks with a stocking filled with sand or a stave off a wooden cask. This punishment was more of an embarrassment than a punishment.

5. Child Punishment:

Many ships employed boys as young as 10 or 11. For boys aged 19 and under caning of their bare butts was the punishment rendered for minor offenses.

For more serious offences the youngster had to "kiss the gunner's daughter." He would be tied to a cannon in front

391

of the rest of the crew, with his pants around his ankles to receive lashes applied to his rear end.

6. Running the Gauntlet:

In most navies, stealing from a shipmate was a cardinal sin. All crew members hated a thief. Thieves were required to run the gauntlet. That way, every crew member was allowed to hit the thief.

The thief would be stripped to the waist, then be forced at sword point to walk between two rows of men who wielded lengths of knotted rope. Each crewman was allowed to bash the criminal as hard as possible while he slowly passed by. There was an officer behind him with a sword to prod him forward through the gauntlet and another in front with a sword at his chest to prevent him from running.

7. Falling Asleep on Watch:

Being on watch was an important job, as it was the watch stander who would first sight an enemy ship on the horizon. The watch stander guarded all the lives onboard. Sometimes, especially on overnight watches, the crewman on watch would doze off. It happened often.

Because falling asleep on watch was so prevalent, punishments were on a graduated scale, so the more often a crewman fell asleep on watch the more severe his punishment:

a) For a first offense, a bucket of cold seawater would be poured over the crewman.

b)   The second time, his hands would be tied up and cold water tipped into his shirt.

c)   For the third violation, a sailor would be tied to a ship's mast and be made to hold up heavy objects with his arms stretched out wide.

d)   The fourth punishment was deadly. The crewman was put in a basket which was hung from the bowsprit and left to starve to death. An armed guard was instructed to shoot him if he tried to escape.

8.   Hanging From the Yardarm:

With the crew assembled on deck to watch punishment, after the offending crewman had his hands and feet tied, a noose was placed around his neck. Upon a signal designated crewmen holding the rope began hoisting the offender's body. He would be "run up the yardarm" and left there to strangle to death.

9.   Keel Hauling:

Keel Hauling was the most barbaric punishment on the high seas until it was banned internationally about 1720. After stripping the prisoner naked two ropes were tied around him, one of which ran under the keel of the ship. He would be thrown overboard then pulled under the keel of the ship and brought to the surface on the other side of the ship. His body would be drug across the bottom of the ship, which was covered in very sharp barnacles. Many drowned in the process. Others' bodies were cut to pieces, causing the offender to die from loss of blood. Those who survived had scarred bodies for life.

The balance of the crossing to Guam was relatively unremarkable. The waters around the

Sandwich Islands were known to be the mating ground of whales, and these behemoths were spotted frolicking in the water daily blowing water up through their blow hole. Also, seeing dolphins playing in the ships wake was a common occurrence.

The captain noted the crossing of the International Date Line on December 18, 1781. The crew had begun decorating the ship for the Christmas holidays. Eduardo was sad. His second anniversary was on December 23rd, and he would again not be with her on either their anniversary or Christmas.

On Christmas all hands of both ships had a day off except for those essential to operations, who each had to work a two hour shift. All hands assembled on deck that morning after breakfast.

As they had no chaplain onboard, Eduardo led them in saying the Rosary and the Lord's Prayer. Each crew member was given a triple ration of beer, and the musicians held forth on the quarter deck for all to hear, enticing the crew to join in song.

After lunch the *Diligence* pulled up to within 50 yards of the *Caca Fuego*. The crews of both ships were allowed to swim in the area between the two ships. Riflemen lined the rails to shoot at any sharks that might want to join the swimming party. Their pork dinner was courtesy of the Sandwich Island[22] king. The officers read, played dominos, wrote letters or took a nap.

---

[22] Current day Hawaiian Islands

New Year's day was celebrated in a similar fashion.
They slaughtered a steer, which not only fed the crews of
both ships, but also gave the crews of both ships beef for
the balance of the trip to Guam.

. . .

On January 20, the officers and crew of both ships toasted
the king on his birthday.

CHAPTER 123

Philadelphia, Pennsylvania

Aboard the *Sharnbrook*

January 4 - 6, 1782

As soon as the *Sharnbrook* docked in Philadelphia, Eduardo dropped into the mail letters to Sara, Bernardo and Eduardo. He told them all of his new agreements with the Gardoqui firm in Bilbao and his new French agent.

He would have loved to visit his friend Benjamin Franklin, but at the time Dr. Franklin was in Paris as the U.S. Ambassador to France.

He visited with his brother Joseph, who managed the ship line to learn its current finances and was very pleased as a result.

CHAPTER 124

Chris arrives home.

Edenton, North Carolina

January 9, 1782

Sara had left the Christmas decorations up both outside and inside. She had gotten Chris's letter posted in Philadelphia only two days before. She was standing on the pier watching the *Sharnbrook* gracefully enter the harbor.

Chris was the first one down the gangway and rushed to hug and kiss Sara. After they exchanged greetings, Chris took her back to his cabin and gave her the perfume and negligee Christmas presents.

When Chris left, they had just moved into a newer and larger home. He was pleasantly surprised at the way Sara had decorated their home. He was also very pleased to see the decorated Christmas tree in the living room and green holly with its red berries decorating the home. The smell of juniper permeated their home. For a long time, they sat in front of their fireplace, drinking egg nog, and talking.

That night for dinner, Chris had the best meal he had enjoyed in one and one-half years: Turkey, dressing, giblet gravy, stuffed deviled eggs, candied yams, green beans, cranberry sauce, with mashed potatoes and gravy. For dessert, Sara had baked a pecan pie.

Chris and Sara went to bed very early as they had many things to discuss. With his hands Chris explored every part of Sara's body. She in turn rubbed her firm breasts on his face, chest, stomach and genitalia. With very little rubbing of her clitoris, Sara became excited. When she reached over to touch his penis, it was already erect. She slipped out of her negligee, and they made love.

CHAPTER 125

Agana, Guam

Aboard the *Caca Fuego*

January 22, 1782

The port of Agana was on the west side of the island. The facilities on this Spanish owned island were designed to replenish and repair Spanish ships. The presidio and the navy base were adjacent and contiguous. Both ships docked at the navy base. All but rotating gun crews were given liberty. It was a small island with only a handful of villages. Most of those villages had a bar, and that is where you could find crew members at any time of the day.

The *Caca Fuego* began unloading mail and cargo destined for Guam, as Eduardo and Fernando walked down the gangway. They were off to pay their respects to the commanders of the presidio and the navy base. Although Agana played no active part in the transfer of goods from Manila, it served an important backup role, the respective commanding officers might have some valuable suggestions. At any rate they deserved the courtesy of a visit from the king's personal representative.

During its three days in port, the ship restocked its larders, purchasing sugar, pineapple, coconut, macadamia nuts, coffee, seafood, beer, wine and liquor. Eduardo restocked his candy supply at the navy base shop.

While in port Eduardo wrote several letters. He updated Toni on the storm they had encountered and how they spent time in the Sandwich Islands. Similar short letters were written to Bernardo and Chris. His report to King Carlos was in greater detail to explain his delay in arriving in the Philippines.

All the crew's mail was placed in a diplomatic mail pouch at the Navy base headquarters.

CHAPTER 126

Sailing between Agana, Guam and

Subic Bay, Philippines

Aboard the *Caca Fuego*

January 26, 1782

On the second day out of Guam, a seaman on *Diligence* fell from the riggings and broke his arm. He was rowed over to the *Caca Fuego* for treatment by the doctor. He was confined to the *Caca Fuego* for a week so the doctor could follow his progress.

Eduardo frequently saw crewmen fishing but rarely saw them catch anything. Today there was a lot of commotion on deck after lunch. One of the seamen had caught a sailfish. It was 9 feet, 10 inches long and weighed about 150 pounds. That night the entire crew dined on sailfish.

While in Agana, the XO had repeatedly complained of a boil on his butt. When he complained about the boil on the tenth day, the captain ordered the doctor to lance it. The XO was only partially literate in Spanish, but he was also partially literate in English and French. However, the XO was an expert in reading nautical charts and in navigating by the stars. The crew respected and liked him. Captain Luna gave him two days of rest following the lancing procedure.

The crew all knew that this lengthy voyage would be over in a few days. This knowledge seemed to lift their spirits. More music was played in the crew's quarters. There seemed to be a dominos game going on at any time of the day. Eduardo continued his Tagalog tutoring with 2nd Mate, Domingo Torres, while nibbling at his last piece of candy.

CHAPTER 127

Subic Bay, Philippines
February 14, 1782

 By flag signal, Eduardo had ordered the officers of the *Diligence* to come aboard the *Caca Fuego* as soon as it docked.

"To Captain Luna and the officers of the *Caca Fuego*, I want to thank you on behalf of me and my staff for all the courtesies extended. We met as strangers and now depart as friends. To Captain Francisco and the officers of the *Diligence*, although we did not get to know each other as well, it was enjoyable getting to spend time with you onboard and in port. My staff and I will always cherish the times we spent together. This is where we part. My staff and I will disembark later this morning. We will remain in the Philippines for a few months. Your two ships will continue sailing in tandem. I wish you fair winds and following seas. You are dismissed."

One by one, each officer said words of farewell and shook hands with Eduardo, Fernando and Javier. Although he didn't show it, Eduardo choked up emotionally.

The main navy base in the Philippines is in Subic Bay. The Presidio, the largest army base is located in Manila, on Manila Bay. As the crow flies Subic Bay is about 50 miles north of Manila Bay. The three day ride to Manila must cover about 70 miles of winding mountainous roads.

Sgt. Blanco had been one of the first down the gangway and had returned with a coach and a two horse team to take Eduardo and his staff with their luggage to the Subic

403

Bay BOQ. Sgt. Blanco remained with the coach as the officers checked in at the BOQ and then took Eduardo's luggage and money chest to his VIP suite. He then assisted Colonel Garcia with his luggage to his BOQ room. When he returned to the coach, Lt. Ramirez had already taken his luggage with him. Sgt. Blanco then drove to the NCO barracks. He checked in and took his luggage to his room. Then he returned the coach.

Eduardo's VIP suite was a bit larger than his nautical quarters. His furniture was all made from bamboo. One of his third floor windows overlooked the harbor. Several warships were docked at the pier which extended from the dock. A huge warehouse where the oriental treasurers were stored between shipments faced the dock. His other window looked out at the mountains that covered the island.

He sent a messenger to the office of Rear Admiral Antonio Carlos Jobim, requesting a meeting the following morning at 10:00 a.m. Later that day a note was slipped under his door that the Admiral would be delighted to meet with him.

The following morning Eduardo and his staff entered the admiral's waiting room. The sign on the door read:

Commanding Officer

Spanish Far Eastern Fleet

Admiral Jobim was a dark skinned, part Arab from Granada, Spain. His mother was born and reared in Tangier, Morocco as a Muslim. After she married his father, she converted to Catholicism. His Arab blood had haunted him since school days. This heritage had caused him to be cold and seemingly without emotion. He was only about 40 years old. For a man to become a two star admiral that young meant that he must be a highly competent officer.

Admiral Jobin greeted the three officers with a smile and offered them coffee or tea. After he read the king's letter, his eyes seemed to shine as he said, "What can I do to serve our king?"

Eduardo advised him that his staff needed to review all documents relating to the purchase, storage and transfer of all goods on the treasure ships. He also requested that his staff be provided with a list of the names and addresses of all individuals or companies that had sold items for transport.

"While our respective staffs are gathering the records, I would like to take you to lunch at your favorite place.

"General, I suggest we eat at Emilio's just outside the gates. I recommend that you order "Pancit", a food favorite in the Philippines.

Twenty minutes later the driver dropped them off at Emilio's Restaurant, which appeared to be a popular place. They ordered and were served quickly.

Eduardo loved the pancit. "What's in this dish," Eduardo asked?

"Pork, Chicken, onion, garlic, cabbage, noodles, carrot, salt, pepper, five spices and lime," answered the admiral.

As they were enjoying their after lunch coffee, Eduardo told the admiral "Part of my job is to inquire of all key people if they have any complaints or concerns about the present manner of the purchase, storage and shipment of oriental goods. Also, I would like to know if you have any recommendations or suggestions to make the operation flow smoother. I would like your comments in

405

writing within three days. I estimate that I will be in Manila for a month or more but when I depart I will travel to Lima. When is the next ship to Lima scheduled to depart," asked Eduardo?

"The *Caca Fuego* will depart in about two weeks. The *Santa Maria* is expected to arrive Subic Bay in late March and depart for Lima in early April.

"Admiral, I will do my best to complete my business in Manila and return to Subic Bay in time to travel to Lima on the *Santa Maria*. Please keep me posted on the arrival of the *Santa Maria*.

Now, if you will, please give me a tour of the base to follow the goods from the time they are received until the time they are shipped out. Talk to me about security."

Over the next few days Eduardo's staff analyzed the records. The great majority of suppliers were based in Manila and its suburbs. They found no discrepancy between the goods shipped from Subic Bay to Acapulco, and those received.

One night Eduardo treated his staff to a Mongolian Bar-b-que at a restaurant in the nearby city of Olongapo. Each diner would fill his bowl with some of the many varieties of noodles, to which he would add beef, pork, chicken, vegetables, and spicy sauces. Cooks would empty the bowl on a huge flat grill, frequently stirring until done. To this hot bowl could be added peppers, salt, chopped nuts, chopped coconut and other spices. The dish seemed to call for beer, which they all enjoyed. Next door was a strip club.

Admiral Jobim was delighted to learn that General Lopez' staff had found no inconsistences in his records. Eduardo made a few suggestions that would enhance security around the warehouse, which the admiral promised would be enacted that day.

"Admiral, it would be appreciated if you would assign a squad of marines to escort us to Manila," Eduardo said.

"General, that is a hard three day coach ride and there are no inns for you to spend the night between here and Manila. I will send a platoon of marines to escort you. They will be supplied with tents, cots and bedding for you, and they will cook your meals. We look forward to your return."

"*Salamat*", said Eduardo, meaning "thank you" in Tagalog.

CHAPTER 128

Manilla, Philippines

Meeting with King's agent. Tour to Cebu & Bohol.

Review of records. Review of warehouse.

February 22, 1782 –

Manila, a city on Luzon Island of the Philippines, was founded in 1571 by a Conquistador,

Miguel Lopez de Legazpl. It lay on the southeastern shore of Manila Bay. It was known as the

"Queen City of the Pacific." Spain viewed Manila as the Capital of the East Indies. Manila was home to people from China, Japan, Indonesia, Malaysia, Spain, Mexico, and India. Those from native tribes that predated the Spaniards spoke Tagalog.

The coast was lined with tall volcanoes, and it appeared that Luzon Island was filled with them. Eduardo had learned from the captain that Luzon Island was one of the most dangerous islands in the Pacific because it suffered eruptions of volcanos, earthquakes, floods, typhoons and tidal waves. He thought to himself that perhaps he should ask for hazardous duty pay.

They drove through several small communities before reaching Manila proper. Manila, the walled and fortified city, was referred to by the locals as Intramuros. It was a quarter of a square mile fortress with limited entrances. Its northern wall overlooked the Pasig River, which divided the city on a north-south axis. All of the Spanish public buildings and almost all Spanish homes and business were within the walls of Intramuros. Those doing business with Spain and all non-Spaniards lived outside the walls.

During the Seven Years War[23], England captured Manila, but was required to relinquish it back to Spain by the 1763 Treaty of Paris, which settled that war. Traffic was entering and exiting the Intramuros freely, as two guards lounged near the gate. Within the gates of Intramuros, they approached the gates of the Presidio. At the gate they were given directions to the BOQ.

Eduardo's coach stopped at the Presidio BOQ. When he asked for a room, he was told that a private residence had been reserved for him, where the commanding general thought he would be more comfortable. The other officers and their luggage were offloaded, and they signed up for their rooms.

The carriage drove down a shady tree lined street and stopped at a small bungalow that was shaded by dozens of large Coconut Palms and some huge trees with diameters 5-6 feet that stood 150-200 feet high. He later learned that these were Dipterocarp Trees. The grounds of this

bungalow had been landscaped beautifully. The air smelled of honeysuckle and trumpet vine. He thought to himself, that this might not be such a bad tour of duty.

---

[23] Currently referred to as the French and Indian War (1756-1763).

Map of Manila Bay 1

The young marine carried his luggage to the front door, opened it with a key, and took Eduardo's luggage to the bedroom. "Here is your key General. Also, here is a note from the Commanding General. I hope your accommodation is acceptable and that your stay is pleasant. "Good afternoon, sir," he said as he saluted smartly and left.

Eduardo, sat on the edge of the bed and opened the note, which read:

Dear General Lopez,

Welcome to Manila. I hope your accommodations are acceptable. I suspect that you are exhausted from your murderously long journey. If you will be so kind as to join me for lunch at noon tomorrow, I will have a driver pick you up. I wish to learn your orders and how I and my staff can be of service to you. If you will look in the

kitchen you will find that my cook has prepared a typical
Philippine dinner for you with a hefty supply of beer,
wine, rum and brandy. Tea, coffee, sugar, bread and
other essentials are in your cabinets with tableware,
plates and cups.

Eduardo thought that the note showed that the General and his staff intended to cooperate with his inquiries. He took off his coat and hung it in the closet. Next came his boots. He opened his bag and took out his comfortable slippers. "Let's see what my home for the next few months looks like," he thought.

Adjacent to his spacious bedroom, was a living room, through which they had walked from the front door. It was furnished with a large sofa, and an overstuffed chair and ottoman, between which there was a table upon which was a candle and a local newspaper. Across the room was another table and four chairs. Two windows with shades faced the street. He thought it strange that there was no fireplace. He would soon discover that although it rarely gets into the 100 degree temperatures, there is seldom a need for heat in Manila.

Between the sitting and eating areas was a door, which opened out to a huge screened in porch. To the left were two rocking chairs with a table (and candle) in between. On the right was a cot, which appeared to be a cool place to sleep. The four strange plants hanging from the ceiling gave off very pleasant odors.

In the kitchen there was a wood cooking stove, a large counter- top, which contained his dinner which was on a tray covered by a large napkin. Above the counter were several wooden cabinets. On the other side of the room was the bar which was well stocked with a small barrel of beer and bottles of liquor. In the corner was a barrel of water, near which hung several towels. "Looks like I will not starve," he thought. The back door led to the outhouse.

The coach dropped Eduardo off at the Presidio Officers Club. Eduardo had to stop for a few seconds to take in the magnitude of this building. It was the largest officers club he had seen outside Europe. Major General Gaspar Valdez was standing in the lobby to greet him. They shook hands and chatted. Eduardo checked his hat and followed General Valdez up the stairs. A greeter escorted them to a private dining room on the corner of the building with picture windows overlooking the Intramuros.

"Over a month ago, I received a letter from the king which informed me of your arrival and instructed me to cooperate with you," General Valdez told Eduardo.

"General, please read this," said Eduardo as he passed the letter from the king to General Valdez.

"Is there a problem in my command," asked General Valdez. "Am I under suspicion for some crime?"

"No, no, General. That's not why I'm here. King Carlos cannot physically visit all his empire. He is very interested in the acquisition of goods from the Orient. Instead of coming himself, he asked me to be his eyes and ears.

During their lunch Eduardo asked the general's assistance in delivering notes to all suppliers that they must come on base and be interviewed by Eduardo's staff at the designated time and place. Failure to appear will result in their company being struck from the list of authorized suppliers.

"General, while my staff is interviewing our suppliers, I would be appreciative if you would assign a junior officer to give me a tour of your entire command – even Corrigedor. And I'll also need a list of your staff, all your subordinate commands, with their location, CO and XO. Also, I will need a coach and driver at my disposal while in Manila.

By 2:00 p.m. Eduardo was on the coach provided by General Valdez. The driver opened the coach door for Eduardo in front of the Royal Palace. He was there to pay a courtesy visit on Philippine Governor General José Basco y Vargas, 1st Count of the Conquest of Batanes Islands. He was a former Spanish naval officer who had been appointed as the 53rd governor of the Philippines in 1778. He was known for his revival of the tobacco industry and his promotion of the production of cotton, spices, sugarcane, and mining, and he encouraged scientific research.

Eduardo showed Governor Basco the letter from the king and outlined his proposed activities in the Philippines. The governor was cordial, offering him a glass of wine. Eduardo assured the governor that he would be provided with a copy of Eduardo's report and recommendation on the Philippines. The governor told Eduardo that he would help in any way he could. Their meeting took less than an hour.

. . .

The following morning at the arranged time a young captain appeared at Eduardo's bungalow with a coach and driver. He introduced the Captain to his orderly and the three boarded the coach.

413

"Sir, just to drive around the bay to Mariveles at the mouth of the bay is 90 miles, which would require four or five nights on the road. Its 35 miles by sea to Corregidor. The general arranged a two masted sloop to serve under your command while you are here in addition to the coach. This way the ship can travel at night while you sleep. If this is agreeable with you sir, I will be glad to assist you while you pack up what you'll need for your inspection tour."

"My compliments to the general. He is very considerate. Please ask the coach driver to take Sgt. Blanco to the NCO barracks; wait for him; and then to return here.

. . .

The *Resolve* was a two masted sloop with 24 guns. Her captain, LT Julien Arocha, was standing at the railing near the gangway. He saluted and introduced himself and his XO, Sub. Lt. Gilberto Flores. Eduardo introduced Captain Acosta and Sgt. Blanco.

"May we step into the captain's quarters, please," asked Eduardo. They filed into the captain's cabin and took a seat.

"Gentlemen, please read this letter," said Eduardo, as he passed the letter to Lt. Arocha. After reading the letter he passed it to Sub. Lt. Flores, who passed it to Captain Acosta.

"King Carlos has a vast kingdom. It is physically impossible for him to visit his realm. As a result, he asks his friends to make inspections. My father and the king's father were good friends. My job is to review the entire Philippine military operation."

"I want to sail along the coast and visit every fortress, gun battery, look-out post, etc. We will stop, and if necessary, I will be rowed ashore to speak with the soldiers at each position. Our first stop will be the gun batteries on the peninsula extending from Novatas, to the north.

The following 8 days Eduardo spent inspecting military positions along Manila Bay. He spent two days in Corregidor and one day on Caballo, Island. Eduardo was concerned with the amount of cannon dedicated to protecting the entrance into Manila Bay.

About halfway through his inspection Eduardo began experiencing both cold chills and hot sweats together with a mean headache.

While Eduardo and Sgt. Blanco were sailing around Manila Bay, Fernando and Javier were busy interviewing the suppliers. To each supplier his staff asked:

Describe your products?

What are the sources of your products?

What other sources are there for your products?

How do you transport your product to Subic Bay?

 If I were to place an order today, how long for you to fill order?

By utilizing another source, can you speed up deliveries?

By utilizing another source could we double deliveries?

If you hired more employees, could we speed up deliveries?

Would it save any time to deliver your products to Manila versus Subic Bay?

Would it save any time to deliver your products to Agana, Guam versus Subic Bay?

Would it save any time to deliver your products to Kwajalein, Marshall Islands versus Subic Bay?

Have you suffered any losses to pirates or thieves while your products are in transit?

Do you have any complaints or suggestions that would improve your sale and delivery?

When the *Resolve* returned Eduardo to Manila, on March 2nd he told them that he planned on going to both Cebu and Bohol and asked them to stand by. He had the coach driver drop him off at the clinic. He ordered the driver to take Sgt. Blanco to the BOQ to drop off his luggage; to return the Sgt. to the NCO barracks and then return to the clinic for him. The doctor diagnosed him with the "Shaking Disease.[25]" He was admitted to a private room in the base clinic. They immediately began treating him with ground bark of a tree from Peru. Eduardo sent notes to Colonel Garcia and General Valdez.

While Eduardo was fighting off sweats, chills, and uncontrollable shaking, two days later a typhoon hit Manila and Subic Bay. The ships in port had to move into Subic and Manila Bay and ride out the storm or suffer damage being dashed against the pier. The bay is partially sheltered by mountains surrounding the bay. The tempest destroyed the Subic Bay navy pier and took the roof off of the warehouse.

During his two week hospitalization he was treated by Rosario "Rosy" Fuentes, R.N. Rosy was pretty, about age 29, single, 5'6'', 120 pounds, with raven black hair, which she normally wore in a ponytail. She had bright hazel eyes. She was an attentive nurse, who fell in love with her patient. She would hold his hand for a minute, then give it a squeeze as she let go. She would touch his face. By the end of his hospitalization, he was also hooked. For the remainder of his time in Manila, Rosy was an overnight guest in his quarters.

Eduardo prepared a separate Final Recommendations for security of the Manila Military Command which he mailed to the king, with a copy to Governor General Bosco:

Construct a fortress on the highest spot on Milinta Hills on the island of Corregidor.

Install 10 gun batteries on the island of Corregidor to protect the entrance to Manila Bay.

Install 3 gun batteries between Morivrtes and Cabcaben on the north shore to protect the entrance to Manila Bay.

Install 3 gun batteries on Carabao Island to protect the entrance to Manila Bay.

Install 5 gun batteries on Grand Island to protect Subic Bay Navy Base.

Install 3 gun batteries on Chiquita Island to protect Subic Bay Navy Base.

Install 3 gun batteries on Camayan Point to protect Subic Bay Navy Base.

Install 3 gun batteries on Binango Point to protect Subic Bay Navy Base.

Reassign a company of army calvary to a new base next to the navy base to provide additional security. To be reinforced by a platoon of Cannoniers, kitchen platoon, and medical unit.

Ensure that the pier at Manila Bay will accommodate a 200 foot long treasure ship that draws 38.5 feet at low tide to guard against future typhoon damage.

Place a look-out post atop the 5,000 ft high southernmost peak of the Sierra de Mariveles, which overlooks the entrance to Manila Bay.

[2525] Malaria had not yet been discovered.

CHAPTER 129

Aboard the *Resolve*

Departing Manila

Sailing to Cebu, Philippines

March 16, 1782

The *Resolve* sailed out of Manila Bay through Boca Grande between Caballo Island and Carabao Island. Sailing the 620 mile route to Cebu, Philippines you were always in sight of one or more of the Philippines' 1,700 islands. The islands were of volcanic origin and are lush with tropical flora and fauna. The voyage took 53 hours.

Eduardo's thoughts were constant about Rosy. She made him tingle. It was the most sexual excitement he had experience since his honeymoon many years ago. He had considered bringing her along on this trip, but it was a relationship he did not intend to advertise.

Cebu is over one hundred miles long but less than 10 miles wide. It is the second largest island in the archipelago. It was the first trading port in the Philippines and has the necessary infrastructure to accommodate treasure ships. Eduardo was thinking in terms of finding a replacement agent in Cebu in the event of a catastrophic event that might prevent the movement of treasure ships.

From the harbormaster he obtained a list of all warehouse operators. From those operators and others on the waterfront he gleaned the names of three possible agents.

He spent the next day, and evening talking to these prospective agents. He discovered that Cebu was the

419

primary grower of aloe vera, which was great for burns, including sunburn. He remembered that aloe vera was not a product in the warehouse receipts. With all three prospective agents he discussed the cost if they delivered in Subic Bay, or if the treasure ship stopped in Cebu for a pickup. A second product not presently being exported to Spain were hand painted floor tiles and paint. Each agent gave Eduardo a list of his producers, the type of product and unit cost.

Eduardo had not recovered from his illness completely. He tired more easily, and his headache was now an everyday occurrence. He invited Sgt. Blanco, Captain Acosta, Lt. Arocha, and Sub. Lt. Flores to spend the day at one of Cebu's fantastic beaches. They had the cook prepare picnic lunches, beer, wine and water for each of them. Eduardo bought each man a wide brimmed straw hats from vendors on the beach to protect their skin from sunburn. He also rented three umbrellas to protect them from sunburn.

Eduardo swam out from shore to where the water was about 30 feet deep. It was amazing, he could clearly see the seashells on the white sand bottom. The weather cooperated with temperatures in the high 80s.

"Tomorrow, we sail for Tagbilaran, Bohol," said Eduardo, as his lifted his beer to his lips.

CHAPTER 130

Cebu to Bohol, Philippines

On the *Resolve*

March 23, 1782

Bohol was an almost round island which lies due east of Cebu. Their voyage took up most of the day. When they arrived in port, they decided to eat at a local restaurant.

The next morning, Eduardo and Javi repeated the process from Cebu. Their island exports many of the same items from Luzon and Cebu. The craftsmen of Bohol create high quality woven goods, purses, hats, bags, mats, etc. and they also have loomed some beautiful colorful cloth.

The question presented was whether it was feasible to deviate from a course from Manila to Lima to pick up a few supplies.

On March 25th, the four men hired a guide. He took them to a viewing point where they looked at hundreds of small perfectly shaped mountains that covered the better part of a valley. Javi said, "They look like a dollop of whipped cream on top of ice cream." Nando said, "Sir, I am looking at a field of women's breasts."

On their way back to the ship, they visited some ancient ruins. Because none of them were impressed with their dinner the night before, they had told the cook they would be eating onboard.

CHAPTER 131

Bohol to Manila, Philippines

Aboard the *Resolve*

March 26-28, 1782

For the next few days, Eduardo was finishing up on his letter to Toni and writing Chris and

Bernardo. He was keeping a "things to do" list, which reminded him to have dinner with General Valdez and thank him for his courtesies. His thoughts kept reverting to Rosy. He was dying to see her – to hold her – to make love to her.

When the ship docked in Manila, Eduardo went directly to the General's office. He told the skipper of the *Resolve*, that he would require transportation for him and his staff to Subic Bay in a few days.

General Valdez brought him up to date on the scheduled departure of the treasure ship *Santa Maria*. It was now scheduled to depart Subic Bay on April 4, 1782. He provided the general with a copy of his report to King Carlos and invited the general to have dinner with him and his staff the following evening. He arranged for a private dinner in his bungalow with Rosy that evening.

The next day he went shopping for newspapers, candy, and a pearl necklace as a gift for Toni.

He had a wood carver make a name plate for his desk with beautiful carvings of water buffalo. He visited the clinic to get a refill of his medicine. At the Presidio uniform shop, he replaced his sword that he had presented to the King of Hilo. He sent a messenger to the *Resolve* to be prepared to depart Manila for Subic Bay on March 30th.

Although he still had not read his encyclopedia past the "r's, he looked for a few more books to keep him occupied for two lengthy sea voyages. He selected *Age of Reason*, by Thomas Paine, *Gulliver's Travels*, by Jonathan Swift, and *Memories of a Cavalier*, by Daniel DeFoe. He mailed Toni's present together with a short note expressing his undying love.

When he returned to his bungalow after dinner with the general, he found that Sgt. Blanco had already gotten him packed and ready for an early morning departure. As he was about to blow out the last candle, there was a knock on the door. When he opened the door, he was pleased to see Rosy.

When he awoke the next morning, Rosy was gone. Eduardo was so conflicted. He loved his wife and felt guilty for betraying her trust. He had been halfway around the world and in the hospital and it had not been a case of his seeking an affair. He had been seduced – yet he was an eager participant.

CHAPTER 132

Manila to Subic Bay

Aboard the *Resolve*

March 30 – April 1, 1782

As the *Resolve* approached the Subic Bay pier, Eduardo saw that the *Santa Maria* was already in port. The loading process had already started. As soon as Eduardo and his staff were ready to disembark, Eduardo released the *Resolve* and thanked her officers for their assistance. He promised them that they would be mentioned favorably in his report to the king.

He had the coach drop him off at Admiral Jobim's office and sent the others to check in at the BOQ. Admiral Jobim had a smile on his face as he arose from behind his desk to greet Eduardo. Eduardo brought the admiral up to date on his activities in Manila, Cebu and Bohol.

Admiral Jobim informed Eduardo that the war ship he had assigned to escort the *Santa Maria* was the *Impulse*, a 38 gun, two masted Galleon, manned by the following officers:

CO	Captain Manuel Soya, Commodore
XO	Fragata Captain Sebastian Monjaras
Gunnery Officer	LT Marcos Montes

Navigator	LT Tomas Macias
Supply Officer	Sub. LT Enrique Duran
Cargo Officer	Sub. LT Santiago Delgado
Midshipman	Luis Cazorla

Admiral Jobim also provided Eduardo a list of the officers of the *Santa Maria*:

CO	Captain Manuel Soya, Commodore
XO	Fragata Captain Sebastian Monjaras
Gunnery Officer	LT Marcos Montes
Navigator	LT Tomas Macias
Supply Officer	Sub. LT Enrique Duran
Cargo Officer	Sub. LT Santiago Delgado
Midshipman	Luis Cazorla

That evening Eduardo sent notes to the captain of both ships asking that all officers join him and his staff for dinner in the Officer's Club the following evening.

. . .

At the start of the cocktail hour before dinner on April 2nd Eduardo introduced himself and his staff. He read the letter from the king so all would be aware of his status. He told the officers of the two ships that the *Impulse* was permanently assigned to escort the *Santa Maria* to protect her cargo against pirates and the British. Since they would be traveling in tandem for four months to Lima he thought it was a good idea for them to get to know one another.

CHAPTER 133

Santa Maria Treasure Ship Departs Subic Bay

Bound for Lima, Peru

April 4, 1782

As the *Santa Maria* exited Subic Bay it fired a cannon salute. The *Impulse*, trailing 100 yards to port likewise fired a salute as it departed.

The configuration of the *Santa Maria* was identical to the *Caca Fuego*, and he was berthed in a cabin almost identical to his VIP Suite aboard the *Caca Fuego*.

Eduardo thought to himself, 'I am finally on my way home."

On their second day at sea Eduardo called the three junior officers into his cabin. "Gentlemen," He said, "As an officer you must constantly strive to improve yourself. Learning about great men is a part of your education. I am giving you each a biography to read. When you are finished, please pass your book, and take the book which was read by your associate. I want each of you to complete all three books before we arrive in Lima.

The *Impulse* sailed south through the Philippine archipelago to Leyte Gulf, where it passed between Leyte and Mindanao Islands into the Pacific. Their voyage passed through the Melanesian Islands, including the Carolines, the Marshals, and the Marquesas, after which it was open sea until Lima.

Eduardo still had medical issues. He would go to sleep with a fever so bad that his whole body was wet with

427

sweat and awake in the middle of the night in a cold sweat. His headaches were almost a daily affair. He thought of Rosy several times every day. He spent much of his time in his VIP cabin reading his new books.

Every Saturday evening the two ships converged and the officers from the *Impulse* were rowed to the *Santa Maria* for dinner and entertainment. Fernando discovered that the *Santa Maria* Gunnery officer, Lt. Marcos Montes also played the guitar. They had been practicing and the first Saturday at sea, they were a hit.

CHAPTER 134

Galvez Captures the three forts in the Bahamas.

6 May 1782

With the English surrender on October 19, 1781, the war was over – or was it? The English still had a large army in New York, Detroit and Florida. George Washington had moved the Continental Army to Newburgh, New York, where he intended to stay until the last English ship sailed out of the New York City harbor.

Peace negotiators for England, France, Spain, Holland and the United States could seem to make no headway. The consensus was that the British were dragging their feet. They were looking at having only Canada, Kingston, Jamaica and Nassau, Bahamas for the western hemisphere in their empire.

The Spanish fleet was under the direction of His Excellency Juan Manuel de Cagigal, Spanish Governor of Havana. His fleet of 64 transports, seven ships of the line and seven frigates supported the army of 2,500 men who sailed from Havana on April 18, 1782.

When the Spanish arrived at Nassau, Eduardo sent a message to the British commander, Vice Admiral John Maxwell requesting his surrender. As Admiral Maxwell peered through his looking glass all he could see was Spanish ships. He wisely surrendered his three forts, 600 men, and 5 ships, including a frigate. This was a boon to American shippers who no longer had worry about an attack from the English. It was now a port where American and allied ships could make repairs and obtain

429

provisions and supplies. Mainly, it denied the British of a port from which they might operate.

Left with only Kingston, Jamaica as their only crown colony in the gulf and Caribbean, the English treaty negotiators rushed to complete the peace treaty which was finally signed on September 3, 1783 – when Galvez was in the midst of their final plans to invade Jamaica.

CHAPTER 135

Kwajalein, Marshall Islands

Onboard the *Impulse*

May 7, 1782

The first stop after five weeks at sea was in Kwajalein, Marshall Islands The *Santa Maria* had no cargo for Kwajalein, as this was only a stop to replenish food and water and crew rest. A messenger to the Presidio delivered mail and packages and picked up the outgoing mail. Most of the crew was given leave. The supply officer and his crew were busy purchasing food, wine, beer and water.

Spaniard Ruy Lopez de Villalobos first discovered Kwajalein in January 1543. It had been held by Spain continuously since that time. It was a small outpost with a population of fewer than 1,000.

Eduardo and his officers went ashore to look around. In addition to the small presidio, the church and the government building there were only a few shops. The bar was clearly recognizable as the building from which came the tumultuous noise of a crew getting drunk. He purchased a newspaper and some candy.

They returned to the ship, ate lunch, changed into swimming attire and walked a short distance to a shaded beach near the pier. A large number of crew members were already enjoying the beach and surfing when they arrived.

That evening the Captain in command of the Kwajalein Presidio and his XO joined them and the officers of the *Impulse* for dinner in the captain's cabin. He reported that there had been a raid by an English war ship on the island of Majuro the month before.

. . .

Three days after departing Kwajalean the ships crossed the International Date Line, which was just another day aboard ship.

CHAPTER 136

Crossing the Equator

Aboard the *Santa Maria*

May 19, 1782

Crossing the Equator a week later was a different story. This ceremony is practiced by navies of every country. A senior crew member, usually the Bosun is dressed as King Neptune, and several of his accomplices are dressed like members of his court. Sailors who have never crossed the equator at sea were called "Tadpoles" or "Pollywogs," whereas those who have crossed it before were called "Shellbacks."

On the morning of the crossing just after breakfast the "Tadpoles" were all lined up and blindfolded below deck. They were led on deck and doused with buckets of water by the "Shellbacks." Some old salts viewed the initiation as a test for inexperienced sailors to see if they could "cut it." Most officers viewed the ceremony as good for morale.

The Tadpoles were subjected to all sorts of embarrassment. One sailor was forced to gut a fish and wear it as a hat. Some had flour thrown in their hair, while others had their faces rubbed with oil or grease. All of them were forced to walk the plank, and then were required to tread water for what seemed an eternity.

After the initiates got back to the quarterdeck they were allowed to wash off. Then King

Neptune had them swear to an oath and announced that they had graduated from "Pollywog" to "Shellback." Then the captain presented each of the new shellbacks a handsome certificate with their name, signed and dated by the captain.

All the while a similar initiation was taking place aboard the *Impulse*. After lunch the two ships were dead in the water separated by about 100 feet and both crews were given a swimming period.

Eduardo and his staff, Captain Soya, CO of the *Santa Maria* and his XO, Commander Monjaras were invited to dine onboard the *Impulse*. A change of venue is always nice. Their cook had prepared a filet of sole, which they all enjoyed. The highlight of the dinner was the bread pudding which was served for dessert.

At four bells that afternoon both ships hoisted their sails and moved on. On both ships that night the crews received a double ration of beer.

CHAPTER 137

Nuku-Hiva, Marquesas

Aboard the *Santa Maria*

June 22, 1782

It had been a monotonous five weeks from crossing the equator, except for a storm that did a bit of damage in the riggings. Almost daily, dolphins played in the bow wake of the ship. The damage had been repaired by the crew. Eduardo continued experiencing night sweats and chills. His thoughts were often of Rosy.

The Marquesas were first discovered by a Spanish sailor but was later colonized by the French. The population was 90% Polynesian, with about 10% French officials. The tallest mountain on Nuku-Hiva was about 4,000 feet high.

In the supplies brought onboard were baskets of breadfruit, mangos, manioc, taro, coconut, bananas and several types of berries. Two live goats and a pig were led up the gangway.

Eduardo paid a courtesy call on the French Commandant of the Marquesas, a Major, who invited him to lunch at a beachside restaurant. The major recommended an island specialty which Eduardo devoured. It was a crab dish with crème cheese, onion, garlic, celery, and peppers which was baked in an oven and sprinkled with black pepper.

After lunch the major's carriage driver drove them around town. They stopped at a shop where Eduardo purchased a newspaper and some hard candy.

CHAPTER 138

From the Marquesas to Lima

Aboard the *Santa Maria*

June 24 – August 8, 1782

This was the longest leg of their voyage – about six weeks, and all out of sight of land. Tedium had set in. Many of the officers played dominos. Many, like Eduardo, spent their leisure hours reading. Eduardo completed reading through his encyclopedia and all three of his new books two nights before arriving in Lima. "Timed that pretty well," he thought. He made a mental note to purchase more books in Lima for the long voyage to Acapulco. Eduardo had been without candy for about two weeks. He couldn't wait to go on a candy binge.

Just out of Manila he had started a letter to Toni. From time to time he would inform her of his activities and life shipboard. At each port stop, he added a paragraph about his experience ashore. Even when in the act of writing to Toni, he often thought of Rosy. He was conflicted.

He also had open letters going to Viceroy Galvez, Bernardo and Chris to all of which he made frequent entries. They all were to be mailed upon their arrival in Lima.

Although he had been making temporary reports to King Carlos, he had compiled those reports, to which he would make entries about Lima and Mexico and place in the mail as his final report upon his return to New Orleans.

The only variance to his hum drum life were the weekly dinner visits to the *Santa Maria* by the officers of the *Impulse*, and the stops to allow the crew to swim.

As they approached Lima about 10:00 a.m. they entered a fog banc. They could see San Lorenzo Island on their starboard side but were unable to see La Punta Peninsula closer to shore. The captain decided to furl his sails and sit dead in the water until the fog lifted. While they were eating lunch the forward lookout knocked on the captain's door.

"The fog has lifted sir."

Commodore Soya got up from the table and proceeded to the poop deck. "Drop the sails, make way to the port of El Callao."

Callao was the main port of the Americas, connecting the colonies with Spain via Acapulco. After several pirate raids took place in the 17th century, Viceroy Pedro Álvarez de Toledo y Leiva ordered the construction of a wall to protect Lima between the years 1640 and 1647. An earthquake in 1746 destroyed most of the fortification. Viceroy José Antonio Manso de Velasco, ordered the contraction of the fortress to bolster the defense of the port. The fortress was named after King Felipe, V de Borbon. The fortress was completed in 1774.

As Eduardo entered the port of El Callao, port city of Lima, he could see that two new fortresses were under construction. That year the viceroy had ordered the construction of two smaller forts; the "San Miguel" and the "San Rafael."

CHAPTER 139

Acapulco Navy Base

Acapulco, Mexico

July 5, 1782

Five officers waited in the outer office of Rear Admiral Adonis Contreras, Spanish Commander of its Central Pacific Fleet. These were the officers of the Spanish Navy ship *Fortitude*. They had been summoned here by the admiral's aide.

The *Fortitude* was a large four masted galleon that boasted 38 guns. She was the queen of the Acapulco fleet.

As Admiral Contreras stepped into the room, each officer rose and stood at attention. "As you were. Please join me in my office, gentlemen," he said. "Please be seated."

"The last treasure ship from Lima was attacked by a pirate ship about 50 nautical miles northeast of the Galapagos. Fortunately, the treasure ship was able to outrun the pirate. Intelligence reports indicate there are a large number of pirates living on Cocos Island, off the coast of Costa Rica. The problem is that our treasure ships must stop on Cocos Island for food and water."

"Your job is to seek out and destroy pirate ships along the west coast of Mexico and Central America. I want you to proceed down the coast to Panama and to go into every gulf, bay, or harbor big enough to hide a pirate ship. When you get to Costa Rica you are to investigate the ships anchored in the harbor and at the pier. I have

439

selected the *Fortitude* because yours is the fastest and best armored ship in my command. Any Questions?"

"Admiral, we should be finished loading supplies by tonight. We can leave on the morning tide," said Captain Tomas Macias, the skipper.

"That will be good. Good hunting. You are dismissed," said the admiral.

The five men rose and left the room.

. . .

July 9, 1782

Today marked the one year anniversary of Eduardo's departure from New Orleans. They were in the middle of the South Pacific Ocean. Eduardo had the ship's cook bake a cake to commemorate the occasion.

CHAPTER 140

Lima, Peru

August 8 – September 15, 1782

Spanish conquistador Francisco Pizarro conquered Cusco, the capital of the Inca Empire The Spanish Crown established the Viceroyalty of Peru in 1543. That viceroyalty included present day Argentina, Chile, Bolivia and Peru to Ecuador, Colombia, and Panama – the western part of South America. Lima, the "City of Kings" was established as its capital. For several years there were revolts of the native population. It was a chaotic time with the conquerors fighting one another over the division of the gold.

This action by the Spanish was not well received by the Inca population. Almost immediately they revolted. Spanish soldiers were killed. Warehouses were looted and set on fire. Donkey caravans from the gold mines were hijacked.

When Francisco de Toledo (1569-1581) assumed the office of the Viceroyalty of Peru in 1575, peace finally arrived. He obtained control of the native population by ordering the native leaders to manage the affairs of the local population and making them responsible for observing the laws, collecting taxes and providing forced labor.

Then, in 1780 the indigenous population, after more than 200 years revolted again. They argued that they had suffered from the strict and harsh oppression of the Spaniards including forced labor, high taxes and the ban on the speaking of their languages and practicing their beliefs and traditions. The bloody rebellion spread throughout the remaining Viceroyalty of Peru and even into modern-day Bolivia and Ecuador causing severe economic disruption. The rebellion leader was captured and executed in May 1781.

Even though the rebel leader had been caught and executed the hatred of the Spanish was uniform throughout Peru. As a result, although not declared, martial law was being applied.

Eduardo's mission in Peru, had just gotten complicated.

Before the *Santa Maria* docked Eduardo and his crew bid them farewell and thanked them for their courtesies over the past several months. They each had letters that they asked to be mailed in Acapulco.

When they docked, Eduardo directed his staff to get checked in at the Navy base. It was 4:00 p.m. when Eduardo arrived at the office of Contra Admiral[24]Marcos Zepeda, Commanding Officer of all Naval forces in Peru.

"Admiral Zepeda, I apologize for barging in here this late in the day. I merely wanted to apprise you of my presence on your base and ask for an appointment with you tomorrow morning." "General, I have been expecting you. I have spies everywhere, he said with a wink. I have reserved a VIP suite for you in our BOQ. I suggest that you and your staff get checked in; take a hot bath and enjoy a nice dinner at the Officer's Club. Sleep in tomorrow and let's get together for lunch at the O Club at noon."

---

[24] Equivalent to Commodore Admiral in the United States - 1 star.

"I ordered you a coach, a supply wagon, and a platoon of marines to provide security for your visit and your travels inland to visit mines. With all the rioting going on, I urge you and your men to be armed at all times. I've alerted the armory to have pistols ready for you and your staff. You should remain on high alert during your entire stay."

"Admiral, do you have the names of the marine cavalry officers who will be escorting us," Edwardo asked?

"The Platoon Leader is Lieutenant Hector Delgado," replied the admiral. "The Assistant Platoon Leader is Sub Lieutenant Emilio Cazoria. They have been instructed to pick up your staff and load all your luggage tomorrow at 1230 hours. Then, at 1330 hours they will pick you up in front of the officer's club.

"Two things," stated Eduardo. "What is the name of the next treasure ship due in port; when is it due and when it is scheduled to depart for Acapulco? What ship have you assigned to escort it, and the names of its officers?"

"General, you must be living right. Ordinarily, only three treasure ships operate in the South Pacific, and your next ship would not arrive until December. One of the warships in port ran into a cargo ship from Manila heading here two weeks ago. The *Singing Lady* is due in port on September 4th and is due to depart for Acapulco on September 10th. I will alert the harbormaster to inform the captain of his new passengers. I don't have the names of the officers of the Singing Lady, but your escort vessel will be the 28 gun sloop, *Infinity*. Its skipper is Captain Jaime Rubio. The XO is LT Esteban Seguin. Their gunnery Officer is LT Micaela Sendejo, and as Assistant Gunnery Officer is sub lieutenant Ygnacio Cruz.

"Admiral, many thanks. I look forward to our lunch tomorrow."

When he arrived at the BOQ his orderly was in the lobby waiting for him. "Sir, I have already unpacked your luggage and put away your clothes. I Just thought I would check in sir, to see if you needed anything tonight," said Sgt. Blanco.

"Sgt. you are a lifesaver. I would love a hot bath. Please start filling the tub."

When his tub was ready, he asked Sgt. Blanco to advise the staff to be packed and ready for pick up at 1230 the next day.

Eduardo luxuriated in his warm bath. He wished that somebody would invent a tub for bathing so that you could lean back, stretch out and relax.

. . .

Eduardo slept late and skipped breakfast. Instead, he had coffee and *pan dulces* delivered to his suite. At noon he walked next door to the Officer's Club, where he was greeted by Admiral Zepeda. After they ordered Eduardo showed the admiral the letter from the king.

"What do you need from me general," he asked.

"Admiral, I need copies of all documentation relating to the receipt of gold and silver ore from all the mines; documentation about storage and handling created by your people and bills of lading of goods shipped from here to Acapulco. If you will please collect those documents, my staff will make the copies. Also, before I leave, I will need a tour of the base and I will want to spend some time looking at the security of the base in general and the gold and silver warehouses in particular.

444

Finally, I would appreciate it if you would provide me any comments, criticisms, or suggestions regarding the mining, storage and shipping of gold and silver oar."

"General, your staff can start tomorrow. I have set aside a suite of office space for your exclusive use while you are here."

"Admiral, my staff has been confined aboard ship for four months. We are going to take a couple of days off before we attack the paperwork."

Eduardo's next task today was to meet with Viceroy Manuel Guirior.

As his coach from the El Callao Naval Base worked its way to the Plaza de Armas in downtown Lima, they were confronted by protestors. Picketers with signs marched at most of the major intersections and in front of the Royal Palace as the coach pulled up in front of it. People on the sidewalk were throwing stones at his coach. A government worker had been stoned to death by rioters a few days before.

"Good afternoon your excellency," opened Eduardo. "I appreciate you seeing me on such short notice."

Viceroy Agustín de Jáuregui y Aldecoa rose to the rank of lieutenant general, and was knighted as a member of the Order of Santiago. He served in Honduras, Puerto Rico and Cuba. In 1772, King Carlos named him Governor of Chile. In July 1780 King Carlos appointed him Viceroy of Peru. His thick black hair had streaks of white which asserted maturity. He was about 6'3" and weighed about 230 pounds, indicating that he had been an athlete in his younger days. He spoke with a Castilian lisp, an affectation of former royal families. He was an immaculate dresser.

"Have a seat General. I had a nice letter from Viceroy Galvez in Mexico City advising me of your anticipated arrival. How may I be of assistance," he inquired?"

"Your excellency, it is my pleasure to introduce my chief of staff Colonel Fernando Garcia and my assistant Lieutenant Javier Ramirez. Gentlemen, please meet His Excellency Augustin de Jauregui, Viceroy."

"Your Excellency, please read this letter," he said, as he passed the king's letter to the Viceroy. "Well, I am impressed. I repeat, how may I be of assistance to you and the king?"

"With rioters at almost every street corner, I need to know what is going on? Will my staff be in any danger?

The four men sat for almost an hour discussing the revolt going on with the natives. Based upon his review of the Peruvian problems in his encyclopedia and what he had been told by the viceroy, he gleaned the following history of the Peruvian natives who were descended from the Incas:

The rebellion of Túpac Amaru sought to improve the rights of indigenous Peruvians suffering under the dictates of Spanish King Carlos, III, which increased their taxes and required more work from each man. It began with the capture and killing of the Tinta Corregidor and Spanish Governor Antonio de Arriaga on November 4, 1780, after a banquet attended by both Túpac Amaru, II and Governor Arriaga.

The crowd hated Visitador General José Antonio Areche. Their demands were for reforms, although many wanted to expel the Spaniards and return to their simple life without forced labor.

The restoration of the Inca Empire meant for them the possibility of an egalitarian society, based economically on the Inca communal agricultural system, the ayllu, and one without castes, rich and poor, or forced labor in haciendas, mines and factories, particularly the dreaded textile mills.

Tupac Amaru, II marched an army of 6,000 natives towards Cuzco. On the way they looted the Spaniards' houses and killed their occupiers. The defeat that marked his fall came in Amaru II's failure to capture Cuzco, where his 40,000 – 60,000 native warriors were defeated by natives loyal to the king and reinforcements from Lima. On his way to Lima, he was captured, tried and sentenced to be executed.

On May 18, 1781, he and several members of his family were taken to the Plaza de Armas in Cuzco to be executed one by one. First, they cut out the tongue of his son Hipólito, and then he was hanged. Next, the Spaniards cut out the tongue of his wife. When they tried to hang her, she was too short for the noose to fit around her neck, so they clubbed and beat her to death.

Tupac's tongue was excised, and he was hung. His dead body was then tied to four horses which pulled his arms and legs from his body. His torso was burned in a bonfire on the top of a hill overlooking the city. His head, arms and legs were sent to other cities to inform the population that their leader was dead.

The rebellion was continued by his cousin Diego Cristóbal Túpac Amaru. Native revolutionaries invaded Spanish towns and beheaded men, women, and children. In one instance, a native army under rebel leader Túpac Katari besieged the city of La Paz for 109 days before troops sent from Buenos Aires stepped in to relieve the city.

"Viceroy, my main reason for being in Peru is to examine the procedures being utilized in the gold and silver mines here; their transport from the mine to the warehouse at the navy base and shipment to Acapulco. From you I need a list with the names and location of all gold and silver mines, their managers and foremen.

The viceroy picked up a small hand bell and rang it. Within seconds the door opened and in walked a well-dressed young man. "Jose, please provide the general with a list of all gold and silver mines with their respective addresses and the names of the manager and foreman of each."

"Yes, your excellency, I'll have that in just a few minutes.

"How well do you know Viceroy Galvez," asked the viceroy?

"Your Excellency, he is the uncle of my best friend, Governor General of Louisiana, East and West Florida, Bernardo de Galvez, and all three of us are from the same small village near

Malaga. I had the pleasure of dining with him in Mexico City a couple of times. Bernardo's father is the Captain General of Guatemala.

"I ran into him when I was stationed in Havana over 20 years ago," said the Viceroy. "We hit it off and were friends until the army separated us."

Moments later the assistant returned with the list of mines. There were five gold mines; one between Lima and the town of Trujillo, and four others near Trujillo. The only silver mine was near Cuzco.

"Before I leave Lima, I would greatly appreciate it if you would give me your thoughts on mining and transportation," said Eduardo.

. . .

His next visit was with the with CO of the *Real Felipe* Fortress, Brigadier General Victor Anaya. The fortress was built on the edge of the harbor at the head of the Punta Peninsula on the other side of the city center of Callao.

"General, this is just a courtesy visit. As you can see from my letter from King Carlos, I am on official business, but I will be staying at the naval BOQ. I thought you would want to know that another general was in your area." Eduardo asked the general to be collecting his thoughts about the production process from mine to treasure ship of both gold and silver mines.

"I would appreciate it if you would designate a junior officer to give us a tour of the fort and interesting spots in and around Lima."

The balance of the day was spent touring the fort and the *Plaza de Armas*, which had military stationed at all four corners and a detachment in the center of the plaza. Protestors with signs were all around the square, many of whom shouted at their coach as they passed by. They visited the cathedral. Lima was a huge city with many monuments, fountains and parks.

CHAPTER 141

Cuzco, Peru

August 10 – 11, 1782

Eduardo's staff had been away from home almost a year, with most of that time being confined aboard a ship. For morale he wanted them to be able to enjoy a day of sightseeing. So, he arranged a trip to Cuzco, high in the Peruvian Andes Mountains.

Cuzco was a beautiful town. The white Spanish buildings of colonial architecture were covered with terra cotta tiled roofs. The streets were all cobblestones. The weather was about 20 degrees cooler than Lima. Smoke slowly rose from chimneys.

There were no miliary facilities in Cuzco, so Eduardo and his staff, and the two marine officers had to stay in a hotel in Cuzco. The marine platoon was camped just outside town. The Hotel Libertador, from the 1600's, on the main plaza was constructed with large dark to medium gray stones. In the lobby was a huge fireplace with a friendly roaring fire. When they checked in each of them was offered a cup of herbal tea and provided with a slip of paper, which said:

Warning, Cuzco is at an altitude of about 11,000 feet. Many who have come before you have developed altitude sickness. Please:

1. Drink a cup of the herbal tea provided and lay down for at least two hours.

2. *Limit your alcohol consumption while in Cuzco.*

3. *Use sunscreen, because at high altitude you can easily get sunburned.*

4. *Avoid exertion.*

When Eduardo entered his suite, he was greeted with the smell of Spring. His open bedroom window overlooked one of six small courtyards. After the bellman had delivered his luggage, he decided that he would follow the hotel's recommendation and lie down for a few hours. As he rested, he heard the sweet singing of birds and the soft sounds of birds splashing in the fountain in the courtyard below.

Eduardo, the two marines and all of his staff ate in the hotel restaurant that night. The streets were brightly lit with torches. This was a treat for them all after eating shipboard food for months at sea. Eduardo told them to order whatever they wanted as he was paying. Steak and lobster were favorites. As they were eating Eduardo warned his men about the possibility of trouble with revolutionaries.

Eduardo suggested "Let's take off tomorrow and look around this beautiful town. He invited all five men to join him for breakfast at the hotel the following morning at 8:00 a.m.

After breakfast the next morning, the six men walked across the Plaza to visit the Cathedral. They all left their

451

side arms at the counter where candles were sold at the entrance. Eduardo was tempted to visit the confessional but wanted to confess when his subordinates were not around. Cuzco was a tourist town for Peruvians, so the shops carried items that made good souvenirs. After spending a couple of hours shopping, they sat to enjoy a beer. While enjoying their beer they smelled the wonderful hot sandwiches of beef, cheese, onion, garlic and tomato. They decided to eat an early lunch and visit the ancient fortress afterwards.

The town of Sacsayhuaman was at 13,000 feet altitude. This small village was home to an ancient temple and fortress. Along the road were many llamas and alpacas. From its heights one could look down on Cuzco and the surrounding valley. The most interesting factor about the fortress were the stones with which it was constructed. They were odd shapes that had been fitted with other stones. The stones were huge – many being 20 feet long by 10 feet high and 10 feet wide and they were fitted with preciseness. Eduardo marveled not only about the craftmanship of the masons who constructed this edifice, but how in the hell did they move these heavy monoliths.

LT Delgado asked Eduardo, "Sir, has anybody told you about the significance of the hats worn by Inca women?"

"No. Please educated me."

"Traditionally, brown or green hats made from sheep's wool indicate an Andean woman, while tall, white ones

452

made of thatch suggest a person of mixed Inca/Spanish heritage. If the hat is worn in a cocked position, that is the sign of a widow. In the weaving village of Chinchero the tribal women who still wear traditional dress, wear a flat hat known as a "montera." The montera is shaped like a shallow fruit bowl. These red-felt hats are worn by Quechua women all across the Sacred Valley. In some instances, the "dish" is filled with flowers or baubles; in others it is kept in place by delicately woven sanq'apa straps adorned with white beads."

Just up the hill they visited a cliff overhang upon which had been erected a white alabaster statute of Christ overlooking Cuzco. A small boy about ten years old approached the group with a large condor on a leash. This bird had a wingspan of at least seven feet. When the boy whistled, the condor had been trained to jump on his shoulders and flap its wings.

They then drove northeast on a winding road through the Valley of the Kings. The path took them across the Urubamba River to the village of Pisac. It was market day. The mayor, in full ceremonial dress led a crowd to the church on the town plaza. Natives from all over the valley were there to sell their wares. Some of them had set up small stalls, while others merely spread out a blanket on the ground. The goods for sale were sometimes joined by a baby on the blanket.

Their final stop for the day was at another ancient ruin, which was carved from facing mountainsides. From that high viewpoint they had a commanding view of the many miles of the Urubamba Valley. Directly across from their viewpoint were the remains of several pre Columbian Inca astrological observatories. They learned from a local

453

guide that the Incas relied heavily on their astrologers to tell them when to plant their crops.

It had been a long, tiring day. The officers and Sgt. Blanco plopped into the overstuffed heavy leather chairs in the hotel lobby. Brightly colored native rugs partially covering glaze tile floors. Lining the walls were large antique oil paintings. Chairs in the comfortable lobby of the hotel faced the warm fireplace. The large room was decorated with warm colors. Dominating this meeting area was a large wrought iron chandelier which bore dozens of candles.

Lt Delgado suggested that they eat dinner at an outdoor restaurant on the Plaza de Armas, called

"*El Meson*." They all ordered the house specialty, the "Parilla Plate," which included broiled steak, chicken, lamb, sausages and fried potatoes. There was enough food on each plate to feed three or four individuals.

As they walked back to the hotel Sub. Lt. Cazoria said "Sir, we haven't seen any protestors all day."

. . .

"Gentlemen, our vacation is over. Today we are going to visit the El Dorado Silver mine. We will take a tour to inspect the mine and storage facilities and copy the records. We will compare what we receive in the next two days with the records from the past few years. The last five years reflect no inventory shrinkage.

They arrived back at the naval base on the evening of August 14, 1782.

CHAPTER 142

Inspecting the Lima Navy Base

August 15, 1782

Eduardo and the staff reported to their assigned offices in the headquarters building to begin sorting through and copying the pertinent records. Admiral Zepeda stepped into their office midmorning and introduced Marine Captain Rodolfo Soto, who would serve as their guide around the navy base. They agreed to meet at the main entrance at 1:30 p.m. for the tour.

"Sir, since it's a warm day, I thought a carriage would be more practical than a coach for our tour. As they drove off, Sgt. Blanco was sitting next to the driver. There were two other warships in port, the *Santa Maria* and the *Impulse* having already cast off for Acapulco. The marine area included headquarters, barracks, mess hall, armory, stables, wagon shed, brig, and firing range. They passed the navy barracks, mess hall, dispensary, chapel, auditorium, NCO club, harbormaster, and special services.

When they approached the warehouses, Eduardo had the coach stop. "Let's go through the warehouse where the gold and silver ore are stored pending shipment. The gold was in a large safe that was housed in a locked fenced-in area of the warehouse. The silver ore was stored in open wheeled metal carts. There were two guards assigned around the clock – one in front and one in the rear.

When the base tour was completed, Eduardo said, "It must be 5:00 somewhere. Why don't you gentlemen join me at the Officer's Club for a drink?" He asked the two marine officers to join them. It was "sing along" night at the club. A pianist played all the well-known songs to the accompaniment of officers singing who drank too much, while the O Club made money. The entire group decided to eat hot sandwiches from the bar.

About 10:00 p.m. Eduardo said, "Gentlemen, I am going to call it an evening. We depart for the gold mines tomorrow at 9:00 a.m., hangovers and all."

CHAPTER 143

Pierna Mine

Muraz, Peru

August 16-28, 1782

Before Eduardo and his staff had landed in Peru, they had already analyzed the records of the mines and discovered that there was widespread pilfering.

Their caravan left Lima on August 16th. It was a day's ride north along the coast to the town of Muraz, where the staff and marine officers found rooms at a local inn. The marines set up camp on a nearby field. A mile west was the gold mine *Pierina*.

The next morning Eduardo and his staff met with the *Pierina* mine manager. They were given a tour of the mine and the storage area for the gold. They obtained copies of all journals which kept up with daily production and receipts for delivery of gold to Lima.

The following day Eduardo, his staff, and the marines traveled further north to the coastal town of Trujillo. There were four gold mines in the suburbs of Trujillo: *Yanacocha, Shahuindo, La Arena* and *Lagunas Norte*. At each mine the procedure was the same: they obtained copies of documentation of daily production and copies of all bills of lading for shipments to the Lima mint. At each mine Eduardo obtained the manager and foreman thoughts about process from mine to the mint.

CHAPTER 144

Cocos Island

Off the west coast of Costa Rica

August 22, 1782

Cocos Island is about 300 nautical miles southwest from Costa Rica and 500 nautical miles northeast of the Galapagos. The island is inhabited by fewer than 1,000 people, including the natives. Perhaps half of the European community on the island are pirates or they are among the innkeepers and tavern keepers who supply pirates with food, drink and women. Cocos Island has been the subject of many articles written about pirates and buried treasure.

Sitting at the corner table of the *Lettuce and Grub* tavern was Captain Bennett Graham. Graham had been a Captain in the English Navy, until he had been caught, tried and convicted for theft in Kingston, Jamaica. He was stripped of his rank, and while in formation, all his gold buttons were cut from his uniform. His associates had broken him out of Kingston jail.

Based upon his education, training and experience when combined with his criminal record, the only job available to him was piracy. He and his confederates overpowered the crew of a 28 gun two masted sloop in port and began a new life in Colon, Panama. For years they lived off the gold and silver captured from Spanish ships sailing from Vera Cruz to Havana. The Spanish had started sending armed escorts with the treasure ships, even reverting to including them in protected convoys. Captain Graham had lost two of his pirate ships and over 20 of his sailors. It was rumored that he had buried treasure on Cocos Island.

Graham, about 50, had grown a long beard, much of it white. His deep set blue eyes were shadowed by bushy eyebrows. Hair grew wildly from inside his nose and from his ears. His teeth were crooked and yellow. His face was tan and wrinkled from long exposure to weather.

The man sitting to Graham's left was the Portuguese Benito Bonito, who had specialized in raiding coastal villages from California to Columbia. Bonito was short, fat and ugly. There was absolutely nothing attractive about him. Even his clothes were dirty. His teeth were also crooked and yellow. His breath smelled like a latrine.

On his right was Jolly Jim Sitgrave, the notorious pirate from Edinburgh, Scotland. Sitgrave was the son of a prostitute who had no idea who was his sperm donor. He grew up on the streets. He had been arrested from larceny and shipped to the American colonies for imprisonment. He and the other prisoners took over the British warship and turned it into a pirate ship. His nickname was because as the British officers were required to walk the plank, he laughed at the death of each. Clearly, Jolly Jim was a sociopath.

These three men each had their own pirate ship and crew. "Captain, I was in Acapulco last year when one of the Spanish treasure ships arrived from Peru. It was sailing alone. With our three ships we should have no trouble in capturing it and divvying up the treasures aboard," said Captain Bonito.

Jolly Jim, chimed in, "And they must stop about midway from Lima to Acapulco for food and water and to let the crew get off and get drunk. There are only two groups of islands that meet that description: The Galapagos and here. The Galapagos has only water and animals for food.

The only place they can get water, fresh fruits and vegetables is here."

Finally, Captain Graham spoke. "Gentlemen, I propose that we just sit here until the next Treasure ship arrives. The day after it arrives the three of us leave port and wait for the treasure ship to depart and then attack at night. We should all be rich the following day.

CHAPTER 145

Lima Mint

Lima, Peru

August 29, 1782

When Eduardo's staff reviewed the records of the Lima mint, they found no apparent irregularities. Their main task was to compare the records of how much gold was shipped from the mines and how much was received by the mint. Secondly, a comparison was made of the coins minted versus the number of coins shipped. With the exception of a couple of irregularities there appeared to be no embezzlement or pilfering.

Eduardo's only suggestion was to increase security to avoid theft.

CHAPTER 146

Navy Base

Lima, Peru

August 30 – September 10, 1782

Eduardo penned his report and recommendations to King Carlos:

Your Royal Majesty

HRM Carlos, III de Borbon

Catholic King of Spain Re: Report on Lima, Peru

Your Majesty.

First let me report that over the past five years we found no irregularities in the El Dorado silver mine. My staff and I toured the mine, reviewed their procedures and analyzed their documentation and compared it with the Navy Base warehouse and found no discrepancies. Accordingly, we are not making any suggestions for change.

In analyzing the documentation for the past five years for the five gold mines, we found that pilfering accounted for almost one-half million Reales loss per year. When we visited each of those mines, we discovered that the amount of gold mined was less than five years ago, yet working hours were the same.

After careful consideration I suggest the following:

1.   Establish two locker rooms for miners.

2. Require all miners to undress in locker room #1.

3. Require all miners to walk naked through the shower.

4. Require all miners to wear uniforms with no pockets stored in Locker Room #2.

5. Require all miners to leave their uniform in locker room #2 after work.

6. After undressing, they'll be required to shampoo their hair and shower.

7. Before entering locker room #1 they open their mouth in front of a guard who will inspect the interior of his mouth and ears for concealed gold. The miner would then be required to bend over and spread his buttock for an inspection.

8. After showering they go into locker room #1, where they put on their personal clothes.

9. Offer a substantial reward for any employee who sees another swallowing or concealing a piece of gold.

10. Lunches must be brought to the mine in a paper bag. The bag and all trash must be placed in the trash can of locker room #2.

11. Place a guard in the restroom to watch each miner to ensure that nobody swallows a piece of gold or inserts it into his rectum.

Discussion:

By requiring the wearing of a uniform, the employee is prevented from concealing gold in his clothing. The uniforms should be washed, and the dirty water filtered through fine mesh. In the mine there is dust in the air, including fine particles of gold. Over time a substantial amount of gold can be retrieved. Similarly, a mesh trap should be placed at the bottom of the shower to collect gold dust from the miner's hair and arms. The uniforms should add to the espirit de corps of the employees, a positive morale factor. Their wives will be happy that they don't have to wash the miner's clothes so often.

The remaining problem is that many miners swallow a piece of gold or insert it in their rectum. It is recommended that a high reward be offered to anyone who sees someone concealing a piece of gold and reports it. If somebody is accused but when isolated is found to have no gold in his body, he is released. To prove his innocence, he must be confined for two days. In the presence of a guard, he must spread his feces to inspect for the gold. The false accuser would be subject to a small fine.

If, however, the accuser is correct and gold is found, the accuser is paid a hefty reward. The accused is given 25 lashes in the presence of all miners and taken to jail, where he would be charged with theft. If the reward is substantially more than what a thief could smuggle, most of the miners would be on the lookout for thieves.

My final suggestion is that the Lima mint should beef up its security. Multiple guards at each

post reduces the likelihood of an inside theft.

The following nine days were busy but not stressful. Except for three group dinners, and loading the gold on their final day ashore, Eduardo gave his staff leave. He planned a dinner with his staff and the officers of the *Infinity.*

After she arrived in port on September 4th, he hosted a dinner with his staff and the officers of the *Singing lady.* On the evening before they departed Lima, he hosted a

465

reception for his staff and the officers of both ships, together with the Admiral and the two marine officers who escorted them.

They were able to spend several days at the beach with the assistance of the Officer's Club cook, who prepared lunches for them.

On a free day Eduardo went shopping. He purchased a soft alpaca sweater for Toni. At a bookstore, a block off the Plaza de Armas he purchased the 4 volumes set of *Don Quixote, The Man of La Mancha*, by Cervantes and *Observations of a Trip Around the World*, by Johann Reinhold Forster (the naturalist who accompanied Captain Cook on his voyage around the world).

At a sweet shop he purchased several kinds of hard candy. He also bought some chocolate covered marzipan. He picked up copies of the three local newspapers and one from Santiago, Chile.

When his shopping was finished, Eduardo went to confession at the enormous Cathedral on the Plaza de Armas. He confessed about his affair with Rosy. The priest gave him his way to atone, which included informing Toni about the affair with Rosy. Eduardo thought "This is something I must do in person. This is not something to discuss in a letter."

On their last day ashore, while his staff was monitoring the loading of the gold coins onto the *Singing Lady*, Eduardo was having his final meetings with the Viceroy, the Admiral and the General.

The Viceroy said, "Eduardo, I wanted you to have a souvenir to remind you of your time in our part of the world." He then handed Eduardo a shiny new 1782 2 Escudo gold coin. "Also, I have a small gift and a letter to Viceroy Galvez in Mexico City. I would greatly appreciate it if you would deliver both to him when you arrive in Mexico City."

"I am deeply honored your Excellency; I shall treasure this coin forever. *Muchas Gracias.* As Eduardo was leaving the Viceroy's office, he said to Eduardo, "*Vaya con Dios, mi amigo.*"

Eduardo thanked both the general and the admiral for their assistance. As he was leaving the admiral's office, he said, "You and your staff should keep the sidearms as you still have lots of territory to cover."

"Thanks admiral. It has been a pleasure working with you."

CHAPTER 147

Onboard Treasure ship *Singing Lady* from Lima to Acapulco

September 10, 1782

It was a beautiful Spring morning in Lima. Sea gulls flew over the *Singing Lady* and occasionally swooped down near the deck. The ship was sitting high in the water because it was only 1/3 full. As a result, they loaded live cows, goats, sheep, pigs and chickens and fresh fruit.

To enhance the ship's cargo, the supply officer purchased sheep hides, wool and alpaca cloth and sweaters, wine, coffee, and tea. This was the old version of the treasure ship. It was shorter and displaced about 2/3 the amount of water as the *Santa Maria* and had fewer guns.

"Single up all lines", ordered Commodore Justo Mireles, from the poop deck. The executive officer, Fragatta Commander Emilio Sosa was on the quarterdeck manning the gangplank.

"Welcome aboard General. Sir, If you will allow me, I will take you to your quarters. Mr.

Serna, please direct these other officers to their quarters," instructed the XO, Commander Sosa.

Eduardo's cabin was a VIP suite, but not as spacious as on the *Santa Maria*. Other than lacking a couch, it was about the same. Fernando was assigned the only other VIP suite.

At dinner that night Eduardo had an opportunity to evaluate his fellow officers:

Captain Justo Mireles was about six feet tall, who appeared to be in good shape for his 50 years. His silver hair was streaked with fine lines of black. His weathered face and hands showed that he had spent his life at sea. He had a good private education in Granada and was well read.

Fragata Captain Emilio Sosa, the XO, had just been promoted. At age 38 he was young to be XO of such a large ship. His rounded face was accented by his small protruding ears. He was about 5' 10" and slightly overweight.

Eduardo's tocayo[25] was Fragata Capitan Eduardo Suarez, the ship's doctor. He was nondescript, average height, average weight, average build. On his right forearm was a large tattoo of a caduceus on an anchor, which he got one night when drunk in port. His eyes were puffy and red. It appeared that he was an alcoholic.

Lt. Juan Serna was a 42 year old gunnery officer. He was a mustang, having worked his way through the enlisted ranks and being directly promoted for bravery in battle. He was ruggedly handsome. With little formal education he felt out of place at the officer's dinner table. Most of his leisure time was spent with the crew.

LT Antonio Segovia, the supply officer, was also newly promoted. He was a 26 year old who still looked like a teenager. His rust colored hair matched the freckles

---

[25] Spanish for a person with the same first name. In many Hispanic countries there is a special relationship between people with the same first name.

469

across his nose and cheeks. His dental hygiene was evident by looking at his clean teeth. There was not an ounce of fat on his lean body. He spoke Spanish and French.

Sub Lieutenant Augustine Zuniga, the Assistant Gunnery Officer was recently commissioned at age 20. This was his first voyage. His home was Bilbao, Spain. His mother was from Denmark, which explained his fair skin, blue eyes and blonde hair. In addition to Spanish, he spoke Danish, Swedish and Norwegian.

The ice was broken well. Because Eduardo had entertained these officers twice ashore there seemed to already be comradery at work. After dinner Fernando played his guitar to entertain the other officers.

The following day Eduardo got his staff to analyze the Lima records with those they brought with them. Since they would be at sea for months, and since there was so little to do, he asked them to devote two hours per day. After lunch he took a stroll on the deck and returned to his cabin to read. No sooner than he had hung up his coat and sat in his easy chair to read than he heard a commotion on deck.

He opened the hatch to the quarterdeck to see two seamen fighting. Other crewmen pulled them apart. One of them broke away and ran through the hatch to the crew's quarters. Moments later the crewman returned to the quarterdeck wielding a large knife. Before anybody could intervene, he had stabbed the first crewman in the heart. When Dr. Suarez arrived, he pronounced Seaman Juan De Siva dead.

Commodore Mireles ordered that the knife wielder, seaman Pablo Ruiz be locked in the brig. After dinner that night the Captain announced that there would be a burial at sea the following day, and asked Lt. Segovia to organize it. He also announced that he would conduct a court martial for seaman Ruiz. "I will serve as chief judge and the two senior officers General Lopez and Colonel Garcia will also serve as judges. Commander Sosa, you will run the ship during the trial. Also, notify the Master at Arms that he must be in attendance. LT Serna, you will serve as the prosecutor. Lt Segovia, you will be defense counsel.

The trial will commence on September 14, 1782 in these quarters at 10:00 a.m.

The next two days LT. Serna was talking with the witnesses about their respective testimony. LT Segovia was scratching his head trying to come up with a defense for seaman Ruiz.

CHAPTER 148

Burial at Sea

Aboard the *Singing Lady*

September 12, 1782

Burial at sea is a solemn ceremony. The deceased's remains are bound in sail cloth which is stitched together. By custom, the last stich is through nose to insure he is really dead. His body is placed on a board. His remains were covered with a Spanish flag. The crew was assembled, and all other activities were halted. All hats were removed. First there was a eulogy by a crewmate. The Eulogy was followed by a prayer by Commodore Mirales:

And I saw the dead, great and small, standing before the throne. And there were open books, and one of them was the Book of Life. And the dead were judged according to their deeds, as recorded in the books. The sea gave up its dead, and Death and Hades gave up their dead, and each one was judged according to his deeds. Then Death and Hades were thrown into the lake of fire. This is the second death—the lake of fire....

After a moment of silence there was a three gun salute. The officers and crew came to attention and saluted. The side boys holding the body tilted the board upward and allowed the body to slide into the sea.

CHAPTER 149

Murder Trial

Aboard the *Singing Lady*

September 14, 1782

Commodore Mirelis sat at the end of the table with the other two judges seated to his left and right. The defendant sat at the other end of the table with his lawyer to his right. Standing behind the defendant was the Master of Arms, who was wearing a sidearm.

As each witness came into the room they were sworn. Each of three crewmen testified they witnessed the stabbing, and that it was seaman Ruiz who stabbed seaman De Silva.

LT Zuniga testified that when he apprehended seaman Ruiz, he still had the bloody knife in his hand.

Dr. Suarez testified that the knife wound was the cause of death.

When the prosecution rested, LT Segovia called seaman Ruiz to testify. He was sworn in by the captain.

"Seaman Ruiz, why did you kill seaman De Silva," asked LT Segovia?

"Sir, we wuz arguin. He said my wife wuz a hore. Sir, that's not rite. I cudden't let him get away with that," responded Ruiz.

"Anything more from the defendant, LT Segovia," asked the captain?

"No sir, the defense rests."

"Very well. Everybody left the courtroom except the judges. Master at arms, take the prisoner back to the brig."

This was a fairly simple case. All three judges found the accused guilty. All hands were mustered to witness punishment. The Captains read the charges and specifications against the accused and announces the verdict. The convicted seaman was hung from the yardarm.

Commodore Mireles continued the custom of inviting the officers of the escort ship to dinner on Saturday nights. All four officers of the *Infinity* were fascinated to learn of the murder, burial at sea, court martial and hanging. Their only excitement had been the spotting of a pod of whales frolicking in the ocean. Fernando played his guitar for an hour after dinner, while the wine flowed.

At dinner that night there was a discussion among the officers as to whether a murderer was entitled to a Christian burial? After a lengthy discussion it was agreed that it was a premeditated murder for which the accused showed no remorse. His body was tossed overboard unceremoniously during the dog watch.

Seaman hanging from ship's yardarm !

CHAPTER 150

Crossing Equator ceremony

Aboard the *Singing Lady*

September 20, 1782

Since the hanging the weather had been blustery. The ship's movements made it difficult to walk on the deck. It was weather like this that caused ship's tables to be made with a large lip around the edge that prevents plates from sliding onto the deck.

By signal flags Commodore Mirales had ordered the *Infinity* to pull alongside so that tadpoles from both crews could be initiated. For about two hours, the crew had their fun with the newbies on the deck. Each ship has its own way of initiating its crewmen. This crew set up a plank. Crew members were blindfolded and forced to walk the plank.

After all the tadpoles were in the water, the remainder of the crew of both ships except the sharpshooters enjoyed a crew swim.

These activities helped get the crew's mind off the murder and hanging. The crew was given double beer rations.

Later that evening one could hear singing in the crew quarters.

. . .

Commodore Mirales had ordered that the crews of both ships have a fire drill, an abandon ship drill and a gun drill. For the gun drill, *Infinity* towed a target for the

Singing Lady, and she in turn towed a target for *Infinity*.

CHAPTER 151

Pirate attack

Aboard the *Singing Lady*

October 15, 1782

The tropical weather had been sultry. The hot muggy days had been cooled by almost daily tropical showers. It was one of those days. The afternoon shower was welcomed. They were scheduled to make port at Cocos Island the next day.

Commodore Mirales was not new to this route. He knew that pirates sometimes used Cocos Island as a base. By flag message he instructed the *Infinity* to lay back over the horizon and not enter port until the following day.

. . .

The following day the *Singing Lady* entered port alone. The crew were given leave while the supply officer planned for food, water and supplies. That afternoon, at different times the three pirate ships left port. Seeing no escort, they assumed that capture of the treasure ship would be easy. They assumed that the treasure ship would set a direct course for Acapulco, which would be 335 degrees. They decided to follow that course for 25 nautical miles and then sail over the horizon to both port and starboard. Each ship would put a lookout in the crow's next to keep lookout for it. Once spotted they would attack.

. . .

The following day the *Infinity* entered port to secure food and water. Her crew was also given leave.

. . .

On October 19th, the Spanish ships departed Cocos Island separately on a heading of 335 degrees bound for Acapulco.

. . .

On the afternoon of October 21st, another tropical rainstorm began, cooling the clammy day. Visibility was limited. The pirate ship *Graham's Folly* was nearby before it was spotted on the starboard bow. At about that time the *La Tormenta* also came into view off the starboard beam.

The *Black Shark* had misjudged and was approaching from the port side trying to catch up with the *Singing Lady*. All three pirate ships were flying the Jolly Roger, but no two flags were alike. As the *Black Shark* sought to get into position to fire at the *Singing Lady*, she was hit by three cannonballs from Infinity. One ball ripped a hole in the mainsail. One ball severed the mainmast, and the other was deadly. It hit the *Black Shark* at the waterline and water began gushing in.

Neither Pirate Captain Bennett Graham nor Captain Binito Bonito had seen the *Infinity*. They both assumed that the *Black Shark* had been hit by the *Singing Lady*. In their minds it was still two to one, so they continued their attack. For the next 20 minutes the three ships exchanged gunfire. *Infinity* had still not gotten the other two pirate ships in its range but was coming up fast.

The *Singing Lady* had fired its port guns and was making a turn to port to make its starboard guns bear toward the pirates. While it was making its turn, there was an explosion onboard *La Tormenta*. A fire raged on the deck which must have been near the gunpowder storage area because its crew members were jumping overboard. Its Captain was standing on the poop deck waving his sword. He was madder than a mule chewing bumble bees.

Looking to the right coming through the rain from the northeast with guns blazing was the 38 gun Galleon *Fortitude*. Captain Graham saw that he was now outnumbered and headed due west through the rainstorm.

Captain Macias of the *Fortitude* ordered the signalman to send the following flag message to the *Singing Lady*:

"*You are buying!*"

Eduardo had the signalman on the *Singing Lady* to signal *Fortitude* to board and take control of the disabled pirate ship, which was to be its prize. He ordered *Infinity* to lay alongside *La Tormenta* and to assist *Fortitude* in coming up with a crew to sail the captured ship. He ordered that carpenters begin making repairs. He instructed officers of both war ships to join him for dinner aboard the *Singing lady* at 7:00 p.m.

At dinner he thanked the crew of the *Fortitude* for pulling their chestnuts out of the fire. Upon questioning him he discovered that the captured pirate ship was sailable. He ordered the *Fortitude* to join his convoy, which now included a captured pirate ship.

"In Acapulco, it will be my honor to buy you all not just a drink, but the best dinner in town, with all you want to drink," promised Eduardo.

CHAPTER 152

Typhoon Near Acapulco

Aboard the *Singing Lady*

November 1, 1782

At sunrise on November 16, 1782 the Officer of the Deck spotted a massive storm to the southeast. The barometer was dropping fast. The sustained wind was already at 30 knots, with gusts up to 40 knots. He immediately awoke the commodore. They watched the movement of the storm, which seemed to be moving due north. Commodore Mireles identified the storm as a typhoon, which usually remain in the western Pacific.

"Helmsman, come left to 310 degrees," shouted the commodore. Signalman, notify the convoy to come left to 310 degrees. As they sailed away from the tempest, the wind subsided, and the seas calmed.

By noon, the storm was due east of the convoy about 40 miles and still moving due north. By 6:00 p.m. the storm was to the northeast and no longer a threat.

"Helmsman, make your course 360 degrees. Signalman, notify the convoy to come right to 360 degrees.

. . .

The remainder of the trip to Acapulco was uneventful.

. . .

On their last night at sea, they were joined by the officers of both the *Infinity* and the *Fortitude* and the officers operating the pirate ship for a gala dinner onboard the

481

Singing Lady. They talked and laughed and listened to the guitar of Colonel Garcia. Before the happy group adjourned, Eduardo offered a toast to the officers of the three ships: "May you each enjoy smooth sailing, fair winds, and following seas."

Each officer knew that these new friends may never be seen again. That's just part of military life.

CHAPTER 153

Arrive Acapulco

November 16, 1782

As they entered Acapulco Bay, Eduardo and his staff were all glad to see Acapulco. It represented the end to countless days at sea for a while; an end to monotonous food at sea; and the addition of all the varieties of life on land. They all hoped there would be mail from home for them.

As their ships tied up at the navy pier Eduardo could see that Admiral Contreras had already followed his recommendation that extra security be positioned inside and around the warehouse.

Eduardo had three letters from Toni. Toni reported that Bernardo was to be a father. She told in detail of Bernardo's involvement in sending military supplies up the Mississippi to George Washington. She mentioned Chris's visit on his return from Vera Cruz. Much of the letter was spent telling Eduardo how much she had been missing him; how boring it was just sitting around and meeting with the other wives a couple of times per week. She gave him news of the American Revolution and news from Spain. In each letter she expressed her undying love for him.

Eduardo also received a letter from Viceroy Galvez:

Dear Eduardo,

We followed your suggestions and found that the Mint Manager had a mistress. He had purchased a small

483

house for her and was supporting her. Because he was spending so much time with the mistress, he had to give expensive gifts to his wife. The Mint Manager worked a deal with the mint garbage man, who made pick-ups at 9:00 at night, when the mint was closed, and no other employees were present. Whenever the garbage man picked up garbage on the loading dock in the rear, the manager would put four cartons of newly minted Reales in the garbage wagon. The guard was stationed between the foundry and the mint and thought nothing of the garbage wagon coming and going. Of the four million Reales missing, the government should be able to recover half by selling of the manager's home, his mistress's home and all the jewelry, etc. Thank you for your assistance in plugging the leak. Plan on joining my wife and me for dinner on your return.

There was a letter from the king:

Dear General,

Thank you for your periodic reports. You are to be commended for not only discovering the embezzlement from the Mexico City mint but devising the plan to catch the thief. You have prevented an annual loss of 2,000,000 Livres per year. Viceroy Galvez advises me that we will be able to recover almost half our loss.

I look forward to your safe return and the receipt of your final report.

HRM Carlos, III de Borbon, Catholic King of Spain

Eduardo also had letters from both Bernardo and Chris. Each of them sought to bring Eduardo up to date on their respective activities.

. . .

The officers of the *Singing Lady* and the *Fortitude* gave him mail to deliver to Vera Cruz for transshipment to Spain, via Havana.

CHAPTER 154

Reviewing shipment procedures

Acapulco, Mexico

November 17, 1782

As the gold and silver was unloaded and stored in the secure Acapulco navy base storage area Eduardo's staff was copying the documentation as it was being created. Their plan was to finish up in Acapulco and to travel with the donkey train from Acapulco to Mexico City.

Admiral Contreras was asked to join the dinner party at Antonio's Restaurant, Acapulco's newest and finest restaurant. Eduardo presented medals to the officers of the *Singing Lady*, the *Fortitude,* and the *Infinity* as well as his staff for their excellence. Eduardo had arranged for Mariachi's to serenade them all evening.

. . .

The next two days was spent unloading the *Singing Lady* and Eduardo's staff kept copying documents as they were created. Eduardo's staff took another two days to compare the documents reflecting how much was received with those created in Lima of what was being shipped. They were all satisfied that there were no irregularities. Eduardo completed his report that evening.

CHAPTER 155

Acapulco Navy Base

Acapulco, Mexico

November 21, 1782

Eduardo's final duty in Acapulco was to provide Admiral Contreras with a copy of his report to the king related to Acapulco's involvement and to get him to assign a Marine platoon to escort the donkey train to Mexico City.

Admiral Contreras was delighted to see Eduardo. He asked Eduardo about his transpacific crossing, his time in the Philippines, his voyage back across the Pacific and his time in Peru. The two men talked for over an hour. The admiral briefed Eduardo on the security changes he had implemented at Eduardo's suggestion.

Eduardo informed Admiral Contreras that he would be leaving with the donkey train the next morning and inquired the names of the Marine officers that would escort them to Mexico City.

"The platoon is commanded by Lieutenant Rodolfo Mayor. His Assistant Platoon Leader is Sub Lieutenant Rafael Mendoza," reported the admiral.

. . .

"Gentlemen, this is probably the last decent meal we will be served until we get to Mexico City next week," said Colonel Garcia. We've been on the way home since we left Manila. We all can now see the rainbow leading us to New Orleans."

CHAPTER 156

Donkey Train from Acapulco to Mexico City

November 22 – 31, 1782

 The donkey train was uneventful except for the buzzing mosquitoes. Eduardo was bothered by chills and fever along the way.

It was not necessary to stop in Taxco on this trip except to add a dozen donkeys ladened with silver ore heading to the foundry in Mexico City.

Eduardo's staff looked forward to stopping for the night in Cuernavaca. They remembered the great La Posada restaurant. Neither of the Marine officers had eaten there before. A great meal was had by all.

CHAPTER 157

Mexico City, Mexico

Dec. 1, 1782

Upon their arrival in Mexico City, Eduardo gave the Marine Platoon liberty for a week, assuming that his business in the capital would be finished by then.

His first order of business was a meeting with the Mint Director. After a brief tour of the foundry, mint, and storage areas, Eduardo's staff began pouring over the records created since they were last in Mexico City.

The director informed Eduardo that the manager had been arrested and was awaiting trial for embezzlement. Both his home and that of his mistress had been seized and sold at public auction. His wife's jewelry had also been confiscated and was now being appraised.

His staff spent the next three days evaluating the recent records of the mint and were satisfied that there was no further theft from the mint. While Eduardo was in the city, the gold coins were stored at the mint.

Next, Eduardo had arranged a meeting with Viceroy Galvez.

"First, your Excellency, I bring a note to you from Viceroy Augustine de Jaurequi of Lima," announced Eduardo.

After Viceroy Garza read his note, he said to Eduardo, "You made a very good impression on Viceroy Jaurequi. He has asked me to join him in recommending to King Carlos that you be considered for an Ambassadorship or

489

some other high post. Apparently, the ship you sailed on from Lima to Acapulco carried a letter from the Viscount to the king making that recommendation. I guess that means that the letter is among the mail you have been carrying on your donkey train and will carry with you to Vera Cruz," he said with a crooked smile. "I am impressed with your intelligence and your efforts, and will gladly join the Viceroy. I will have a letter to King Carlos, seconding your nomination in your mail pouch when you depart.

The two men went over Eduardo's final recommendations:

1.   Close the entrance to the foundry road. Maintain only one entrance for the foundry and the mint.

2.   Maintain a full time gate guard 24/7. He must inspect the inside of each coach, carriage, wagon or cart exiting the mint to ensure that no bullion is being carried away.

3.   Place a permanent Guard Station at the rear entrance to the mint.

4.   Establish a roving patrol inside the mint.

5.   Establish a Sergeant of the Guard positioned in the lobby of the main building.

CHAPTER 158

Mexico City

Treatment in the hospital for malaria.

December 7-19, 1782

Eduardo's "Shaking sickness" had attacked him again. One minute he was wringing wet from sweat, while the next minute he was shivering from being chilled. His headaches were so unbearable he was confined in the military hospital in Mexico City for 12 days treatment.

Viscount Galvez visited him on December 18th.

"Eduardo, I have spoken with your doctor. You will be dismissed tomorrow. I want you to be my guest at the royal palace for at least until after Christmas. My Christmas day gala will be in your honor. Invite your staff – even Sgt. Blanco, and the two young marines whose platoon escorted you here."

"On Christmas Eve, I am entertaining all the government officials for a private dinner. On the 23rd my wife and I will be hosting the senior military officers in the area for dinner. On the 21st we have invited all the business and religious leaders to a dinner party at the palace."

"Because I want to introduce you to all these important people, I forbid you to leave before the day after Christmas," said the Viscount, as he patted Eduardo on his shoulder with a smile on his face.

. . .

Eduardo moved into the Royal Palace on the 19th. The next day he took a carriage to town and purchased *Les Liaisons Dangereuses,* a French novel by Pierre Choderlos de Laclos, which had been published in four volumes in March 1782. He purchased his required quota of hard candy and newspapers from Mexico City.

CHAPTER 159

Christmas Gala. Eduardo the guest of honor.

Governor's Mansion

Mexico City, Mexico

Dec. 25, 1782

Eduardo had enjoyed the luxury of living in the royal palace. Every few minutes a servant asked if he needed anything. Because for over a year he had been living aboard cramped ships or on military bases he enjoyed being spoiled. He enjoyed the lavish parties thrown by the Viceroy.

On Christmas Day the priest from the Cathedral said mass in the palace chapel. Festivities started early. Children of high ranking civilian officers were brought to the Royal Palace to meet with Santa Claus. Santa sat next to a giant decorated Christmas tree. Each child received a wrapped gift and a piece of candy. For lunch the children had the option of eating several foods that were not good for them, but which they enjoyed, followed by a table of pastries.

While the children were eating the adults had a choice of *huevos*[26] *huevos, rancheros, huevos benedictos or huevos revueltos,* with bacon, ham and sausage. The bar was open all day. The children were entertained by clowns, jugglers, ventriloquists, and magicians. Before the children were taken home, they were offered a pony ride around the palace.

---

[26] Eggs.

The evening guests began arriving about 6:00 P.M. The palace was illuminated by thousands of candles. Five candelabras illuminated the dining room, together with the candles on the dining room tables, the hearths of both fireplaces and the side tables. Poinsettias and holly were used to decorate with the Christmas spirit. The light from those candles was magnified by mirrors strategically place throughout. A string quartet played on the balcony over the banquet hall. Roaring fires were at both ends of the hall, in fireplaces that were tall enough for a man to walk into without bending over.

As the guest of honor, Eduardo stood next to the Viscount, and his staff by rank stood to his right. As each guest entered, the Viscount introduced Eduardo and his staff, including Sgt. Blanco. After all the guests had been introduced to the guests of honor, an announcement was made that dinner was served. Liveried footmen stood behind the table to serve each guest.

Before the guests were served, Viceroy Galvez offered a toast to Eduardo, his staff and the two Marine officers. Afterwards, Eduardo offered a toast to King Carlos.

The group assembled ate like royalty. For entrees they could choose between ham, turkey, beef steak, and tuna. Vegetables included potatoes, sweet potatoes, carrots, cucumber, jicama, green beans, and tomatoes. Dozens of types of homemade breads were available with butter and cheese. There were so many choices of desserts each diner was asked to get up, go to the dessert table and select their own dessert.

At 9:00 p.m. the party moved from the dining room to the ballroom, which was also brightly illuminated and contained another beautifully decorated Christmas tree.

At the far end of the ballroom a full orchestra began playing dance music.

Eduardo was still not 100% physically, so he said good night to the Viceroy and his wife about 11:00 p.m. while the party was still in full swing.

Eduardo's group and the donkey convoy was scheduled to depart Mexico City for Vera Cruz on December 27th. A separate donkey train from the mint with minted coins joined the convoy.

He wondered what Toni had done for Christmas. He pondered if she missed him as much as he missed her. His thoughts also were about Toni, the love of his life.

CHAPTER 160

Coach and Donkey train

from Mexico City to Vera Cruz, Mexico

December 27, 1782 - January 7, 1783

Glad to be back in a coach after days on horseback over mountainous terrain, Eduardo was in good spirits as they departed Mexico City. "One step closer to home," he thought.

Even though it was winter, the Mexican jungle was hot and humid. The donkeys were making better time on the road than on the steep mountain trails.

They arrived in Vera Cruz on New Year's day. They had missed the celebration the night before. They learned that they would have to spend a week in Vera Cruz waiting on the treasure ship *Reliable* to arrive, unload, load and depart.

They stored the silver, gold and other valuables at the Navy storage facility. The Marine platoon camped out near the warehouse.

Eduardo and his staff had time on their hands. He hired a guide to take them on an overnight trip to see the Tajin prehistoric ruins. They borrowed tents, cots, etc. from the Marines.

When they returned to Vera Cruz on January 4, the *Reliable* had already made port and was unloading its cargo. Three days later it was loaded and ready to depart.

Eduardo reassigned his Marine escort to accompany the donkey train carrying the cargo of the

Reliable back to Mexico City. He thanked them for their service.

CHAPTER 161

Voyage from Vera Cruz to New Orleans

Aboard the *Reliable*

January 8, 1783 – January 28, 1783

Eduardo could not believe that he and his men were on the final leg of their year and one-half expedition. He looked forward to spending time with Toni, and long talks with Bernardo. He wondered if he would hear from Chris soon. Over the next 20 days he

1. finalized his report to King Carlos and sent copies to both Viceroy Galvez and Viceroy de Jaurequi and kept a copy for Bernardo.

2. prepared efficiency reports on his officers, recommending each for promotion.

3. granted his staff 30 days leave.

4. prepared efficiency reports on the two groups of Marine officers who escorted them.

5. prepared efficiency reports on the officers of all the ships that had carried him or escorted his vessel.

6. promoted Sgt. Blanco to master sergeant.

7. wrote a long letter to Chris, bringing him up to date on his travels.

8. made a list of things to do when he returned to New Orleans.

CHAPTER 162

Arrival in New Orleans

January 25 - 28, 1783

Eduardo was impatient. The *Reliable* had turned into the Mississippi River three days ago, and they still had three days to go before docking in New Orleans. When he arrived in Vera Cruz, he had dispatched a letter to Toni advising her of his travel plans, but it was unlikely that she had already received it. The weather was cold and overcast. The wind aggravated the cold.

. . .

As the *Reliable* edged near the assigned pier Eduardo found no familiar faces. No one was there to meet him or any of the other members of his staff. They said their good-byes to the officers of the *Reliable* and boarded a coach. It took a few minutes to secure all their luggage, including Eduardo's strong box.

Rank has its privileges, so Eduardo was dropped off at his home first. Sgt. Blanco helped him with his luggage to the front door. He knocked. Toni was stunned – for many seconds she looked at Eduardo in Amazement. Was it really him?

Following her shock, she laughed and with both hands reached up and pulled his face down to her and kissed him on the lips passionately.

"Darling, it's been over a year and one-half since you left. I have so much to tell you. But I want to hear about where you have been and what you have been doing. I loved your detailed letters. They helped me justify in my mind because it was so important to the king for you to be gone so long. Sweetheart, please promise me you will never leave me for so long ever again, please," Toni demanded.

"Tomorrow I will go to the office. I'm sure Bernardo will have a million questions and I have copies of my report to the king for him. I'm sure he will have a new position for me. I gave my staff 30 days leave. I'm hoping that the two of us can slip off to Havana for a few weeks to bask in the sun, drink rum on the beach, take naps and have dinners with music. How does that sound, sweetheart," he asked?

"If we can step into the bedroom, I have something I wish to discuss with you that has been bothering me since you left," she said as she tugged at his shirt and motioned with her fingers to follow her.

. . .

"I love your darling." "I love you, too."

CHAPTER 163

Office of the Governor General

New Orleans, Louisiana

January 29, 1783 –

"The world traveler returns," said Bernardo to his friend Eduardo. Are you any wiser," asked Bernardo?

"I'm older, I'm more experienced, and I am tired of traveling," replied Eduardo.

"Before we talk, I would think you would first want to read my report to King Carlos," said Eduardo as he passed the document to Bernardo. It took Bernando about five minutes to read the report.

"Lalo, King Carlos is already very pleased that you were not only able to direct the Mexico City Mint embezzlement investigation, but that your plan broke up what had been a 2,000,000 theft each year, and that you directed the recoupment of almost half the loss. That alone would be enough to ensure that you'll have a good position for the remainder of your life."

"Then, day before yesterday I got a letter from my uncle, the Viceroy of New Spain telling me that he had received a letter from the Viceroy of Peru asking him to join in recommending you for an ambassadorship or other high office. Looks like I may be the one saluting you in the near future."

"Any idea of what you would like to do now that your back," asked Bernardo.

"I gave my crew 30 days leave and I was talking last night to Toni about spending some time on Havana's beaches and eating to the tune of a Cuban band. So, when you can do without me, we would like to vacation in Havana."

"By the way, here is the money chest I been carrying half-way around the world. There is a receipt for each expenditure. I had money enough for about 14 months' salary for me and my staff, but each of us is owed about three month's pay.

"What would you like for me to do," asked Eduardo.

"I want you at my house tonight at 7:00 for dinner with me and Felicite. Tomorrow, I want you to take Toni to the best dress shop in New Orleans and buy her some new clothes, shoes, hats, etc. This coming Saturday there will be a reception, dinner and dance in your honor and that of your staff. The remainder of the week I don't want to see you.

"You are now the Liaison Officer between me and the Governor General of Cuba. You and Toni are to be on the next ship to Havana. You are on official business, so I will present you with a different money chest for your expenses. For your first 30 days I want you to reconnoiter Havana. Your leave will not begin until your first full day in Havana. To do your job properly, you must investigate every beach, every bar, every night club, and every restaurant. I want you to be in top physical shape, so you are instructed to avoid stress, sleep late, take naps and drink too much.

"After your first 30 days you are to report to the Governor General and request that he assign you an office suite and staff. If he gives you any problem, I will send you your recent staff. You and Toni are to continue checking out the beaches, clubs and restaurants around Cuba."

Finally, it will be your responsibility to organize the meeting of "The Warriors" at a resort in Havana.

"I have a stack of musty old newspapers from around the world. Shall I bring them with me tonight," asked Eduardo?

CHAPTER 164

Guarico, Haiti

February 24, 1783

General Bernardo de Galvez and 10,000 Spanish troops were on standby in Guarico, Haiti waiting to invade England's last possession in the Caribbean. Additional Spanish troops were being marshalled at the port in Cadiz, Spain, awaiting orders to sail to the Caribbean.

General Galvez had already been designated as the overall commander of the invading forces. It

was this imminent threat of the loss of British holdings in the West Indies that forced the English to sign the peace treaty.

CHAPTER 165

Edenton, North Carolina

May 6, 1783

Sara had been enjoying Chris at home. With his new customers in Spain and France, Chris's empire was growing. He was now operating 15 ships. All of his new captains were required to speak English, French and Spanish. His gift shops were expanding into department stores and his warehouses were doubling in size. Chris gave more responsibility to his younger brother Joseph, who ran the day to day operation.

With the war almost over, Chris felt that there would be a need for luxury passenger ships to transport people to the Caribbean tropical islands for a vacation. He had been spending his spare time working with a nautical architect to draw plans for a cruise ship. Chris's idea was not to just deliver the passenger to a tourist destination. He wanted to make the cruise the vacation. His plan was to stop at an island, row the passengers ashore, give them a tour of the island, have a picnic lunch on the beach with native entertainment; followed by a nice dinner onboard to the musical accompaniment of a small orchestra. Other passengers might prefer to sit around a roaring bonfire on the beach. Chris already had a toe hold on all the French and Spanish islands in the Caribbean.

"Darling, a letter has come for you. Looks like it's from your friend Eduardo," said Sara.

Chris opened the letter:

March 28, 1783

Dear Fellow Warrior,

As you know I returned to New Orleans a few months ago. Bernie has me as his liaison to the Governor General in Havana. He also assigned me to plan our next meeting of the Warriors. I hope you and Sara can join us in Havana from July 1- July 8, 1783. Our reservations are at the luxurious Half-Moon Bay resort.

Warm regards,

Eduardo

Chris passed the letter to Sara for her to read.

"Sweetheart, how would you like to go to Havana," Chris asked?

"You know, I think a cruise to the tropics would be great. I am more interested in meeting your friends and their wives."

Chris looked at a shipping journal for a few minutes. "We have a ship departing Philadelphia in late May bound for New Orleans that would get us to Havana on June 29th. When it arrives in Edenton, on June 6th, we can occupy the VIP suite. We would stop in Charleston, Savannah, and

Nassau. We would be dropped off in Havana and be picked up after our ship makes a run to

New Orleans and back."

CHAPTER 166

Edenton, North Carolina

Aboard the *Sara*

June 6, 1783

How fitting that Sara's first ride on one of her husband's ships would be on the ship named for her. The *Sara* was the newest and largest in the fleet. The Captain was one of Chris's first masters, Captain Henry "Hank" Simmons. Hank had owned a small coastal cargo ship until it was confiscated by the English for evading taxes. He was about 40 years old with salt and pepper hair around his temples. Like most men who spend their lives at sea, his skin was tanned and wrinkled. Hank loved to read in his off hours and was a good conversationalist.

When Chris and Sara entered the VIP suite, they found that Hank had placed cut flowers on their table. Chris laid a satchel on the table, which peaked Sara's interest.

"What do you have in the bag," Sara asked?

"Newspapers for Eduardo and Bernardo, and hard candy for Eduardo," replied Chris.

The couple enjoyed smooth sailing with brief stops in Charleston and Savannah.

CHAPTER 167

Nassau, Bahamas

June 20, 1783

While the *Sara* was unloading its cargo in Nassau, Eduardo met with their agent.

"Jose, the rumors I am hearing about the peace negotiations going on in Paris is that Spain will be restored to ownership of both East Florida and West Florida, but that the Bahamas will be given back to England. So, we may be out of business here soon." "As I see it Jose, you have two options:

1. We will be back here in about a month after making stops in Havana and New Orleans and back to Havana. You can close up shop and have everything in our warehouse ready to ship to the states when we return; or

2. You can wait until the British reoccupy the island and then speak with the commanding officer. The island is going to need food and supplies. They can either rely upon supplies coming from England across the Atlantic or they can do business with us and acquire fresher items quicker. They don't have to reinvent the wheel.

"You need to decide in time to have the cargo ready next month should you decide to close up shop. If you elect to stay, we will have fresh cargo for you from New Orleans and Havana.

CHAPTER 168

Half Moon Bay Resort

Baracoa Beach, Cuba

June 30, 1783

The Half Moon Bay Resort was on Havana Bay just a few miles west of Havana. It had a pier that extended about 50 yards out to the dark blue water. The pier had been extended so that supplies could be delivered directly by ocean going vessels without having to be processed through the port downtown.

Hank had agreed to drop Chris and Sara off at the resort before unloading his cargo in Havana. The resort had a carriage awaiting their arrival at the end of the pier.

The resort covered about 10 acres on the beach. As they were driven to their cabin, they passed the beach. Lined up in a row were lounge chairs and tables under straw palapas. Near the beach was a beach bar and outdoor restaurant. Native vendors of straw hats and crafts silently offered their wares on colorful blanket laid out on the beach. Between the beach bar and the main building was a large swimming pool. A sign directed them to the tennis courts off to the west and horseshoes and badminton to the east. In the main building was the office, a cocktail lounge, dining room, gift shop and sightseeing office. Connecting the main building with the beach in a wide semi-circle were individual bungalows, like a half-moon.

The carriage driver drove them to their palm tree shaded bungalow and carried their luggage into the bedroom.

They entered through a large screened in porch about 15' by 20' with a couch and four rocking chairs in bamboo and wicker furniture. The living room was about the same size. It was also decorated in bamboo and wicker furniture, including a couch, side table, two lounge chairs with ottomans, coffee table, and a dining table with four chairs. One painting was of a tropical sunset, while the other was of a sailing ship at sea. The bedroom contained a large bed with a bench at the end, side tables with candles, a lounge chair and ottoman and a chest of drawers. There was a small closet where Sara could hang her dresses and the small room with the wash pan and pitcher and the chamber pot.

Chris thought to himself, "This could be a stop on my cruise ship idea."

There was a note on the bed from Felicite that she and her two children had already arrived. Bernardo's wife and Children arrived the day before on a mail ship from New Orleans. From the note it appeared that the three couples had adjoining bungalows, with Bernardo and Felicite in the middle. When Chris and Sara knocked on the door, they were greeted by Maria Matilde de Galvez, age six, and her little brother Miguel de Galvez, who was born last year. Maria was clutching a red headed doll while the baby was nursing a bottle.

Chris introduced Sara to Felicite and Maria. Sara was taken by the beautiful child in front of her. She had shiny black hair and emerald colored eyes. Her skin was fair, and she almost always wore a smile on her face.

"Bernardo is due late tonight or early tomorrow," said Felicite. Eduardo and Toni should check in tomorrow morning. Shall we dine in the resort restaurant tonight," inquired Felicity?

510

The conversation at dinner that night was mostly about problems during pregnancy, babies' colic, childhood diseases, postpression, diets and recent fashions. Chris was delighted that Felicite and Sara were getting along so well.

Bernardo left Haiti for this meeting on the early tide. His 10,000 troops had been ready to attack Jamaica for months but had been held back by the crown. He had been assured by the palace that the peace treaty was going to be signed, and it should create no problem for him to be a day's sail away from his troops.

By noon the following day Eduardo, Toni and Bernardo had all checked in. They all decided to put on their swimsuits and go to the beach. After a couple of rum drinks each, they ambled over to the bamboo hut with straw roof. The special of the day was pork ribs basted with a lemon molasses sauce and fried potatoes. Little Maria had a wonderful afternoon playing in the surf and making a sandcastle with her dad on the beach.

At 4:00 p.m. it was nap time – not just for the children.

At dinner that night Toni revealed that she was pregnant and expecting in mid-September. Sara and Toni were seated together so they could get to know each other quicker.

Chris said, "I checked with the office today. They provide babysitting services. I suggest that tonight we all go to one of those international floorshows that Havana is so famous for. All six seemed to agree.

"I'll call and make a reservation for the 10:00 p.m. show and reserve two carriages for 9:30," responded Chris."

At 10:00 p.m. they were being seated at a table for six near the stage. The band was playing its opening number. It was an Afro-Cuban group, with an array of drums: congas, bongos, and timbales, as well as a wide selection of noise makers: gourds, cymbals, cow bell, wood block, castanets and a tambourine.

For the next hour and one-half they were entertained with comedians, magicians, jugglers, dog acts, singers, dancers, knife throwing, and musical solos. Chris loved the Afro-Cubano music.

. . .

The following afternoon Eduardo and Chris were alone on the beach enjoying a beer. "Lalo, are you still keeping a daily journal about your travels," asked Chris?

"I have made a journal entry every day since I left for school," answered Eduardo. "Why do you ask?"

"You have seen the information that I have been adding to the back of my charts about each port. It occurred to me that when the war is over, people are going to start traveling for enjoyment. But where will they go? How long will it take them to get there? What will they do once they get there? Will there be a comfortable hotel at their destination? Are there good restaurants there? It appears to me that we could combine the information the two of us have recorded and create the first book for travelers."

"This sounds great Chris. I'll have my journals copied and mail them to you. What's our next step," asked Eduardo?

"I plan to see Dr. Franklin in Philadelphia. I will make him a proposal that he would become a

1/3 partner in this book by organizing and printing it and advertising it in his chain of newspapers. Dr. Franklin has created an inter-colonial network of newspapers. He sponsored two dozen printers in Pennsylvania, South Carolina, New York, Connecticut and even the Caribbean. By 1753, 8 of the 15 English language newspapers in the colonies were published by him or his partners. In addition, he has work-around agreements with other newspapers to exchange free advertising. Our book could be famous in the colonies."

. . .

For the next week, the six "Warriors" relaxed, talked, ate, drank, napped, swam, basked in the sun and had a wonderful time.

Their conversation on the last night turned to the reality of what was about to happen to them. With the war almost over, nobody knew if either Bernardo or Eduardo or possibly both of them might be ordered back to Spain, Mexico, Honduras, or possibly to Peru. Chris wondered if after the war it would be profitable for him to continue his business with agents in New Orleans and Havana. By the end of the Warrior Week Sara had firmly embedded herself into the Warrior group.

CHAPTER 169

George Washington Victory

Yorktown, Virginia

Oct. 19, 1781

 Following British defeats on the Mississippi, loss of Mobile and Pensacola, and American victories at Kings Mountain and Cowpens, General Cornwallis retreated to Yorktown, on the Virginia Coast. He had lost his supply line to Charleston. He was low on ammunition, food and water and hoped to be resupplied and/or rescued by the English Fleet.

By the time Cornwallis' troops were settling into Yorktown, the area offshore was blockaded by the French Fleet.

The uprising of the French troops under Genera Rochambeau who had been threatening to desert were finally paid their salaries for the past three months, courtesy of Spaniards in Havana, whose arms had been twisted by General Bernardo de Galvez to loan 500,000 pieces of eight to the French government.

The Battle of the Capes occurred near the mouth of the Chesapeake Bay on 5 September 1781. The British fleet was led by Rear Admiral Sir Thomas Graves, while the French fleet was commanded by Rear Admiral François Joseph Paul, the Comte de Grasse. The French were able to prevent the Royal Navy from reinforcing or evacuating General Lord Cornwallis from Yorktown, Virginia even though the two fleets were almost evenly matched with men and ships.

With no prospect of rescue and supplies at a minimum, General Cornwallis surrendered. It is interesting to note that General Cornwallis did not participate in the surrender ceremony. He sent a junior officer and feigned sickness to avoid public embarrassment.

CHAPTER 170

American Revolutionary War is Over

Paris Peace Treaty

September 3, 1783

Under the terms of the treaty signed in Paris on September 3, 1783 it was to become effective in six months after being signed by all the parties. The treaty provided that West Florida and East Florida were to be returned to Spain. The Bahamas was to be returned to England. England and the U.S. were given free access to the Mississippi River.

Pirates were still successfully attacking treasure ships. Louisiana could not pay its debts and was facing bankruptcy. King Carlos asked Bernardo and others for suggestions. King Carlos advised Bernardo that the fate of the Louisiana colony depended on a plan.

Bernardo discussed the problem with Eduardo. Both Bernardo and Eduardo suggested to the king that a treasure ship from Vera Cruz be diverted to New Orleans and unload gold and silver there to pay creditors and allow those with "worthless" paper money to exchange it for gold and silver.

. . .

Baby boy, Eduardo, Jr. was born to Eduardo and Toni in Havana on September 14, 1783 with no complications to mother or child.

CHAPTER 171

Havana, Cuba to New Orleans

Boarding New Orleans Mail Ship

November 28 – December 25, 1783

Bernardo received a note from King Carlos that he had approved Bernardo's recommendation. Galvez ordered Eduardo back to Vera Cruz to oversee loading, security and transport of the treasure ship to New Orleans.

The Havana Mail ship was ordered to pick up Eduardo, Toni, and Eduardo, Jr. in Havana and drop them off in New Orleans. Toni and the baby were to stay there while Eduardo was away.

. . .

On the night of their arrival back in New Orleans, Eduardo and Toni had dinner at the Officer's Club with Bernardo and Felicite. Beforehand they had stopped at the Galvez home to visit Maria and her little brother and to leave Eduardo, Jr. with the Galvez babysitter. They had not seen one another in four months, so they had a lot to talk about. They stayed at the club until closing time.

Both couples begin to decorate their homes for Christmas. At least this year Eduardo would be home for Christmas. Unfortunately, he was scheduled to ship out the day after Christmas.

All three of Eduardo's former staff members were ready to get back into the saddle and signed up for the journey. He told them that they would have no duties while at sea and suggested strongly that they bring along a lot to read. He told Fernando, "Don't forget your guitar."

The officers of the *El Cazador* were invited to participate in the Presidio Christmas Party. Galvez ordered huge tents be erected and that all the crews and enlisted soldiers and marines be invited for food, booze and entertainment all day on Christmas.

To read on his long journey, Eduardo purchased *Wealth of Nations* by Adam Smith, *History of London* by John Cooke, and *A Journey To The Western Islands of Scotland*, by Samuel Johnson. Sara had already purchased for him a bag of candy and all the latest newspapers.

It was a sad Christmas for Toni because Eduardo was leaving the next day and would be gone for about seven weeks.

. . .

Bernardo announced that he had been appointed Governor and Capitan General of Cuba and scheduled to move to Havana. He named Eduardo as his Deputy Governor and Captain General of Cuba.

CHAPTER 172

El Cazador

New Orleans, Louisiana to Vera Cruz, Mexico

December 26, 1783 – January 8, 1783

Eduardo and his staff met Captain Emilio Ponce at the Presidio party on Christmas Day. He was from Bilbao, Spain. He knew and respected the Gardoqui family. He had met Chris when both their ships were in port in Bilbao at the same time. Captain Ponce was a stout 5' 10". He was bald except for a patch of hair over his ears that circled his head. For a man his size, he was very quiet.

The *El Cazador* was a large treasure ship of the latest model. Both Eduardo and Fernando had VIP suites.

Eduardo and his staff met the other officers at dinner on the first night out. Fragata Captain Danielo "Flaco" Rodriguez the XO from Madrid was about 40. He was a very slim 6' 2" with long brown hair. He had served with Captain Ponce for the past eight years.

The ship's doctor was Antonio Hernandez, M.D., who held the rank of Fragata Captain. He had a long white beard which matched his lengthy white hair. His cheeks were red. With his 5' 9" frame on his 250 pounds, he looked like Santa Claus. He could regale the officers with interesting sea stories for hours.

The Navigator was LT Pedro Ruiz, from Gran Canary Island. He was a very average looking 30 year old except for his glasses. He was a book worm, who could navigate by the stars.

LT Andres Sevilla, the Gunnery Officer was a 28 year old bachelor, from El Escorial, who was trying to have a girl in every port. He was rakishly handsome with a perfect physique. He was always involved in the conversation around the dinner table.

The Supply Officer was LT Nicolaza Texado, age 27, from Cadiz, graduated from one of Madrid's finest private schools. He intended to get out of the navy when his enlistment was up. He planned to become a lawyer by going to work for his lawyer uncle. He played the guitar.

LT Pedro De Los Santos, age 32, from Saragoza, served as the Cargo Officer. He had been passed over for promotion and exhibited a sour disposition. He never participated in the conversation at the dinner table. He did his job and kept to himself.

Three young men Sub Lieutenant Santiago Sequin, age 19, the Assistant Gunnery Officer from

Barcelona; Sub Lieutenant Josef Serna, age 19, the Assistant Supply Officer from Cartagena; and

Midshipman Antonio Losoyo, age 17, Assistant Cargo Officer, spent most of their spare time together. It was only natural that these young men would become friends as they were the three youngest officers.

After dinner the first night at sea, Fernando got his guitar and began to entertain the other officers. Lt Texado went to his cabin and retrieved his guitar and joined Fernando. The two officers played their guitars until late that evening. Eduardo, Captain Ponce and Doctor Hernandez played dominos.

. . .

Although their ship was on a desperately important mission, a relaxed atmosphere spread through it. For the next 20 days the weather was good, there were no accidents onboard and no disciplinary problems were encountered.

Eduardo continued to make daily entries into his journal. He spent his time reading and reminiscing about their adventure.

CHAPTER 173

Loading Cazador in Vera Cruz

January, 1784

 The treasure ship that would transport Eduardo and his staff back to New Orleans was being loaded with the contents of the mule train with gold coins from Peru, the Oriental treasurers from the Philippines and the silver coins from the Mexico City, Mexico mint.

El Cazador, a Spanish treasure ship 1

Carlos, III, King of Spain, decided to replace the worthless currency with valuable Spanish silver coins. On 20 October 1783 Charles, III of Spain sent her on a mission to bring much-needed hard currency to the Spanish colony of Louisiana in order to stabilize the, currency. In Veracruz, Mexico, under the watchful eyes of Eduardo and his staff, she was loaded with approximately 450,000 Spanish *Reales*. To be more precise, she was loaded with silver Spanish coins, mostly 8 *Reales*, "Pieces of Eight," It carried 400,000 silver pesos and another 50,000 pesos worth of smaller change, of various dates. At one ounce to the peso, and 12 troy ounces to the pound, that's 37,500 pounds of silver.

It was a 90-foot-long Brig. A brig is a sailing vessel with two square-rigged masts. During the age of sail, brigs were seen as fast and maneuverable and were used as both naval warships and merchant vessels. It carried 18 high quality bronze canon and was like an 18th century "Armored Car."

Silver was being mined in the Mexican Mountains between Mexico City and Acapulco. It was shipped by mule train to Mexico City, where the Spanish coins were minted. The Spanish coins of 1783 were minted in this building in Mexico City. The coins were shipped to Veracruz, Mexico, by mule train where most of it was shipped by sea back to Spain, with scheduled stops in Havana for repairs and supplies for the transatlantic voyage. In the case of the *El Cazador*, it was destined for New Orleans.

Cutaway diagram El Cazador being loaded 1

Eduardo had a platoon of Marines to join his staff in following the precious cargo from the warehouse to the hold on the ship to ensure that there was no pilfering. That platoon of Marines was relieved at 7:00 p.m by a fresh platoon, who guarded the warehouse and pier throughout the night.

CHAPTER 174

Sinking of the ship *El Cazador*

Feb. 1784

When *El Cazador* left Vera Cruz, she was sitting low in the water, meaning her cargo holds were full. It was a warm tropical day. For the first two weeks of the journey the weather remained tropical.

On the 17th day out of Vera Cruz the weather turned. The barometer began to fall. To the north Eduardo could clearly see the dark line of clouds announcing a cold front. Huge black clouds formed a solid line across the sky. The balmy tropical temperature was steadily falling. The sky beneath these monster clouds was dark, indicating that it was raining hard under those clouds. The wind picked up and the seas became angry.

"XO, prepare for a blow," shouted Captain Ponce!

"Aye, Aye Sir.

"Bosun, rig a jack line on all decks,' ordered the XO. "Furl the sails on the mainmast and the mizzenmast. Batten all hatches and prepare for a storm. Prepare the sea anchor for deployment. Anyone not working on this deck should get below and stay below.

Just as the officers were sitting down to dinner they passed through the front. The fall of heavy raindrops pelleting the ship sounded like gunfire. The raging head wind howled. The ship rolled, pitched and yawed barely making headway. For hours it was bombarded with hail the size of a grape. Huge waves washed across the quarterdeck. Had it not been for the jackline stretched across the deck, a sailor would have been washed overboard. The ship helplessly bobbled in the ocean like a cork.

By morning, the tempest had subsided. The officers and crew found themselves in the midst of a winter storm. The sea had calmed itself considerably, but it was far from smooth. A strong northerly wind had dropped the temperature to about 20 degrees, which was unseasonable for the Gulf. There was constant heavy snow. As they neared the mouth of the Mississippi River, they began to see large chunks of ice. Presumably, the ice was floating down the river from Illinois. The closer they got to the river, the larger the chunks of ice.

Eduardo noticed that the ship was sitting dangerously low in the water, with only a few feet of freeboard. When he mentioned it to the captain, Ponce ordered the XO to get all hands busy chipping ice off the ship. Overnight the ship had accumulated over 2 inches of ice. Within minutes the decks were covered with crewmen chipping ice off the railings, the decks, and hatches, while other crewmen swept the ice off the deck. Several members of the crew found themselves hanging over the railing to chip ice from the side of the ship. On the lower decks sailors were knocking ice off the side of the ship through gun ports. A third group of seamen climbed into the riggings to break the ice of the masts and cross members.

After about two hours the ship was sitting about a foot higher in the water.

That afternoon the storm worsened. There was a winter mix of sleet, hail and snow. The wind howled. Ice continued to accumulate all over the ship. Overnight she was sitting just a few feet above the waterline. The temperature had remained in the 20s. It was so noisy that Eduardo could not sleep. He was sitting at his desk updating his journal. As they were about to enter the mouth of the Mississippi River, they were hit by a huge slab of ice.

At about 3:00 a.m. the ice hit *El Cazador* at the water line knocking a huge hole in the bow of the ship. At the moment of impact there was a loud noise that could be heard throughout the ship. As the ship made its way through the water, its hold began to fill with water. Eduardo could feel the ship going down by the bow. He grabbed his coat and ran to Fernando's cabin. He knocked on his door and shouted for him to wake him up. He then ran to Javi's cabin and did the same. He continued through the hatch to the quarterdeck where he could see that the ship was already down by the bow.

He rushed to a lifeboat secured on the deck when he was hit by falling riggings from above.

He was knocked out and didn't remember anything until he awoke in the hospital.

Painting of El Cazador sinking 1

En route to New Orleans, the El Cazador was sunk in a winter storm. Historical records indicate that January and February 1784 were one of the two worst winters in New Orleans. The lower Mississippi River froze, and the area experienced two feet of snow. The El *Cazador* could have been struck by ice from the river that entered the Gulf of Mexico. Sea ice could have covered the ship, making it un-maneuverable. Ice would also add to the weight of the ship, causing it to sit deeper in the water and increasing the likelihood that it would sink.

Colliding with one of the large ice floes (reported to be 30 feet in diameter by 5 feet thick) would have been similar to having a 22-ton railroad box car filled with 80 tons of concrete ramming you. The contact point would have been fairly sharp, at the waterline, and due to the flatness of the ice only 10%, or about 5 inches, above the water. Even at only a few knots combined speed, this would have been devastating to a wooden vessel. Working against this ship were :

1) Long winter nights

2) Frequent fog along the Texas and Louisiana coasts

3) Frequent winter rainstorms.

4)   Possible crew deaths due to exposure.

. . .

Eduardo had washed up on the beach near Houma, Louisiana. He was the Sole Survivor.

CHAPTER 175

Eduardo Shipwrecked

El Cazador

February 1784

Eduardo was found on the beach covered in snow by a Cajun fisherman. He was taken to a Cajun doctor and treated for exposure. He was kept at the doctor's home for 3 days. He remained knocked out for the entire time. On the fourth day he was taken to the New Orleans hospital by wagon. When he was admitted, a clerk sent a message to Toni.

Toni dressed the baby and took a carriage to the hospital. When she arrived, he was sitting up in bed enjoying a cup of hot chocolate. His left arm was in a cast and there was a large bandage on his forehead.

"Looks like my military career is over. I failed to get the money to New Orleans. Louisiana is bankrupt and I failed," Eduardo lamented.

"Sweetheart, nobody in their right mind will blame you for the worst winter storm in history. I'm just so happy that you survived. Have you heard anything about your staff? Did any of them make it off the ship?

Before he could answer, Bernardo walked into the room with grave concern on his face.

"What do the doctors say? Are you going to be OK," Asked Bernardo?

"I had 8 stiches on my forehead, and I have a broken left arm. I was suffering from exposure, but my core temperature is getting back up and running. Even so, I am still trying to warm up. I have vague recollections of floating on a large piece of wood. There was a mixture of rain, sleet hail, and snow. There were large pieces of ice in the water. It was a large chunk of ice that knocked a hole in the bow."

"Here," said Bernardo, as he handed Eduardo a flask filled with brandy, "this ought to warm you up. When you get time, you might want to read your publicity in the *Crescent City Dispatch*. Lalo, you are now a local hero. Look at this headline: ***Local Officer Lone Survivor***.

. . .

When Eduardo was released from the hospital, he conferred with Galvez. Creditors were demanding payment of debts. Citizens wanted to exchange their worthless paper money for gold and silver coins. Eduardo sadly wrote his report of the loss of the cargo to the king. Both the U.S. and New Spain – particularly New Orleans, were suffering from a depression. England had set up an embargo on the import of American goods to both England and her Caribbean colonies. Spain now possessed both East Florida and West Florida but had to return the Bahamas to England.

. . .

"Bernardo, I would like to arrange a memorial service at the chapel for my staff and the officers and men of El Cazador.

"By all means. Let me know if you need my help.

531

CHAPTER 176

Gardoqui Appointed Ambassador to US 1784

Don Diego de Gardoqui, of the Gardoqui trading company in Bilbao, Spain that had greatly assisted the rebels during the war, was appointed as Spain's first ambassador to the United States of America in 1784. Gardoqui became well acquainted with George Washington, stood immediately to the right of George Washington when he took his oath of office, and marched in the newly elected President Washington's inaugural parade. King Charles, III of Spain continued communications with Washington, sending him two mules from Spain that Washington had requested for his farm at Mount Vernon.

Don Diego was the most famous member of the Gardoqui family, who was the first Ambassador of Spain to the United States and Spanish Finance Minister in 1792.

Spain made loans to the United States to be used to furnish war supplies through the House of Gardoqui, which "supplied the patriots with 215 bronze cannon - 30,000 muskets - 30,000 bayonets - 51,314 musket balls - 300,000 pounds of powder - 12,868 grenades - 30,000 uniforms - and 4,000 field tents during the war.

. . .

The U.S. Congress formally cited General Bernardo de Galvez and Spain for their aid during the American Revolutionary War.

CHAPTER 177

Edenton, North Carolina

Ship to Havana for Warrior's meeting.

September, 1784

Sara was excited about going to a meeting with the Warriors. She and Chris had gone shopping.

They both bought new outfits. They purchased baby gifts for the Galvez and Lopez children. For Lalo and Bernie, they purchased newspapers and silver handled walking sticks. Obviously, a supply of candy was purchased.

Knowing that they were always in the market for a good book, for Bernardo, Chris purchased *A Voyage to the Pacific Ocean,* by Captain James Cook. For Eduardo, he selected *Sketches of History* by William Godwin.

CHAPTER 178

Havana, Cuba

October 1784

Galvez arrived in Havana and assumed his duties as Governor and Captain General of Cuba.

Felicite was delighted with the upgrade to the Governor's mansion. Eduardo was promoted to Deputy Governor and Captain General of Cuba, with a military promotion to Lt. General (3stars).

The Warriors met in Havana, Cuba for the last time. Bernardo and Eduardo were both delighted with two new books to read. Toni and Felicite loved the baby gifts. These six people had a wonderfully relaxing week at the same Half Moon Bay Resort of their first meeting.

Chris reported to Eduardo that Dr. Ben Franklin had agreed to his proposal to become a 1/3 partner in the publication of their new travel book. Franklin had agreed to print the book and to promote it by advertising it in all eight of his newspapers and to exchange free ads with a dozen other newspapers. He will also print flyers for my gift shops.

. . .

Galvez' uncle, Mathias de Galvez y Gallardo, Viceroy of New Spain, died in Mexico City in November 1784. Shortly thereafter, Bernardo Galvez was named as the Viceroy of New Spain. Eduardo was named Deputy Viceroy and promoted to Captain General. They arrived in Mexico in February 1785. Eduardo and his wife moved to Mexico City about the same time.

During his administration two great calamities occurred: the freeze of September 1785, which led to famine in 1786, and a typhus epidemic that killed 300,000 people the same year. During the famine, Gálvez donated 12,000 pesos of his inheritance and 100,000 pesos he raised from other sources to buy maize and beans for the populace. He also implemented policies to increase future agricultural production.

Bernardo and Felicite got out and met the people. He began construction of Chapultepec Castle and greatly enlarged the Cathedral. A typhus epidemic hit the city. They both tended to patients in the hospital. On November 30, 1785, Galvez died in Mexico City of typhus.

. . .

Eduardo replaced Galvez as the Viceroy of New Spain.

CHAPTER 179

Cruise Line Formed

1784

 The travel book written by Chris and Eduardo and printed by Dr. Franklin was a success. Chris was convinced that Americans – at least wealthy ones – wanted to travel. He decided to execute the second part of his plan.

Chris contacted his agents in the French islands he had been visiting. On each of five islands he purchased a 10 acre beach front lot where the water was clear and there was a reef to attract fish. On each property he built a bar and restaurant and built small palapas for people to relax in the shade.

His plan was to advertise a cruise where each day the passengers were either shopping in an island town or relaxing on the beach with a fancy rum drink in their hands. Some might want to go deep sea fishing or sailing with the independent contractors, who would be obligated to rebate a portion of the fees paid. His agent would line up local entertainers to regale his guests.

Chris already had a steady source of income from those islands carrying mail and cargo. He and Dr. Franklin founded a new company to promote cruising. In the beginning they dedicated one ship to cruising, which required some modification to add suites and reallocate some space.

By 1785 there were three ships carrying tourists, from New York, Philadelphia and Charleston. As business began to improve, they added a small hotel on the island of Martinique. With nightly entertainment, the bar and restaurant also catered to residents of the island. People would ferry over from another island to spend the weekend. In 1785 they ordered a specially made ship for cruising. It contained a large dining room, a library, card room, gift shop, bar and weight room. It was designed for transatlantic crossings.

In July 1788, the *Adventurer* made its maiden voyage carrying passengers from New York City to Dublin, Ireland; London, England; Le Havre, France; Bilbao, Spain; Oporto, Portugal; San Miguel, Azores and Hamilton, Bermuda. Dr. Franklin was named as the onboard speaker, who promised to regale the passengers with some of his interesting adventures. Each cruise also carried one or more entertainers including singers, dancers, comedians, jugglers, magicians, etc. They found the best chef available, and the onboard orchestra played every night for dinner. A string quartet played for tea, which was served every afternoon, and a jazz group played late. At each port local groups were brought onboard to entertain. In some ports, the passengers were transported to visit important sights, like the Book of Kells in Dublin, London Theatre, a winery in Oporto, etc.

CHAPTER 180

Inauguration of George Washington

New York City

April 3, 1789

Christopher received an invitation to attend the inauguration of George Washington as U.S. President on April 30, 1789, at Federal Hall in New York, City. He also received an invitation to a private reception afterwards at Fraunces Tavern, just a block away. He also received a note from Benjamin Franklin urging him to attend the private reception.

Dr. Franklin had asked Chris to meet him 30 minutes before the swearing in ceremony at the Masonic Temple. Franklin presented Chris a commission as a Rear Admiral in the U.S. Navy, signed by George Washington.

"Chris, this is an honorary commission. There will be no salary. At that moment, George Washington entered the room. He walked directly toward Chris and Dr. Franklin. Washington thanked Chris for risking his life and his ships to transport war materials from Spain.

At that time Don Diego Gardoqui entered the room and joined General Washington, Dr. Franklin and Chris. Don Diego praised him for delivering the military supplies. Diego also thanked him for using his other 8 ships for continuing the journey from Gardoqui's ship to New Orleans. "You have the heartfelt thanks of a grateful nation," said General Washington.

Ambassador Gardoqui stood to his right, in the position of honor, as General Washington was sworn in by Robert Livingston. Gardoqui marched next to Washington in the parade that followed and sat next to him in the church service at St. Paul's Chapel.

That evening at the reception at Fraunces Tavern, just a block from Federal Hall, George Washington told Chris that Fraunces was his best spy during the war as all the British officers ate there daily and he was a good listener.

In addition, Chris met and briefly chatted with Vice President John Adams; Secretary of State, Thomas Jefferson; Secretary of the Treasury, Alexander Hamilton; Secretary of War, Henry Knox; and Attorney General Edmund Randolph.

Before dinner George Washington toasted the Kings of France, Spain and Holland. After a long pause Washington said:

Without the contributions of each of you in this room our fortunes in this war would have been reversed. Each of you made a vital impact. The people in this room are the individuals primarily responsible for our victory. Gentlemen, I salute you.

Chris was saddened to learn that in 1801 King Carlos was forced to sell Louisiana to France to pay off the large debts they incurred in assisting the United States. He was shocked to learn in 1803 that Thomas Jefferson had purchased Louisiana from Napoleon and had sent off explorers Lewis and Clark to investigate what lay in that vast land, which once his friend Bernardo had ruled.

EPILOG

The U.S. Congress formally cited General Bernardo Galvez and Spain for their aid during the American Revolutionary War.

Galveston, Texas, Galveston Bay, Galveston County, Galvez, Louisiana, and St. Bernard Parish,

Louisiana were, among other places, named after him. The Louisiana parishes of East Feliciana and West Feliciana (originally a single parish) were said to have been named for his wife Marie Felicite de Saint-Maxent d'Estrehan.

The Cabildo, a branch of the Louisiana State Museum located on Jackson Square in New Orleans, has a portrait of General Gálvez accompanied by a display of biographical information. Spanish Plaza, in the Central Business District of the city, has an equestrian statue of Gálvez adjacent to the New Orleans World Trade Center. There is also a Galvez Street in New Orleans. Mobile, Alabama, also has a Spanish Plaza with a statue of Gálvez.

In Baton Rouge, Louisiana (present-day state capital), Galvez Plaza is laid out next to City Hall and used frequently as a site for municipal events. Also, the 13-story Galvez Building is part of the state government's administrative office-building complex in the Capitol Park section of downtown Baton Rouge.

In 1911 in Galveston, the Hotel Galvez was built and named after him; the hotel is located on Bernardo de Galvez Avenue. The hotel was added to the National Register of Historic Places on 4 April 1979.

In 1980 the U.S. Post office issued a commemorative U.S. Postage stamp in his honor.

On December 14, 2014, Galvez' portrait hung in the U.S. Senate Foreign Relations room in the nation's capital.

U.S. postage stamp honoring Gen. Galvez 1

On December 16, 2014, the United States

Congress conferred honorary citizenship on Gálvez, citing him as a "hero of the Revolutionary War who risked his life for the freedom of the United States people and provided supplies, intelligence, and strong military support to the war effort." He is one of only seven individuals to be named honorary citizens. In 2019, the Spanish Government placed a 32-inch-tall (80 cm) statue of Galvez in front of the Spanish Embassy in Washington, D.C.

541

Galvez, by Judge Ed Butler named by Amazon.com Editorial Board as one of the "Best History Books in 2018."

Portrait of Gen. Bernardo Galvez. 1

QUESTIONS

1. If the *Cazador* had reached New Orleans with its treasure, would Spain have still been forced to sell Louisiana to France?

2. If the *Cazado*r had reached New Orleans with its treasure, what would have happened to the desire of the U.S. to expand westward?

3. After Cornwallis' defeat, the British still had several large concentrations of troops at

St. Augustine, Florida; Charleston, South Carolina; New York City; and

Detroit. Why didn't Britain use these troops to reinvade? It has been suggested that they were about to lose Jamaica with the massing of Spanish and French ships and troops and that it was better to negotiate than to lose all its Caribbean possessions.

ABOUT THE AUTHOR

Judge Edward F. Butler, Sr. is a retired U.S. Administrative Law Judge, before which position he served as Presiding Municipal Judge for South Padre Island, Texas. He is an honor graduate of the Vanderbilt University School of Law, and was a board certified civil trial lawyer before assuming full time duties on the bench. He is the author of 14 books, three of which are on family history. He has a 10 vol. set of books that traces his great grandfather's ancestors back to Charlemagne, which are scheduled for publication later this year..

Judge Butler retired from the U.S. Naval Reserve in September 1990 at the rank of Commander. His military career encompassed 35 years, during which he was awarded two Navy Commendation Medals and three Armed Forces Reserve Medals

Judge Butler is a frequent seminar and after dinner speaker on historical and genealogical topics, and is a regular contributor to national and state legal, historical and genealogical society journals and magazines. For several years he has been a speaker on cruise ships.

Since his retirement in 1997, he has devoted a considerable amount of his time and energy to the Texas Society of the Sons of the American Revolution (SAR), where he held the office of President General.

Judge Butler is an active member of the National, Texas, and the San Antonio Historical and Genealogical Societies; as well as numerous other state and local genealogical societies.

He previously served as Genealogist for the Texas Society, SAR; for three years as a member of the National SAR genealogy committee; and for two years as genealogical editor of *The Texas Compatriot*, magazine of the Texas Society of SAR. He also published a monthly column for SAR chapter newsletters, entitled "The Genealogy Corner".

In May 2010 he had a private audience with HRM Felipe de Borbon, King of Spain. The king asked judge Butler to write a book about Spain's assistance to the United States during the American Revolutionary War. In late 2014 judge Butler published *Galvez,* which won seven awards. The editorial committee of Amazon.com ranked *Galvez* as **"one of the best history books of 2018."**

Judge Butler has received several national awards for his community service, including:

1. The SAR **Gold Good Citizen Medal** (2010)

2. The Daughters of the American Revolution's **Medal of Honor** (2017)

3. **Legion of Merit**, highest award of the Order of North America (2018)

4. **Legion of Merit,** highest award of **the Knights Templar** (two awards)

5. Selected for inclusion in the **Texas Genealogical Hall of Fame (2017)**

This is his first attempt to produce an award winning novel. He has previously published both an award winning family history book and an award winning history book.

Photo of Author

Figure 1 Judge Edward F. Butler, author

Other Books By the Author

Royals, Nobles, Warriors and Leaders of the Western World, Southwest Historic Press, San *Antonio, 2023.* This 10 volume set contains the ancestors and descendants of Pvt. Benjamin F. Lovelace.

Butler Arms, Southwest Historic Press, San Antonio, 2017. This Butler family book documents the arms of the family of Thomas Boteler, the authors direct ancestor, through each generation back to 1129 AD: together with other documentary evidence of the family tree using DNA and historical documents. ASIN: B07C4NSVSC

George Washington's Secret Ally, Southwest Historic Press, San Antonio, 2016. ISBN 978-1-5323-1601-2 50750; ASIN: B07BZGHV9X

Galvez / Spain - Our Forgotten Ally in the American Revolutionary War: A Concise Summary of Spain's

Assistance, Southwest Historic Press, San Antonio, 2015 (5 Awards). ISBN 978-0-692-03088-2; ASIN: B07C9W4JM8 **"One of the best history books of 2018,** "according to Amazon.com editorial committee.

Wanderlust, Butler Family Limited Partnership, San Antonio, (covers a series of travel articles from 2000-

2010, including Central America, Mexico, Caribbean, Eastern Europe, Western Europe, Greenland, Iceland & islands. ASIN: B07CCB4C74

Pacifica, Butler Family Limited Partnership, San Antonio 2005 (covers a series of travel articles from Jan. – Aug. 1998 through Hawaii, the islands of the South Pacific, Australia, New Zealand, Indonesia, Singapore, China, Taiwan, Philippines, Korea and Japan). ASIN: B07CFWS62K

Contributing editor, *Colonial America: An Encyclopedia of Social, Political, Cultural, and Economic History, Vol. Two, Edited by James Ciment*, "Inheritance" by Edward F. Butler, Sr., (2006), M.E. Sharpe, In, Armonk, NY.

History of The Irish Kings, Ancestors of the Lovelace, Marshall and McClanahan Families, Compiled by E.F. Butler, , Butler Family Limited Partnership, San Antonio 2000.

1997 Around-The-World Adventure, Butler Family Limited Partnership, San Antonio 2004 (covers a series of travel articles from Jul. - Dec. 1997 through Western Europe, Eastern Europe, Scandinavia, the Baltics, Russia,

Belarus, Oman, The United Arab Emirates, India, Nepal, Singapore, Myanmar, Malaysia, and Thailand).

ASIN: B07C4QL3JH

Travels with the Judge, Butler Family Limited Partnership, San Antonio 2003 (covers travels around the world from 1963 – 1997). ISBN 9781980763338; ASIN: B07BZJXMN4

The Texas Genealogist's Handbook, Butler Family Limited Partnership, San Antonio, Jan. 2001.

The Descendants of Pvt. Philip Nicholas Myers, American Revolutionary War Patriot, jointly with Robin Myers Butler, Butler Family Limited Partnership, San Antonio, Dec. 2000.

The Ancestors and Descendants of Diana Parker Martin, of Lane, DeWitt County, Illinois, jointly with Robin Myers Butler, Butler Family Limited Partnership, San Antonio, Dec. 2000.

The Descendants of Thomas Pincerna, Progenitor of the Butler Family, GenPub, Dallas, 1997 (First Prize, Best Family History Book, Dallas Genealogical Soc., 1997). ASIN: B07C5BGF2H

Texas Litigator's Handbook, Butterworth, Austin, 1989 (ISBN 040925432-0).

Family Law in Texas, co-author, Legal Education Institute, Naples, FL, 1988.

Cultural Behavior Handbook: Australia/A Guide for Defense Attaches, U.S. State Dept., Washington, Nov. 1986.

USN Atlantic Fleet Special fleet intelligence publication, *Soviet Incursion into the Caribbean (COMNAVFLT- Norfolk, VA., 1970, UnClassified)*.

Reviews

I thoroughly enjoyed reading The Warriors. In his first historic novel, after numerous genealogy and

non- fiction books, Judge Butler did a wonderful job of weaving fact and fiction. The style reminds me of

Michael Sharra, author of Killer Angels, where the characters speak in plausible terms regarding the

proven facts and circumstances that surround them. The Warriors is a perfect mixture of historical facts,

and plausible fiction, so that readers who are fans of history and readers who are fans of fiction will both

be equally pleased.

I was very impressed by the details of relationships, food and drink consumed, and places visited by

the characters. Judge Butler relies heavily on these enjoyable details based on the journals of Eduardo

Lopez and his staff. That such journals have survived is, in itself, an astonishing fact, as they are truly a

treasure and a great glimpse into the 18th century life and founding of our nation.

I look forward to Judge Butler's next historical novel.

David Nels Appleby, Jr., Attorney at law

Grand Master, The Sovereign Military Order of the Temple of Jerusalem ("Knights Templar")

President General, National Society Sons of the American Revolution (2008-2009)

First, congratulations on your excellent work that produced such an interesting and readable novel. I enjoyed it all the way. The characters you chose show interesting and intriguing personalities, which Is challenging when you are presenting such a large number of people.

The plot starts with a focus, placed in time and place, and then, slowly evolves introducing situations and actors who come into the story in a very natural way, finding their place seamlessly. The novel then expands from places where the action started to the nation, to countries, and from continent to continent in a versatility of somehow Tolstoian deployment.

It seems to me that a central character, the ship Captain who has a side-role to start with, evolves along to attain his well-defined role, at the core and heart of the novel: the story of real warriors.

Bernardo, after his courageous military experience in Algeria, Portugal, France and Texas-Coahuila seemed to the Court - including HM Carlos III himself-   a most adequate man to carry out -from the Government of Louisiana- the important help to the Americans, starting with a delicate undercover assistance while Spain was nonbelligerent, and later, in open war against England.

The character Eduardo is very interesting; and in several aspects reminds me of Coronel Ezpeleta (later General and Conde de Ezpeleta) who was Galvez's friend, comrade and essential in bringing desperately needed land troops to help take Panzacola (later Pensacola). I should add that the description of the bay of Acapulco and the Spanish defenses are particularly well described.

I very much enjoyed the fully detailed narratives of naval maneuvers, as well as

descriptions of warships of the time... etc.. very rich in the positions onboard, the usage, etc..

You could easily dream that you were aboard! Even the different penalties imposed on guilty sailors are most vivid. And the same applies to the various scenes in

551

restaurants, in Officers Rooms, in many places.
(Michelin's Stars!)

Initially -I think- you wanted to focus on the historical
facts about Galvez; then later in the book you explore
events in the Philippines, the "Galleon de Manila", the
Acapulco Veracruz transits , etc.. , the "Tagalog" words !
You then add the connection with the Viceroyalty of Peru,
etc..: that was the Spanish tricontinental trade route. I
think these events add to the idea of a "story of The
Warriors", and it's interesting.

The character of Captain Butler is a key piece of the
story; your book is full of interesting people and novelized
biographies; all the intricacies of the ship captain in his
fantastic career and business are surely an inspiration to
his great-grand-grandson Judge Ed Butler.

Hon. Miguel Mazarambroz

Miguel Mazarambroz was the **Ambassador of Spain** to
three countries. He was appointed to this position by the
King of Spain. He has also served as the **Consul General
of Spain in Houston** from 2009 to 2015, where he was
involved in promoting the cultural and historical ties
between Spain and Texas, especially the **Camino Real de
los Tejas**. He is a career diplomat with extensive
experience in international relations and diplomacy. He
has a degree in law from the Complutense University of
Madrid and speaks Spanish, English, French, and Arabic.

Figure 6 Galvez, by Judge Ed Butler, $29.00 at Amazon.com

Figure 7 George Washington's Secret Ally, by Ed Butler, $7.50 at Amazon.com

553

Appendix

NAUTICAL TERMS FOR LAND LUBBERS

By

Edward F. Butler, CDR, USN, Retired

SHIP or BOAT - A ship is any vessel which is capable of carrying a boat. Ships are larger than boats.

FORE AND AFT - These terms deal with the direction on the ship from where you are standing. Fore, or "Forward" is toward the front, or bow of the ship. Aft, is toward the rear, or stern.

BOW and STERN - These terms describe a part of the ship. The bow is the forward most part of the ship, while the stern is the end of the ship.

PROW - The prow is the most forward part of the bow, forward of where it leaves the water line.

AMIDSHIPS - Amidship is the center of the ship.

PORT and STARBOARD - As you face forward toward the bow of the ship the left side of the ship is Port, while the right side of the ship is Starboard.

DECK - The deck is the floor. Each deck on a ship has a name, like Sun Deck, Main Deck, Upper Deck, etc.

ABOVE DECK - You are above deck if you can see the sky.

BELOW DECK - If you are on any deck other than an outside deck you are below deck.

POOP DECK - A ship's aft deck.

QUARTERDECK - Generally, where one boards a ship. The quarterdeck is usually amidships.

ANCHOR - A large heavy metal object placed on the end of an anchor chain and lowered to the seabed below. Used to keep a ship in place in the harbor. When a ship is resting in a harbor with the anchor out, it is "at anchor".

BOUY - A floating device used as a navigational aid by marking channels, hazards and prohibited areas.

CAPTAIN - The senior officer on any ship. He is charged with the safe operation of the ship. The captain is the Master of the Vessel and in charge of discipline.

CREW - Any person who works on the ship.

555

MATE - A mate is an assistant to the Captain. The First Mate is sometimes called the Administrative Captain or Assistant Captain or Executive Officer

STEWARD - The person who cleans your cabin is the "Cabin Steward". The waiter who serves you meals in the dining room is the "Dinner Steward".

PURSER - The purser is the chief cashier on the ship. He or his staff run the currency exchange where you can buy Mexican Pesos, and where the bill is paid for drinks and tours.

HEAD - The head is the toilet or bathroom.

CABIN or STATEROOM - A room inside the ship.

BRIDGE - Where the movement of the ship is directed. The Helmsman on a large vessel is always on the bridge. The bridge is usually in the forward part of the ship, but some oil tankers and container cargo ships have the bridge in the stern.

BERTH - Each individual on the ship is berthed in a cabin or stateroom. Their bed is their individual berth. In small cabins there are bunk beds. One is called the upper berth and the other is the lower berth. The ship is berthed (parked) on the pier or dock.

CAST OFF - To detach mooring lines (ropes), as when the ship is leaving a dock.

CATAMARAN - A twin-hulled boat. Catamaran sailboats are faster than single-hulled boats (monohulls) in some conditions, and harder to turnover.

CHART - Charts are maps for boaters. Usually, a chart includes mostly water, whereas a map covers mostly land.

GALLEY - The kitchen on a ship or boat. On a small vessel the galley may also be where meals are served.

GMT - GMT means Greenwich Mean Time. Greenwich is a suburb of London, England. GMT is used to determine what time it will be in each of the world's 24 time zones. The time in San Antonio is GMT minus 6, meaning it is six hours earlier in San Antonio than London. In the military GMT is the same as ZULU time.

HELM - On larger ships the helm is the wheel used to steer the ship. On smaller boats the helm is the tiller or rudder.

HELMSMAN - The helmsman is the person who is steering the ship.

557

HULL - The hull of the ship is the main body of the ship, not counting the keel, deck or mast.

LATITUDE - Imaginary horizontal lines drawn around the earth used to measure distance north and south of the equator.

LONGITUDE - Imaginary vertical lines drawn around the earth to measure distance around the world to the east or west.

LEEWARD - The direction away from the wind.

WINDWARD - The direction toward the wind.

NAUTICAL MILE - Distance at sea is measured in nautical miles, which are about 6,067.12 feet, or 1.15 statute miles. Nautical miles have the unique property that 1 minute of latitude is equal to 1 nautical mile. Measurement of speed is done in **knots**, where 1 knot equals 1 nautical mile per hour. A statute mile is used to measure distances on land in the United States and is 5,280 feet.

PILOT - An individual with specific knowledge of a harbor, canal, river or other waterway, qualified to guide vessels through the region. Some areas require that boats and ships be piloted by a licensed pilot. When arriving at a harbor requiring a pilot, a small pilot boat will pull alongside the ship and the pilot will jump from his boat to the ship. When leaving port, the pilot boat will come for the pilot and the process is reversed.

RUNNING LIGHTS - Lights that are required when a ship is moving at night. Red and green lights denote port and starboard. Lights are also affixed to the upper rigging of the ship so that from a distance one can tell the direction the ship is pointed from looking at the running lights.

SWELL - Large smooth waves that do not break. Swells are caused by the wind over large distances.

UNDERWAY - A ship is underway when it is in motion. The captain might say we plan to get underway at 1930 Hours (7:30 p.m.)

WEIGH AND AWEIGH - Weigh and aweigh both mean to raise, such as to weigh the anchor.

Retired Texas Federal Judge Complies with Request from HRM Felipe VI de Borbon, King of Spain To Write Book About Spain's Assistance During the American Revolutionary War

---

"*Galvez*: Best Revolutionary War History Book for 2014"

In May 2010 Judge Ed Butler and his first lady, Robin, who reside in San Antonio led a group of 35 members of the National Society Sons of the American Revolution on a tour of Spain. During their visit to Madrid, then Crown Prince Felipe granted the SAR members and their wives a private audience at Zarzuela Palace, the royal residence. During that audience King Felipe asked judge Butler to write a book about Bernardo de Galvez and Spain's assistance to the U.S. during the American Revolutionary War.

Judge Ed Butler and First Lady Robin visit with King Felipe VI of Spain

Gently poking judge Butler on the shoulder King Felipe, with a broad smile on his face said:

"I want you to write a book about Spain's assistance to the United States during the American Revolutionary War; then I want you to write a screen play, and get Hollywood to make a movie. I would like Antonio Banderas to play the part of General Galvez."

Judge Butler replied: "I can write the book, and I can write the screenplay, but it will be up to Hollywood to decide if they want to make a movie."

561

The 360 page book with 214 footnotes, and 37 pages of Appendices, contains the names of hundreds of Spanish patriots. It documents the significant support rendered by Spain, and allows our Hispanic community to feel proud that their ancestors played a vital role in the formation of our nation.

History Books by Judge Ed Butler:

Available on Ancestry.com in soft back, CD or audio.

Galvez / Spain –

Our Forgotten Ally in the American Revolutionary War: A Concise Summary of Spain's Assistance.

George Washington's Secret Ally.

So far, these books have won eight awards:

1) The Texas Connection To The American Revolution presented the **"Best American History Book about the American Revolutionary War in 2014;**

2) Readers' Review gave it its **"7 Star Award;"**

3) The Sons of the Republic of Texas presented its **"Presidio La Bahia Award; "**

4) Texas Hill Country Chapter of Colonial Dames - **"Best History Book in 2015."**

5) International Latino Book Award for Best History Book in 2016

6) Daughters of the American Revolution highest award – **The DAR Medal of Honor.**

7) The Order of the Founders of North America 1492-1692 highest award – The OFNA Legion of Merit.

8) Amazon.com editorial committee: **"One of the Best History Books in 2018.**

Travel Books by Judge Ed Butler:

Travels With The Judge: This covers travel in Europe, Japan, Soviet Union, South

Available on Ancestry.com in soft back, CD or audio.

1997 Around The World Adventure: This covers around the world travel through Western Europe, Eastern Europe, Scandinavia, The Boltics, Russia, Belarus, Oman, United Arab Emirates, India, Napel, Singapore,

Above two books bound in hardback together: $69.00

Pacifica: This covers travel Circle Pacific, Travels through Hawaii, Islands of the Pacific, Australia New Zealand, Indonesia, Singapore, China, Taiwan, Philippines, Korea, and Japan.

Above two books on CD: $ 39.00

Wanderlust: This covers travel in Central America, Mexico, Caribbean, Eastern Europe, Western Europe, Greenland, Iceland, and The North Atlantic Islands.

Also Available from Southwest Historic Press, LLP:

In hardback/softback book format:

1. *The Descendants of Pvt. Philip Nicholas Myers, A Revolutionary War Patriot*, by Edward F. Butler and Robin M. Butler, 200, 204 pps. - $39.95 + $5.00 P & H = $44.95.

2. *The Descendants of Thomas Pincerna, Progenitor of the Butler Family*, by Edward F. Butler, GenPub Dallas, 1997. First Prize Award, 1997, Dallas Genealogy Society. 643 pps. $89.00 + 7.50 P & H = $96.50.

3. *Butler Arms*, by Judge Ed Butler. 2017. Full color printed on archival paper. $250.00 + $7.50 = $257.50

4. *George Washington's Secret Ally,* by Judge Ed Butler, 2016. $7.50 + $4.00 = $11.50.

In CD format:

1. *The Descendants of Pvt. Philip Nicholas Myers, A Revolutionary War Patriot*, by Edward F. Butler and Robin M. Butler, 200, 204 pps , $24.95 + $3.50 P & H = $28.45.

2. *The Descendants of Thomas Pincerna, Progenitor of the Butler Family*, by Edward F. Butler, GenPub Dallas, 1997. First Prize Award, 1997, Dallas Genealogy Society. 643 pps. $49.95 +3.50 P & H = $53.45.

3. *The Ancestors and Descendants of Diana Jean Parker, of Lane, DeWitt County, Illinois*, By Edward F. and Robin M. Butler, 2000. $19.95 + $3.50 = $23.45.

4. *Butler Arms*, by Judge Ed Butler. 2017. Full color. $39.00 + $3.50 = $46.50.

5. *George Washington's Secret Ally*, by Judge Ed Butler, 2016. $5.00 + $3.50 = $8.50.

TO ORDER BOOKS OR CDS FROM SOUTHWEST HISTORICAL PRESS:

8830 Cross Mountain Trail, San Antonio, TX 78255-2014

Or

Sarpg0910@aol.com

A NEW AND INNOVATIVE SERIES OF
FAMILY HISTORY BOOKS

Judge Ed Butler announced today that a new series of family history books will be available soon. The new series is entitled *Royals, Nobles, Warriors and Leaders of the Western World*. Although the series is currently being edited, it now is divided into two parts:

Part 1 is entitled "The Ancestors of Pvt. Benjamin F. Lovelace." He was conscripted into the Confederate Army at age 16, taken as a prisoner and was confined in 10 Yankee prisons. At 6,300 pages, this series will be contained in about 8 volumes.

Part 2 is entitled "The Descendants of Pvt. Benjamin F. Lovelace, which is currently 1242 pages, will be printed in two volumes. As there are many photos and other digital documents to include, it is estimated that these books will total about 1400 pages. The set will include all 10 volumes.

FREQUENT FAMILY NAMES IN THIS SERIES:

Aragon, Ascher, Barne(s), Beard, Berrost, Beauchamp (De Beauchamp), Beaufort, Beaumont, Berenger, Bigod, Bohun (De Bohun), Boon, Boteler, Bruce (De Bruce), Brooks, Burgundy, Campbell, Capet, Castile, Clare (De Clare), Courtenay (De Courtenay), Crost(e), Chrichton, D'Anou, De Bourgogne, De Burgh, De Ferrers, De Firmus, De Grey, De Holl(and, De Keith, De Montfort, De Mortimer, De Percy, De Quincy, De Ros, De Vere, De Vermandois, De Warren(e), De Welle(s), Douglas, Erskine, Ferrers, Fitz Alan, Fitz Hugh, Fitz William, Garrard, Gascoigne, Gordon, Graham, Gre(a)y, Hail, Haute, Hay, Henry, Herbert, Holl(and, Horne, Howard, Keith, Kerr, La Zouche, Lovelace, Loveless, Markham, Marshall, Milton, Mortimer, Mowbray, Neville (De Neville), Palmer, Peckham, Percy, Plantagenet, Proctor, Rich, Savoy, Seton, Sinclair, Standish, Stanley, Stapleton, Stewart/Stuart, Stover, Talbot, Touchet, Tudor, Tyrrell, Valois, Vermandois, Welles, Wentworth.

569

9102 individuals covering 42 generations.

*58 Gateway Ancestors – 89% from Great Britain

Discusses over 1,000 Royals: *33 Emperors & Empresses; *521 Kings & Queens; *449 Princes & Princesses; and *96 Dukes.

Includes over 1,000 Nobles: Margraves, Earls, Viscounts, Marquess, Barons and Knights.

Covers over 1,000 Aristocrats, Governors, Judges, Sheriffs, Lord Mayors, Esquires, Gentlemen and high Public Officials.

Encompasses many Bishops, Archbishops, and church leaders.

Describes the life of legions of warriors, including Crusaders, Knights, Admirals, Generals, and common soldiers.

Adds an article about the history of the times at the end of each of the 40 detailed generations, which allows the reader to place his ancestor in a moment of time. What were the pressures that led to them leaving for the colonies? Were they affected by the Black Plague? The Burning of London? Hundred Years War? Depression? Politics?

Utilized all credible "Hints" from Ancestry.com, which yielded copies of: Church records of christening, Marriage, death & burial; Portraits & copy of Arms; Photos of castles, monuments, plaques, tombs, and graves; Maps & copies of pages from history and genealogy books & magazines; Public record of births, marriages, & death; & Military records – muster rolls, prison records, promotions, battles

*Lists of the Gateway Ancestors, Emperors & Empresses, Kings & Queens, Princes & Princesses, and Dukes can be viewed at

SouthWestHistoricPress.com

ABOUT THE AUTHOR – Judge Ed Butler

Award winning author family history book. Author of 14 books - 3 on genealogy - 1 on heraldry - 2 on history - 4 on travel. Has visited many of the castles, manors, tombs of & monuments to ancestors listed in these books.

Award winning author of history book ("Gasto; won one of best history books in 2010", Executive Committee, Amazon.com).

Texas Genealogical College's "Roll of Fame" member.

B.A.R." Medal of Honor", S.A.R. "Gold Good Citizenship Medal."

President General, National Society Sons of the American Revolution. Shipboard enhancement speaker.

Founder & Charter Grand Viscount General, Order of the Founders of North America. Recipient of its highest award: "OFNA Legion of Merit."

Who's Who in the World, Who's Who in America & Who's Who in the Law. Seven writing awards.

At the end of each generation the author has included an historical article about what was going on at the time that might have influenced your ancestor. War, famine, disease, floods, depression are just a few of the events that affected our ancestors. The author has included these historical accounts to make your ancestor come alive.

WRITTEN USING NEW SOFTWARE

This series of books was created using *Family Book Creator, 2019*. First, the author spent over a year reviewing "hints" from Ancestry.com. Only "hints' from reputable sources were used and synced into *Family Tree Maker*. There is a photo gallery following many individuals, where copies of important documents, church records of baptisms, marriages and funerals, portraits, copy of arms, castles, tombs, monuments, etc. can be displayed. A copy of any document is better than a mere footnote.

The Author:

Judge Edward F. Butler obtained his BA degree from the University of Mississippi in 1958, which he attended on a scholarship. He was the Ford Foundation Scholar at Vanderbilt University School of Law, from which he graduated with honors in 1961. Before becoming a judge, he was a Board Certified Civil Trial Attorney. He has served as a judge at the city, county, state and federal levels.

Judge Butler is an outstanding genealogist, having served as Sons of the American Revolution genealogist at the chapter and state levels, and was elected for two terms as **Genealogist General** of the National Society. Subsequently, he served as President General of the National SAR. In 2010 he was awarded the SAR's Highest award, the **Gold Good Citizenship Medal**. In 2012, he was the founder and organizing Grand Viscount General of the Order of the Founders of North America and co-founded the Texas Genealogical College.

In 2017 the National Daughters of the American Revolution bestowed its highest award to him – **The DAR Medal of Honor**. This award was predicated upon the books and articles written by him about American History. The following year, the Order of the Founders of North America awarded him its highest medal, the **OFNA Legion of Merit**. His history books have garnered 7 awards. In 2017 he was inducted into the Texas Genealogical College's "**Hall of Fame**."

Judge Butler has published 2 award winning history books, 4 travel books, 3 family history books, one of which won 1st place in the Dallas Genealogical Society, one book on Heraldry and 2 law books. In addition, he has published dozens of articles on family history, history and law.

He has also served as a national officer in the General Society of Colonial Wars, Order of the Founders and Patriots of America, Sons of the Revolution, General Society of the War of 1812, Washington's Army at Valley Forge, Military Order of the Stars and Bars, and First Families of Maryland. Judge Butler served in the U.S. Navy and retired as a Commander.

572

Made in the USA
Middletown, DE
27 October 2023

41384380R10340